Understanding Educational Complexity

Educational Leadership and Leaders in Contexts

Founding Editors

Tony Townsend (*Florida Atlantic University, Boca Raton, Florida, USA*)
Ira Bogotch (*Florida Atlantic University, Boca Raton, Florida, USA*)

VOLUME 6

The titles published in this series are listed at *brill.com/ellc*

Understanding Educational Complexity

Integrating Practices and Perspectives for 21st Century Leadership

By

Brad Kershner

BRILL
SENSE

LEIDEN | BOSTON

All chapters in this book have undergone peer review.

The Library of Congress Cataloging-in-Publication Data is available online at http://catalog.loc.gov

Typeface for the Latin, Greek, and Cyrillic scripts: "Brill". See and download: brill.com/brill-typeface.

ISSN 2666-7746
ISBN 978-90-04-44784-4 (paperback)
ISBN 978-90-04-43506-3 (hardback)
ISBN 978-90-04-44783-7 (e-book)

Copyright 2021 by Koninklijke Brill NV, Leiden, The Netherlands.
Koninklijke Brill NV incorporates the imprints Brill, Brill Hes & De Graaf, Brill Nijhoff, Brill Rodopi, Brill Sense, Hotei Publishing, mentis Verlag, Verlag Ferdinand Schöningh and Wilhelm Fink Verlag.
All rights reserved. No part of this publication may be reproduced, translated, stored in a retrieval system, or transmitted in any form or by any means, electronic, mechanical, photocopying, recording or otherwise, without prior written permission from the publisher. Requests for re-use and/or translations must be addressed to Koninklijke Brill NV via brill.com or copyright.com.

This book is printed on acid-free paper and produced in a sustainable manner.

Advance Praise for
Understanding Educational Complexity

"Our educational institutions are undergoing multiple unprecedented transitions right now. These are both exciting times for educators to re-envision educational practice, as well as scary times, as the fate of education faces more uncertainty than ever before. *Understanding Educational Complexity* provides a much needed vision and set of practices for current educational leaders and researchers to guide us through these complex times. Kershner draws on numerous case studies and practical examples to present an integrative path forward that can allow our educational systems to meet the planetary age we are now entering."
– **Sean Esbjörn-Hargens**, author/editor of *Integral Education, Integral Ecology,* and *Metatheory for the Twenty-First Century*

"A masterpiece of big picture thinking that is also firmly rooted in rich descriptions of leadership practice. Brad Kershner, a proven teacher and school leader himself, is among the very first to portray how complexity theory can illuminate what it is like to lead schools in times of rapid and turbulent change."
– **Andy Hargreaves**, Professor Emeritus, Boston College, author of *Professional Capital, Sustainable Leadership,* and *Uplifting Leadership*

"Dr. Kershner has written an immensely important book, not just for educators, but for anyone interested in how to think in a more complex and adequate way about organizations, learning, and culture. This is one of the best uses I have seen made of Integral Theory, providing a path breaking application, demonstrating the power of truly comprehensive frameworks. All school leaders should read this book, and most sociologists and philosophers as well."
– **Zachary Stein**, author of *Social Justice and Educational Measurement* and *Education in a Time between Worlds*

"If education is about growth in knowledge in a wide and deep sense, shouldn't the educational systems, cultures, and practices be informed by the best possible maps of the different fields of knowledge and their interrelations? Moreover, if education is about psychological growth and the development of the entire personality of children, youth, and adults, shouldn't education follow the steps of the best developmental psychology, and align with our knowledge of how the human mind and personality learns, grows, and prospers? In today's world, neither of these two things is true. Education-as-we-know-it is informed by rich academic and research traditions of pedagogy, but not by developmental psychology, by systems perspectives, or by a holistic theory of the fields of human knowledge.

Brad Kershner offers us this fundamental upgrade in his book. Well-read in growth and development, the varieties of systems theory, and holistic meta-theories of knowledge, he ventures into sensitive and detailed case studies of American schools and projects—with the gaze that only the experience and ethos of a teacher who truly cares about children can grant—and unpacks their potential. No single blueprint is offered, but the rich timbre of commentary, reflection, and explication opens doors and pathways to an entirely new world of education.

Of all theorists in the interrelated fields of development/systems/metatheory, Brad Kershner is, to my knowledge, the foremost in his grasp of schooling and the teacher's perspective. Of all teachers and educational theorists, he is the foremost theorist in said fields, able not only to apply them but to synthesize and comment upon their limitations and uses. And these fields can and will reshape the future of education. Indeed, they must. And society cannot transform to sanity and sustainability without a fundamental reform of education. For this reason, I believe that Brad Kershner's book plays an indispensable role in the future of society as a whole. It is a rare and impressive achievement that marries the teacher's heart to the theorist's mind."
– Hanzi Freinacht, author of *The Listening Society, Nordic Ideology,* and *The 6 Hidden Patterns of History*

"True reform in any school community involves structural changes which emerge from shifts within each human participant. New ways of being dance with new ways of doing, forming new narratives about the community. *Understanding Educational Complexity* is the rare book that is able to shine light on such complexity. In these pages are deep lessons drawn from the experiences of a true reformer—someone who is able to form and reform their own ideas about a subject. Dr. Kershner uses concrete examples to show how an adult learner who celebrates the process of change has a greater impact than a leader who views reform as a discrete set of policies or practices."
– Nadav Zeimer, author of *Education in the Digital Age*

To the process of education itself—to the perpetual learning and growth that constitutes the path and purpose of every human being on planet Earth

Contents

Preface XI
List of Figures XIII

1 The Complexity of Everything 1
  1 Two Schools, Two Principals, Myriad Challenges 3
  2 Wicked Complexity and Integral Theory 4

2 Complexity Leadership 9
  1 Distributed Leadership 18
  2 The Complex Systems View 19

3 Jeffrey Jackson School: Repetitive Reform and the Slow Process of Adaptive Change 25
  1 Culture, Climate, and Collaboration 29
  2 Distributed Leadership: Consistency and Structured Collaboration 34
  3 Instructional Leadership: Principal Presence in the Classroom 41
  4 Reform Is in the Eye of the Beholder 49

4 Saint Catherine's School: Collective Urgency at the Edge of Chaos 57
  1 DREAM BIG: Creating a Common School Culture 62
  2 Distributed Leadership: Creating Structures for Organizational Learning 66
  3 Instructional Leadership: Challenging and Supporting Teachers 72
  4 Guiding Emergence through Challenge, Support, and Balance 74
  5 Case Study Summary: Contextualizing Processes and Outcomes 80

5 Perpetual Learning in an Integral Ecology 86
  1 Post-Postmodern Pluralism: Integrating Perspectives on Leadership and Change 88
  2 Subjective Realities: Understanding the Spectrum of Perspectives 102
  3 Social Realities: Surfacing System Infrastructures and Ideological Influences 119

6 Methodological Hindsight: Reflections on Systems Thinking, Integral Theory, and Educational Research 135
  1 Fostering and Assessing Development in Complex Systems 143
  2 Plea for a Post-Postmodern Paradigm of Practice 149
  3 Positionality as a Kosmic Address 151

Postscript: Phronetic Social Science and Methodological Metacognition 163

References 167

Preface

There is so much happening right now. There is so much to do. We are all overwhelmed by the enormity and implications of world events, and by the sheer quantity of media and information available to us—so many videos to watch, so many articles and blogs, and so many books to read. In a world of surveillance capitalism and social media, our attention has become our most valuable resource and commodity, and what we attend to is both an expression of what we value and a factor that influences our future thoughts, beliefs, and behavior. The fact that you are holding this book in your hands is an expression of care, interest, and value—for me, for the ideas that this book presents, and/or for the importance of education—and that is incredibly meaningful. Everything matters, everything counts, every moment is precious, and I appreciate you taking time to read this book.

The research for this project was done in conjunction with the Lynch School of Education at Boston College, where I completed my doctoral work. My intention for shaping this research into a book is to offer an accessible exploration of the problems and insights of educational research, practice, and policy, along with an introduction to the frameworks of complexity theory and Integral Theory that is grounded in the real and meaningful stories of urban schools. In addition to that, an even deeper impetus for this text is to model a process of reflection, and to broaden the context in which we interpret education, beyond what is typically included in academic discourse. I do not want only to share my research and conclusions—I want to share my reflections on them. I do not want only to explain what happened in these schools—I want to point toward what we would have to understand and account for to begin to be able to explain what is happening in schools. Not just analysis, but meta-analysis; not just theory, but meta-theory; not just practice, but social praxis.

The purposes of the book are therefore manifold: to share concrete examples of the very real challenges facing educators and leaders in urban schools; to connect those challenges to the deeply flawed and short sighted policies associated with education reform; to show how we can use the interpretive frameworks of complexity theory and distributed leadership to make sense of some aspects of life in schools; to offer important reflections on the limits of educational research, and on the frames of complexity and educational leadership; and to point educators, researchers, and all readers toward the vast, interdependent, dynamic, emergent context of human life that envelops and constitutes our processes and interpretations of schooling, education, and research. I wrote this book not to demonstrate or embody the norms of educational research, but to point beyond them; not to argue for the use of complexity theory or Integral Theory as the answer to interpretive questions, but to point toward the ultimate necessity for interdisciplinary and transdisciplinary sense making and meaning making. This book exists in service of the movement toward inhabiting and understanding process-oriented views of what is happening in schools and in society, and toward views that self-consciously and meta-cognitively account for the ongoing development and growth of everything: students, teachers, leaders, researchers, schools, cultures, and societies. We are experiencing the process of evolution, *in medias res*. Our education systems should embody and facilitate this process of development, and educational theory and research should help to orient us toward how to do that as best we can, as consciously as possible.

That is our context—now to the content. The structure of the book is such that the insights I hope to convey build cumulatively, from theory (Chapters 1 and 2), to practice (as revealed in two case studies, Chapters 3 and 4), to broader reflections and meta-analysis (Chapters 5 and 6). While I believe every word in this book is worth reading, if at any time a reader feels that they may not read the entire book, I implore them to focus on Chapters 1, 5, and 6. Chapter 2 offers a short and selective summary of leadership and complexity research, which can be skimmed for general ideas (especially if one is already familiar with notions of complexity). Chapters 3 and 4 offer meaningful summaries of life in two schools, which for some may be the most compelling aspect of the text. But if you are primarily interested in big ideas and insights, you can find my summative analysis of both cases at the end of Chapter 4. Chapters 5 and 6 present the main ideas that I want the reader to consider, and represent the *raison d'être* of this book.

Again, thank you. We are all on this journey of life and learning together, and I appreciate your interest in learning from this part of my journey, as I continue to learn from so many others.

Figures

1. The four quadrants. 6
2. Networked teams at JJS. 36
3. Networked teams at SCS. 68
4. Evolution in four quadrants. 94
5. Evolution of operating systems (adapted from Smith, 2018). 94
6. Four-quadrant perspective taking. 95
7. Theorists in four quadrants. 96
8. Quadrant absolutism. 96
9. Eight zones of Integral Methodological Pluralism. 97
10. Methodologies in the eight zones (from van Schaik, 2016). 98
11. Comparison of mental complexity stage models. 111

CHAPTER 1

The Complexity of Everything

Education in the United States is a complex and contested arena. Its complexity emerges from the confluence of many factors, including socioeconomic inequality, racial and economic segregation, misguided policy and competing agendas for reform, technological and demographic change, and—at the root of it all—the inherent challenges of establishing institutional cultures and practices that align with the principles of human learning and development. These and other factors combine to create dilemmas and crises that can be readily observed in both educational scholarship and mainstream media. Despite ongoing reforms, research, and rhetoric, both the achievement gap and the opportunity gap remain persistent social problems, and the challenges of society and schooling remain interdependent and irresolvable (Ladson-Billings, 2006; Rothstein, 2004).

But wait, there's more! The unresolved tensions embedded in our educational systems constitute just one constellation in a broader panorama of meta-crises enveloping our world. If we want to understand what is happening in our schools, and what we need to do to respond adequately to the pressures and demands of 21st century education, we need to understand the broader context of our lives as we move into what some are calling the "fourth industrial revolution," which is co-emerging with the tremendous challenges of global climate degradation, unsustainable production and consumption habits, widespread species extinction, job automation, decentralized media, and the development of artificial intelligence (Schwab, 2017; Tegmark, 2018). This is the water in which we swim. Any discussion of education in the 21st century that fails to account for this context and point helpfully forward is wasting our time.

The complexity of education is such that our efforts to address the challenges of policy and practice embedded in the operations of our school systems perpetually fail to accomplish their goals. There are always residual effects, unintended consequences, and collateral damage. Public education has become, in some ways, tragically, a form of iatrogenic dis-ease in society. On one hand, there are persistent achievement gaps between students of different races, social classes, and linguistic backgrounds, and a college degree remains an unattained aspiration for many young people. On the other hand, many policies and practices that ostensibly seek to address these and other problems create other, perhaps even more pernicious difficulties for teachers and students. These problems include: narrowed curricula, test-focused preparatory school cultures that limit the ends and means of the learning process, teacher accountability practices that encourage test-focused instruction and militate against the development of professional cultures of practice, and limited time, money, and support for the arts, physical education, and play. As many have documented, this confluence of systemic pressures and the responses of education reform, largely constituted by standardization, corporate management models, and test-based accountability policies, is widespread both in the US and around the globe (Howe & Meens, 2012; Ravitch, 2013; Sahlberg, 2011).

In this environment of test-based accountability and reform, school leaders face tremendous challenges. It is well known that school leadership is a stressful, high-pressure, high-stakes endeavor (Meier & Wood, 2004; MetLife, 2012). The "work intensification" of school leadership has increased in recent years, and has been described as "long hours, endless demands, punishing pace and continual frustration" (Gronn, 2003, p. 68). School leadership puts one at the fulcrum of macro-, meso-, and micro-level demands and pressures—from educational policy to school management to the nuances of curriculum and instruction—and the cognitive, emotional, and interpersonal demands of the position have never been greater than they are now, especially in urban schools where the injustices of society are felt most severely (Fullan, 2007; Kozol, 2005; Noguera, 2003, 2009). However, beyond this sobering consensus, there are many ways to interpret the challenges of educational leadership, and there are many factors to account for in the quest to understand how leadership shapes schools, how school leaders should respond to the bureaucratic, cultural, and pedagogical challenges of 21st century education, and how to shape the outcomes of these interdependent relationships.

It is also evident that school leadership is not simply an issue for school leaders; schools and school systems are matrices of interaction, and shared leadership is essential (Hallinger, 2011; Heck & Hallinger, 2010; Spillane, 2005). Good schools are constituted by positive, professional, and healthy school cultures, and providing high-quality education is a whole system affair—a principal cannot create it alone (Fullan, 2007; Senge et al., 2000; Bryk & Schneider, 2002; Hargreaves & Fullan, 2012; Saphier & King, 1985; Sarason, 1971).

Given what we know about the influences of education reform, the problems and pressures of leadership, and the distributed and interdependent characteristics of cultural leadership at the school level, attempts to guide and assess educational leadership should strive to understand the context of schools and school systems as fully as possible. But how? What methodologies and theoretical frameworks allow us to disclose, interpret, and understand the reality of leadership in schools in ways that are adaptive, helpful, and enlightening? How do different perspectives on education shape and influence both what happens in schools and how we judge what happens? What perspectives are crucial to enact at the various levels of school leadership in order to ensure that the complex challenges of 21st century education will be responded to adequately?

This book seeks to answer these questions through the analysis of two case studies. I will share examples of school leadership and educational change in order to assess the processes and outcomes of leadership at these schools, and I will then use these cases as a foundation from which to reflect upon the methodological and theoretical complexities involved in assessing and interpreting school leadership and educational success. The purpose of this book is primarily to present and encourage broader and deeper thinking about schooling—how we understand it, how we enact it, how we assess it, and how it needs to change in response to a changing world.

1 Two Schools, Two Principals, Myriad Challenges

The examples of educational complexity presented here emerge from the experiences of two urban schools: St. Catherine's School (SCS), a pre-K to 8th grade Catholic school, and Jeffrey Jackson School (JJS), a pre-K to 5th grade district public school on the other side of the same city.[1] The case studies focus on the leadership of two principals: Helen Matthews at SCS and Harold Weatherbee at JJS. Both Matthews and Weatherbee were participants in a university-based professional development program for school leaders, which I will refer to as the School Leadership Academy (SLA). The research began in conjunction with the SLA, with an intention to examine how three strategies for reform—creating a common school culture, distributing leadership, and providing instructional leadership to improve teaching and learning—worked in concert to impact the experience of each school community.

As a researcher working on this project over the course of six years, I continued to reflect on and learn from my experiences at these schools over time. This learning came not just from ongoing efforts to collect more data, but from a continued refinement of my thinking about, interpretation of, and theorizing about the leadership and change I observed. It came, as well, during the course of my own work as a school leader in the city where this research took place. Though it may appear counterintuitive, this ongoing work in schools led me deeper into theoretical inquiry, not away from it. As a leader embedded in the complex and multi-faceted network of causality and interdependence noted above, I continued to seek vistas of interpretation that made sense of my experience and the experience of the principals I studied. I sought to develop helpful, useful, and practical theory—not just mid-range leadership theory, but big-picture theory that helps to put mid-range leadership theory in a clarifying context of meaning.

It has been said "there is nothing so practical as a good theory" (Lewin, 1943, p. 118). And as Morgan (2006) argued (in reference to effective leadership): "in times of change, it is vital to be in touch with the assumptions and theories that are guiding our practice and to be able to shape and reshape them for different ends" (p. 364). I agree with these sentiments wholeheartedly, and I believe that as an educator it is important to work with and through multiple theories in the effort to achieve a comprehensive and meaningful understanding of the noble, challenging, daunting, and seemingly Sisyphean work of schooling in America. Therefore, this book seeks not only to describe and interpret school leadership and educational change, but also to discern and describe meaningful and applicable insights about the ways that we think about, approach, and understand education, in all its complexity. As should be clear from this brief introduction, grappling with the complexity of education is not easy to do. It is challenging work, and requires sophisticated tools. The tools that I found most helpful in this work were complexity theory and Integral Theory.

2   Wicked Complexity and Integral Theory

> A system is a set of things—people, cells, molecules, or whatever—interconnected in such a way that they produce their own pattern of behavior over time.
>
> DONELLA MEADOWS

> The project of formal education cannot be understood without considering, all-at-once, the many layers of dynamic, nested activity that are constantly at play.
>
> BRENT DAVIS & DENNIS SUMARA

Complex systems have diverse components that interact in diverse ways producing diverse outcomes that are difficult to predict (Page, 2010). They therefore give rise to what are known as "wicked problems"—emergent and interconnected problems with no final solution, which are unpredictable and rapidly changing, involving complex social arrangements (Barnard, 2013; Skabursis, 2008). From the perspective of complexity science, educational change appears as a wicked problem involving many layers and dimensions of influence and interdependence. Wicked problems are never "solved"; they can only be "re-solved" over and over again, and the broader context of such "solutions" is a world that is increasingly volatile, uncertain, complex, and ambiguous (VUCA) (Finkelstein, 2004; Watkins & Wilber, 2015).

In my work with SCS and JJS, I enacted the lens of complexity in order to understand the systems and processes of change that took place at each school. In any human system, changing the dominant ideas, assumptions, beliefs, and values—the shared culture—can be a powerful leverage point for change. In systems thinking, as in complexity theory, changing cultural values and beliefs can serve as a tool to transform the system, because values and beliefs "are the sources of systems" (Meadows, 2008, p. 163). Moreover, "solving wicked problems requires significantly more than behavioral change, both on an individual and collective level. It requires a change of mind or attitude that underlies behavior, otherwise the change won't stick" (Watkins & Wilber, 2015, p. 13). Therefore, in my work at SCS and JJS I attend to both the systemic operations of the schools as well as the mindsets and discourses from which those systems arise.

In addition, I recognize that in human systems changes can cause disequilibrium, and symbiotically, the experience of disequilibrium can promote growth. To grow, people must experience significant change, and such change most often generates a sense of disequilibrium. In the context of schools, the status quo of education needs to be disrupted, and this change is bound to cause disequilibrium for teachers. It is the principal's task to both instigate change and ensure that teachers are supported. For while disequilibrium is necessary for change and growth in any system, too much change, and the disequilibrium it provokes, can lead to rejection, resistance, or retreat (Nadler, 1993). Thus, change is also a matter of balance: intensity matters, and effective growth and change requires each school to find the most effective enactment of reform for its particular context (Opfer & Pedder, 2011).

However adept the frameworks of systems and complexity may be in enabling an understanding of schools as socio-cultural/human systems, the imperative to attend to both the systemic operations of each school as well as the mindsets out of which the systems arise led me to realize that it was necessary to also have a framework for understanding the mindsets of educators and school leaders. In order to understand the thinking and behavior of the individuals who constitute these school systems, and to assess the robustness and comprehensiveness of the systems view of school leadership and educational change, I sought an even broader framework within which to conduct a meta-analysis of the case studies. As I worked to understand leadership and change through the lens of systems thinking and complexity theory, I also tried to account and correct for what I perceived as their interpretive shortcomings; I sought to understand and use these frameworks in a way that acknowledged and clarified the conceptual limits and tensions they exposed, thus moving beyond a complex systems view.

Several philosophers and theorists have attempted to develop comprehensive meta-theories, or integral theories, to integrate the findings and frameworks of others in order to develop a coherent and comprehensive framework for a given field of study (Bhaskar, 2002, 2012; Chaudhuri, 1977; Edwards, 2010; Gebser, 1991; Habermas, 1984a, 1984b). In my analysis of these case studies I will utilize a particular lineage of meta-theory, developed initially by Ken Wilber, noted with capital letters as Integral Theory (IT) (Wilber, 1995, 2000a, 2006d). As Kegan and Lahey (2016) highlighted in their research on Deliberately Developmental Organizations, Wilber's model is "a valuable heuristic for a more comprehensive view of any complicated psychosocial phenomenon" (p. 242).

According to Integral Theory, there are at least four irreducible perspectives to be consulted when attempting to understand a complex system: subjective, intersubjective, objective, and interobjective. Put differently, there are four dimensions that should be accounted for when attempting to understand something like a school: the interiors and exteriors of individuals and collectives. These four dimensions can be represented as four quadrants.

INDIVIDUAL

	I Subjective	IT Objective	
I N T E R I O R	thoughts, emotions, memories, states of mind, perceptions, immediate sensations	material body (including brain) and anything that you can see, touch, or observe in time and space	E X T E R I O R
	WE Intersubjective	ITS Interobjective	
	shared values, meaning, language, relationships, and cultural background	systems, networks, technology, government, and the natural environment	

COLLECTIVE

FIGURE 1   The four quadrants

This four-quadrant framework can be utilized to organize and interpret data concerning the interior, subjective, intentional dimension of teachers' and principals' beliefs and worldviews; the intersubjective, cultural, relational dimension of shared meanings and values; the objective, empirical, behavioral dimension of actions and practices; and the interobjective, structural, systemic dimension of each school context. This framework also allows us to see how different approaches to leadership emphasize particular quadrants, while ignoring others, thus making their interpretations inherently partial.

For instance, leadership that emphasizes particular qualities, behaviors and characteristics are bringing their attention to the upper two quadrants. Whether discussing leadership behavior or the importance of certain leadership dispositions, a focus on "the leader" addresses only the individual "half" of reality, while bracketing the insights of a more complex, network-oriented view. Conversely, discussions of complexity leadership, generative leadership, or distributed leadership are focusing their analysis on the lower two quadrants. Discussions of school culture attend to the lower left (LL), while discussions of group behavior and the workings of complex systems and networks attend to the lower right (LR) quadrant. Being aware of all four quadrants simultaneously can allow us to broaden our understanding of leadership in complex systems, by offering us an interpretive check-point to assess the degree to which our analysis is coherent and comprehensive.

In addition to the four quadrants, the integration of developmental-constructivist psychology is a key component of Integral Theory, and is used to interpret the meanings of discourses, beliefs, and worldviews of individuals and groups (Beck & Cowan, 2006; Cook-Greuter, 2004; Kegan, 2001, 2003; Wilber, 2000b, 2006d). IT also sheds light on the socio-cultural aspects of school research, as every social group is understood to be constituted by the internality codes and rules of discourse that enable it to remain cohesive, and allow its members to identify with it (Wilber, 2006c).

In particular, given the central and important role of principals in school systems, I draw upon IT and developmental-constructivist leadership theory to help me interpret the discourses of both the principals and the social groups at each of these schools. Much work has already been done in the area of development and leadership, and in relation to educational leadership in particular (Harris & Kuhnert, 2008; Rooke & Torbert, 2005; Helsing, Howell, Kegan, & Lahey, 2008; Wagner & Kegan, 2006). This work draws on a vast and impressively consistent research base, and aligns with the following principles of human development:
– Growth occurs in a logical sequence of stages or expanding worldviews, which evolve from simple to complex, from static to dynamic, and from egocentric to group-centric to world-centric.

- Later stages are reached only by journeying through earlier stages. Each later stage includes and transcends the previous ones, while earlier perspectives remain part of our current experience.
- Each later stage is more differentiated, integrated, flexible, and capable of functioning optimally in a rapidly changing world.
- A person's stage of development influences what they notice or can become aware of, and what they can describe, influence, and change.
- As development unfolds, autonomy, tolerance for difference and ambiguity, reflection, flexibility, and skill in interacting with the environment increase, while defenses decrease.
- Development occurs through the interplay between person and environment. It is a potential that can be encouraged and facilitated by appropriate support and challenge.

As Watkins and Wilber (2015) point out, "part of the problem with wicked problems is that they tend to be approached solely through an objective, materialistic, scientific, systems view" (p. 23). Therefore, it is imperative to realize that "part of the solution to wicked problems will involve the actual growth and development of the consciousness of the change agents themselves" (p. 41). Wicked problems require wise answers, and wise answers require interior development and an understanding of the ways in which complexity evolves in all four quadrants simultaneously. This book offers a window into a process of inquiry that encapsulates one attempt to ensure that the insights and contributions of systems thinking and complexity theory are not limited by a materialistic, objectivist approach, but rather are enabled to open out into helpful, enlightening vistas of understanding that can serve to catalyze the development of school leaders.

In Chapter 2 I present a summary of complexity theory as it relates to educational research and leadership. In Chapters 3 and 4 I present in-depth case studies of Jeffrey Jackson School and Saint Catherine's School, and share insights and conclusions from my time at those schools that are meaningful and applicable to many other school contexts. In Chapters 5 and 6 I take a deep dive into some of the bigger questions and problems related to my work in education, and to the broader field of educational research and schooling in the 21st century. Readers who are not interested in the theory of systems and complexity can safely skip Chapter 2 and fully benefit from the stories and lessons from the two cases, as well as from the two concluding chapters.

Note

1 The names of all schools, programs, and participants are pseudonyms.

CHAPTER 2

Complexity Leadership

> The more we study the major problems of our time, the more we come to realize that they cannot be understood in isolation. They are systemic problems, which means that they are interconnected and interdependent.
> FRITJOF CAPRA

∙∙∙

> When we try to pick out anything by itself, we find it hitched to everything else in the universe.
> JOHN MUIR

∙∙∙

> I think the [21st] century will be the century of complexity.
> STEPHEN HAWKING

∙∙
∙

Recognition of the need to understand schools as complex systems is increasing, and new notions of leadership have emerged that align with systems- and complexity-perspectives. Complexity theory and systems thinking are not the same thing, and have distinct academic lineages, but together they have spawned overlapping leadership theories that explain interactive dynamics across a wide range of research. Complexity theory also overlaps significantly with chaos theory, both of which can be understood as branches of New Science and postmodern inquiry. Along with Fleener (2005), we can understand the story of the New Sciences of chaos and complexity as a postmodern logic of relationship, and an interpretive framework for understanding complex and emerging relationships from a systems perspective.

"Complexity" is an umbrella term for work that has been performed in numerous fields of research, and over the past 30 years the title "complexity theory" has become "the name for the work in systems theories that explores the concepts of feedback loops, interrelationships, dynamic systems, parts and wholes as interactively involved that cannot be separated" (Smitherman, 2005, p. 163). According to the New England Complex Systems Institute, "the field of complex systems cuts across all traditional disciplines… [and] is a new field of science studying how parts of a system give rise to the collective behaviors of the system, and how the system interacts with its environment" (NECSI, 2000).

Davis and Sumara (2006) outline several features of the relationship between complexity thinking and education, noting in particular a distinction between "complexity thinking" and "complexity science." The work of applying complexity thinking to educational concerns is not an attempt to utilize the "hard approach to complexity science," but rather the "soft complexity science" of social science, the latter being more pragmatic and more conducive to educational research. They work as well to bring attention to networks, and the ways in which systems are constituted by "a situation of collective-possibilities-arising-in-the-mutually-specifying-activities-of-autonomous-agents" (p. 58).

Thinking about the emergence of intelligence in systems, Davis and Sumara relate emergence to self-organization and note that the collective intelligence of a human system relies on a shared identity—which can be noted in a shift from "I" statements to "we" statements—and that each individual should act as independently as possible, because "intelligent group action is dependent on the independent actions of diverse individuals" (p. 85). Overall, they argue that the evidence in favor of decentralization in school systems is clear and consistent. This strand of thinking, which connects emergence in complex systems with the themes of decentralization and distributed leadership, is elaborated below.

A complex system is a learning system. All complex relations "embody their histories," and in order to understand any complex system one must identify its ethos: its "collective character or community disposition," and/or "the coherence that renders a collectivity both distinct and distinguishable" (Davis, Sumara, & D'Amour, 2012, p. 378). As a researcher in a school or school system, one must seek to understand how people seem to be connected to each other, how ideas might be networked, how people see themselves as a learning system, and how they conceptualize their work and understanding of learners and teachers. They note that shared vocabulary in a group shows the importance of redundancies at the level of collective actions. In their study of school districts, they found that each system had its own "core narrative" that is coherent, stable, rooted in history, and informs collective action. In their view "decentralized networks must be in constant disequilibrium," and there must be stressors that compel systems to adapt and learn, i.e., "triggers for transformation" (p. 396). However, "dynamic learning systems cannot be forced or legislated into existence," and leaders should therefore seek to create and maintain porous and flexible communicative linkages to orient and connect, not control, because "culture cannot be borrowed or imposed, but arises organically in the day-to-dayness of communication and shared work" (p. 398).

While systems perspectives on leadership and management cover a wide range, they are not a meta-discipline or meta-paradigm. Systems thinking is not above or free from paradigm conflicts. Rather, its main ideas are interpreted differently according to the paradigm from which they are viewed. For instance, in a functionalist systems approach, systems appear as objective aspects of reality, and people tend to be treated mechanistically to achieve pre-defined ends. Based in the language of math, it ignores problems that are not easily quantifiable, or distorts them in a quest for quantification.

> The attempt by systems dynamics to model social reality as though it were something external to humans is misguided. The subjective intentions of human beings, which are crucial, cannot be captured in "objective" models.... Rather it is necessary to respect the significance of human consciousness and to examine the worldviews and actions of the individuals who continually construct and reconstruct them. If we are to change social systems we must intervene in the process of meaning construction. (Jackson, 2000, pp. 154–155)

This is a critique of "hard systems thinking," which aligns with the positivist and functionalist approaches that dominated the field prior to the emergence of "soft systems thinking" in the 1980's. In "soft systems thinking," systems are seen as mental constructs rather than as entities with objective existence in the world, and the focus is transferred from the world to the process of inquiry about the world. This shift overlaps in many ways with the even broader shift from modern to postmodern approaches to social science, where "postmodernism seeks to puncture the certainties of modernism, particularly the belief in rationality, truth and progress" (Jackson, 2000, p. 36). This distinction also touches upon the difficulties of transcending the barriers between different areas of science, and reinforces the reality that the social sciences must be understood in light of meaning and intersubjectivity, and therefore not modeled on the natural sciences. Human systems depend on shared understandings and shared cultures, and this acknowledgment points toward the difference between the modernist, cybernetic approach to systems and the more postmodern approach, as characterized by theorists like Wheatley (2006).

One takeaway from surveying systems leadership discourse is that systems thinkers need to be aware of different paradigms in the social sciences, and of how different methodologies can serve different human interests. What

Jackson (2000) calls "critical systems thinking" attempts to integrate technical, practical, and emancipatory interests by seeking the best of what each paradigm has to offer. Ultimately, "critical systems thinking is about constantly reflecting on the limitations and partiality of our understanding" (p. 424). This critical, metacognitive integration of methodologies—a post-postmodern, or metamodern metatheory—is precisely what I am striving to develop as I seek to understand and explain the realities and complexities of education.

Further connections between complexity, systems, and leadership are important to note. Duffy (2008) argues that the ability to identify patterns in systems allows high leverage interventions, and that leaders with a systems approach can work to balance feedback loops to stabilize a system after change and disequilibrium have taken place in order to avoid entropy. Duffy also notes that a systems approach helps one to avoid quick fixes that have unintended consequences that cause original symptoms to potentially get worse.

Reigeluth (2008) explains that in complex systems positive feedback often takes the form of disturbances that cause disequilibrium in the system and subsequently provide information about opportunities to change goals: "Disequilibrium creates a state in which the system is ripe for transformation, which is reorganization on a higher level of complexity" (p. 27). In order to achieve such emergent reorganization, "transformation of an educational system requires simultaneous changes in the core work processes (teaching and learning), the social architecture of the system (culture and communications), and the system's relationships with its environment" (p. 28).

Reigeluth also touches on the importance of "strange attractors." An attractor can be understood as "a pattern or equilibrium that under certain conditions is very likely to emerge and stabilize within a dynamical system, such as a society [or school]" (Freinacht, 2019, p. 21). These patterns are not always directly connected to conscious ideas or beliefs, but Reigeluth argues that ideas and beliefs can have the power to organize a system and functions as attractors. Attractors are symbiotic with culture—neither simply the outcomes of culture nor the impetus of culture—and offer a way of describing patterns of cultural behavior. Establishing widespread norms and beliefs across a school culture can enable the emergence of established patterns of behavior, and when leaders do this consciously and intentionally they can enact a process of cultural cohesion in the direction of desired patterns. Such work is not so much designing or establishing a system—that would be a linear approach, and could lead to undesired, nonlinear outcomes—but rather cultivating new processes that target culture itself to facilitate the emergence of desired social patterns. In such a culture, a leader can use an awareness of desired attractors to influence the organizational process, but must constantly adjust and adapt to emerging reality.

When we see the power and influence of cultural norms, beliefs, and attractors, we can move toward helping stakeholders to expand their mindsets about education and about the ideal kinds of educational system they would like to have, which entails helping people uncover the mental models that often unwittingly influence their views of education. In this view, strange attractors are needed to create a force of support for key leverage points of change, working against the forces of the status quo.

The formation of committees and teams plays an important role in the self-organization of schools, and can serve to pull people into the culture of a system, because collective sense making emerges from working in a group that provides a means to understand individual work in a larger context. As Bower (2008) argues,

> Much of what we want and need in our schools... will not be gained by mandates. Renewal, sustained change, growth, and creativity emerge from within. We cannot create these qualities by fiat or by devising lists of goals and objectives. We can, however, help to create the conditions that allow for these qualities to emerge and grow naturally. (p. 110)

Dialogue is key to this process, while a safe and supportive environment encourages and values risk taking, creativity, and personal choice.

A main point here is that we foster emergence by indirect efforts: "we can only replicate the conditions that support innovation or reform, not the innovation or reform itself" (Bower, 2008, p. 123). In this view, leaders must force communities to face their problems and internal contradictions, and the situation in which problems are surfaced, disequilibrium is created, and all stakeholders are impelled to share responsibility for emergent outcomes is conceptualized as the "edge of chaos." At this point,

> If people make sense of an organization at the microlevel, then new members of the organization make sense of where the organization is in terms of value, vision, or focus through their relationships with others. This process of sense making reinforces the new culture and supports self-organization. (Bower, 2008, p. 129)

Pratt and Stringer (2008) point out the interchangeability of chaos theory and complexity theory, connecting both to an analysis of open systems, which are living systems that must change, adapt, and transform to stay alive. They also connect these overlapping approaches, and what I will refer to as a complex systems view, to a "postmodern view" (Doll, 1993), which embraces multiple perspectives, uses difference productively, eschews rigidity, and thrives on questioning. When our leadership is aligned with this view we allow others to influence our thinking, even when there is fundamental disagreement. Central ideas that emerge from this approach are that small changes can make a big difference, and systems are sensitive to initial conditions. In summary, "a leader in complex, dynamical interactions acts as a facilitator by asking questions to which the answer is not yet known and inviting different perspectives, all the while promoting ownership for everyone who has influence in effecting change" (Pratt & Stringer, 2008, p. 143).

Torre and Voyce (2008) refer to such systems leadership as a "relational model," where some kinds of resistance are indispensible in generating productive tension. Further, there is a need "to provide processes designed to encourage sincere consideration of new thinking and change and means for clear, honest, and meaningful communication and interaction among all constituents," because ultimately the process of decision making is at least as important as the content of the decision (p. 162). As Gomez (quoted in Torre & Voyce, 2008) argues, "Educational reform is essentially a cultural transformation process that requires organizational learning to occur: changing teachers is necessary, but not sufficient. Changing the organizational culture of the school or district is also necessary" (p. 213).

Another way to approach the relationship between complexity, leadership, and educational change is through the themes of perturbance and turbulence, closely related to the notion of disequilibrium, noted above (Nadler, 1993). According to Beabout (2012), disruption of the status quo is key to change, and educational change can be understood as a cycle of turbulence and perturbance, where turbulence is "the perception of potentially disruptive forces in an organization's environment or operating conditions" and perturbance is "a social process in which people respond to turbulence by considering organizational practice" (p. 17). He notes that in complex adaptive systems, planned turbulence is a problematic reform strategy, because there are bound to be unknown and complex consequences. Therefore, a "human-centered conception of change" is needed, and continuous learning by groups of educators is necessary for sustainable improvement (p. 18). "A school that can engage in perturbance requires specific cultural conditions that promote collaboration among teachers in solving the problems of practice," and this requires a culture of risk-taking, support, and collaborative learning (p. 20).

Another recurring theme in the literature on complexity leadership is the distinction between leadership and leaders. As Uhl-Bien, Marion, and McKelvey (2007) argue, "leadership theory has largely focused on leaders—the actions of individuals. It has not examined the dynamic, complex systems and processes that comprise *leadership*" (p. 299). For them and others, leadership in the context of complex adaptive systems is "an emergent, interactive dynamic that is productive of adaptive outcomes," and leaders are those who "act in ways that influence this dynamic and the outcomes" (p. 299). Understanding leadership in complex systems means understanding that "leadership is an emergent event, an outcome of relational interactions among agents" (Lichtenstein, Uhl-Bien, Marion, Seers, Orton, & Schreiber, 2006, p. 2). The complexity leadership approach "recognizes that leadership transcends the individual by being fundamentally a system phenomenon" (p. 3). This distinguishes complexity leadership from individual-centered theories of leadership, and "suggests a form of "distributed" leadership that does not lie in a person but rather in an interactive dynamic, within which any particular person will participate as leader or a follower at different times and for different purposes" (p. 3).

Lichtenstein et al. (2006) describe how complexity leadership dramatically expands the potential for creativity, influence, and positive change in an organization. More than simplistic notions of empowerment, this approach encourages all members to be leaders—to "own" their leadership within each interaction, potentially evoking a much broader array of responses from everyone in an organization. Complexity leadership theory provides a pathway for driving responsibility downward, sparking self-organization and innovation, and making the organizational system much more responsive and adaptive at the boundaries (p. 8).

In sum,

> A key contribution of a complexity leadership theory is that it provides an integrative theoretical framework for explaining interactive dynamics that have been acknowledged by a variety of emerging leadership theories, e.g., shared leadership, collective leadership, distributed leadership, relational leadership, adaptive leadership, and leadership as an emergent organizational meta-capability. (pp. 3–4)

Lichtenstein and Plowman (2009) contribute to this conversation by noting that while emergence occurs through the interaction of a group, and not through the behavior of a leader, there are certain leadership behaviors that foster emergence, namely: disrupting existing patterns of behavior (surfacing conflict and creating controversy), encouraging novelty (allowing experiments and fluctuations and encouraging rich interactions), creating collaboration through language and symbols, and stabilizing feedback. They emphasize that "the more that leaders and members embrace uncertainty, the more likely that a Dis-equilibrium state will be initiated and/or heightened in the system," and that "once a system is pushed to a Dis-equilibrium state, the more that its leaders and members surface conflict and create controversy, the more likely that the system will generate novel opportunities and solutions" (p. 6). The more leaders allow experiments and fluctuations, and/or encourage rich interactions, and/or support collective action, the more likely that "Amplifying Actions" will be present in the system. And "the more that leaders and members create correlation through language and through symbols, the more likely that Recombination/"Self-organization" will be initiated and expanded in the system" (p. 8). Interestingly, they also emphasize that it does not matter if leadership is top-down or bottom-up, stating "we simply do not yet know the right role and degree of influence that formal leaders do and perhaps should have in enacting a leadership of emergence" (p. 12).

This view can be seen to go against the overwhelming correlation between complexity leadership theory and notions of distributed leadership, and yet it can also be seen as a way of naming the tension inherent in all of these pluralistic, bottom-up views, namely that they all do indeed call for leadership actions from individuals in leadership roles to foster or encourage system emergence. We will return to this important point again when we look at principal leadership in our two case studies.

Goldstein, Hazy, and Lichtenstein (2010) understand "complexity and the nexus of leadership" as demanding the creation of "ecologies of innovation" supported by "experiments in novelty." They develop the notion of "generative leadership" in complex systems, in which the primary objective is to allow the emergence of innovative practices that enable organizations to be adaptable to the unprecedented challenges of the 21st century. In this view, interactions are the seeds of creative collaboration, and "continuous effort is needed to strengthen, widen, and *deepen* the capacity of the relationships, so as to transport resources and knowledge more quickly and effectively" (p. 31). In building ecologies of innovation, generative leadership calls for exploration and experimentation, where productive diversity is possible "only if there is freedom to depart from what is expected" (p. 29). Therefore, "leading a successful, thriving... and adaptive organization means *setting up conditions for positive interactions and interdependence*" (p. 42).

In the context of a complex system, the complexities of the environment must be met with equally complex organizing efforts, so that opportunities for system growth, or "opportunity tensions," can be catalysts for development (Goldstein, Hazy, & Lichtenstein, 2010, p. 53). In this view, an opportunity tension is felt as the perception that there is a high-potential opportunity or problem, and there is an internally generated pressure to organize in a way to capitalize on or deal with it. How an organization responds to an opportunity tension will be determined in part by the norms and attractors of that system. Underlying "standard operating procedures" in every organization is a core set of assumptions and values, and these lead to a "dominant logic" for how things are done; "the dominant logic is an *attractor* for employee behavior, managerial decisions, and organizational action" (p. 58). This behavior is driven by implicit rather than explicit forces that tend to be tacit and difficult to surface—and this is a major reason why desired changes can be so difficult to achieve.

While attractors draw individual decisions into patterns of expected behavior, "generative leadership encourages experiments in novelty in order to generate and share informational differences in ways that will move the organization's members from an old organizing attractor toward a new one" (Goldstein, Hazy, & Lichtenstein, 2010, p. 64). For an organization to change, the attractors must change, and leaders must see what is behind organized action. "Generative leadership therefore works on this meta-level; it *works on the level of attractors* as well as on the content level of day-to-day management" (p. 71). In practice, this means

> the job of generative leadership is to develop and nurture an intercohesive social network structure, in which silos of specialized expertise are broken down, and closely knit teams from prior projects are reconfigured in ways that challenge shared assumptions but retain hard-won trust and learning from experience. (p. 118)

In this view, leading for emergence entails four crucial steps: (1) create disequilibrium conditions, (2) amplify actions and experiments, (3) nurture new seeds of change, drawing attention to promising possibilities, and (4) stabilize feedback, institutionalize new structures, and increase feedback loops (pp. 185–186).

Self-organization, emergence, strange attractors, perturbance and turbulence, disequilibrium, and feedback loops are concepts that constitute the parameters of the complexity leadership field. In my review of the literature, in relation to my study of urban schools, two aspects of leadership in complex systems stand out as particularly important: (1) the distributed, shared, and relational implications of leadership, and (2) the ways in which such leadership relies on and presupposes a specific structure of perception and thought, which can be called complex systems thinking.

1 Distributed Leadership

Distributed leadership can be seen through at least two lenses: it can be understood normatively or descriptively (Hargreaves & Fink, 2006, pp. 110–111). On one hand, distributed leadership can be seen as an injunction to do something: we *should* distribute or share leadership in a more decentralized fashion. This would be taking "a normative position" on distributed leadership, where an increase in distribution and a concomitant decrease in centralization is seen as a good thing (Harris, 2008). There is some debate about the merits and results of increased distribution of power, decision-making, and school leadership, but on the whole the evidence appears to favor decentralization and leadership distribution (Hallinger, 2011; Harris, 2008; Heck & Hallinger, 2010; Wallace Foundation, 2011).

On the other hand, distributed leadership can be seen as a description of leadership, regardless of what form or structure it takes. In this view, the distributed nature of leadership is not so much an injunction to do something as it is a theoretical lens through which to view any system of social relations, e.g., the relationships in a school (Spillane, 2005). To see leadership from a distributed perspective is to put interpretive emphasis on the connections and relations between people, and not on the characteristics and behaviors of individuals in particular leadership roles; it is to acknowledge and highlight networks and interactions across a system as a basis for understanding power, leadership, influence, and change. This view of distributed leadership has much in common with the view of leadership as "influence" (Supovitz, 2008), as well as to the related fields of social network theory (Daly, 2010), systems thinking (Despres, 2008; Meadows, 2008) and complexity theory (Davis & Sumara, 2001, 2006). And of course, distributed leadership is not an either/or question, but rather there is a continuum of distributed leadership, from autocracy to anarchy, along which we can situate any organization (Hargreaves & Fink, 2006).

As should go without saying, these two approaches are not mutually exclusive. We can and should aspire to describe the relational nature of work and leadership in schools, and we can advocate for and work to foster approaches to leadership that align with and utilize complex understandings about how social systems operate, change, and transform. We should be concerned with the empirical results of different approaches, but as noted above, there is much evidence in favor of sharing leadership, and we should not lose sight of that broad consensus in the name of any particular counter-example (Egan, 2002). Ideally, we can understand and describe the relational character of school leadership, utilize research to inquire into the effects of certain responses to that relational reality, and develop and advocate for approaches that are both effective and cognizant of relational leadership.

The distribution of leadership in the context of complex systems also overlaps with insights from other related fields, such as network analysis and democratic organizations. As Daly (2010) elucidates, dense work-related relationships support the development and maintenance of innovative climates, and high levels of trust within dense networks enhance opportunities for teachers to learn together, share innovative ideas, and take risks on novel instructional practices: "the opportunity to learn and innovate comes from residing in densely connected, trusting, work-related networks" (Daly, 2010, p. 12). While some respond to increasing complexity with a "command and control model," it is better to involve stakeholders in establishing non-negotiable goals, then enable autonomy in how to reach them (Murgatroyd, 2010, p. 260). This follows the finding that the people closest to teaching and learning are the ones best suited to respond to complexity in schools (Stone, 2010).

Following this logic, one could also argue that democratic forms of governance are best suited to complex systems. As Cunningham (2014) maintains, "Democracy is cybernetic. Thus democracy is the best way to organize complex adaptive systems" (p. 111). A manager in a complex system is therefore wise "to focus on giving individuals and groups within the school autonomy, so they can manage the complexity they are facing with more flexibility or agility" (p. 74). Importantly, such wisdom may entail the need for personal transformation—a transformation that hinges on the development of the "complex systems view," discussed below.

2   The Complex Systems View

When individuals encounter moments of uncertainty, they frame their experience through an interpretive mental model in order to make sense of what has occurred (Kegan, 2003; Stone, 2012; Weick, 2009). The ways in which we think about and understand our experience are of crucial importance, for as many theorists and philosophers argue, "one of the greatest problems we face is how to adjust our way of thinking to meet the challenge of an increasingly complex, rapidly changing, unpredictable world" (Morin, 2001, p. 5). For Senge (1994),

> Complexity can easily undermine confidence and responsibility.... Systems thinking is the antidote to this sense of helplessness that many feel as we enter the 'age of interdependence.' Systems thinking is a discipline for seeing the 'structures' that underlie complex situations, and for discerning high from low leverage change. That is, by seeing wholes we learn how to foster health. To do so, systems thinking offers a language that begins by restructuring how we think. (p. 69)

Alhadeff-Jones (2010) agrees: "the development of a paradigm of complexity goes beyond its conceptual and formal dimensions. It requires the adoption of a specific state of mind and a way of being" (p. 35).

In *Images of Organization,* Morgan (2006) argues that "one of the most basic problems of modern management is that the mechanical way of thinking is so ingrained in our everyday conceptions of organization that it is often very difficult to organize in any other way" (p. 6). In order to manage in the midst of complexity, one must learn to navigate changing contexts, live with continuous transformation and emergent orders as a natural state of affairs, and use small changes to create large effects. "Managers functioning in the midst of this kind of complexity are part of the flux. They need mind-sets that allow them to facilitate the process and flow with the change, rather than try to pre-design and control in a more traditional way" (pp. 256–257). Morgan notes how the "theories of autopoiesis, chaos, and complexity... invite managers to think more systematically about this context and the evolving patterns to which they belong" (p. 263), and that "reality has a tendency to reveal itself in accordance with the perspectives through which it is engaged" (p. 339).

Reviewing the literature, it becomes clear that a recurring theme of leadership in complex systems is that it denotes a particular perspective or range of perspectives on leadership; such leadership requires what Opfer and Pedder (2001) call a "complex systems view." While principal leadership is important for teacher learning and growth, in the context of complex systems, where relations are always nested, the system as a whole is always learning, and system change is unpredictable yet highly patterned, professional development should be collaborative and collective, and the appropriate intensity of cognitive conflict and cognitive dissonance is the key to teacher learning. In this view, "complex systems thinking," or "complexivist thinking" is crucial, where a leader is not just seeing multiple perspectives and/or thinking analytically in systematic ways, but rather is seeing a unitary whole and thinking in "complex systems ways" (p. 380). One cannot enact these qualities and strategies without establishing a "complexity thinking perspective" (p. 396).

As the phrases "complexity thinking perspective"/"complexivist thinking"/"complex systems view" should make clear, what is being referred to is a *view*, or perspective, which perceives reality in particular ways, i.e., as nested, self-organizing, emergent systems. Therefore, it is important to note that complexity and systems theorists are making a twofold claim: that reality makes sense when seen from this view, because the view illuminates patterns and characteristics of the reality of systems (i.e., referring to the Lower Right quadrant in IT), and that this reality, while present, is only discerned, apprehended, perceived, and/or appreciated from a certain point of view: a complex systems view (or "complexivist thinking," or "complexity thinking," or "systems thinking") (i.e., referring to the Upper Left quadrant in IT). As Morin (2008) states in *On Complexity*,

> We need a kind of thinking that reconnects that which is disjointed and compartmentalized, that respects diversity as it recognizes unity, and tries to discern interdependencies. We need a radical thinking (which gets to the root of problems), a multidimensional thinking, and an organizational or systemic thinking [in order to understand complex contemporary problems]. (p. vii)

However it is described, systems and complexity thinkers make connections between the complexity of human and social systems, the increasing demands of leadership in those systems, and the modes of thinking, relating, and being that effective leaders manifest. In short, complex systems perspectives denote the presence of consciousness in context; they present multiple ways of describing the vantage point from which complexity makes sense, and from which one can lead in a "generative" and more conscious way (Davis, Sumara, & Iftody, 2010; Surie & Hazy, 2006).

The ability to perceive the changes taking place in schools from a complex systems perspective illuminates the role and character of leadership in particular ways; it changes the meaning of leadership, because interpretations are always framed by a particular context of meaning (Forman & Ross, 2013; Kegan, 2001; Wilber, 2000a, 2006d). In the context of complex systems, various mainstream approaches to leadership do not make sense. Top-down, linear models of simple cause-and-effect relationships fail to register as either compelling or accurate, and romantic notions of leaders as "heroes" fail to account for the fundamentally relational nature of leadership in systems, the role of networks in establishing the initial conditions and path-dependent responses of actors in systems (Atteberry & Bryk, 2010; Cole & Weinbaum, 2010), the way that complex systems "embody their histories," and the collective identity, agency, and learning that can and does take place in schools (Davis, Sumara, & D'Amour, 2012, p. 375). Complex systems thinking is helpful for disclosing the self-organized, emergent, nested, interdependent, ambiguously bounded and yet structure-determined aspects of experience, and it "helps us actually take up the work of trying to understand things while we are a part of the things we are trying to understand" (Davis & Sumara, 2006, p. 16).

Capra and Luisi (2014) argue that thinking about systems "means a shift of perception from material objects and structures to the nonmaterial processes and patterns of organization" (p. 79). Similarly, Senge (1994) states

> systems thinking is a discipline for seeing wholes. It is a framework for seeing interrelationships rather than things, for seeing patterns of change rather than static 'snapshots'.... And systems thinking is a sensibility— for the subtle interconnectedness that gives living systems their unique character. (pp. 68–69)

St. Julien (2005) makes a distinction between the complex analytic and the reductive analytic, where analytic refers to "our habits of inquiry, to the actual activity that we habitually engage in when we attempt to understand" (p. 104). Noting how "the particular way the world is understood is profoundly important in the way people live their lives," he describes "the complex analytic... [as] more a predisposition to a set of habitual perceptions and actions than a set of rules that must be followed," and emphasizes that "education is an area in which the value of a reductive analytic is quite limited" (p. 108). It is also important to remember that all systems are seen from a socially and politically situated perspective, so the definition and interpretation of systems always involves issues of power (Williams & Hummelbrunner, 2011).

Checkland (1999) asserts that systems thinking is "an epistemology which, when applied to human activity, is based upon four basic ideas: emergence, hierarchy, communication, and control as characteristics of systems. When applied to natural or designed systems, the crucial characteristic is the emergent properties of the whole" (p. 318). Arnold and Wade (2015) state that systems thinking is "a set of synergistic analytic skills used to improve the capability of identifying and understanding systems, predicting their behaviours, and devising modifications to them in order to produce desired effects. These skills work together as a system" (p. 675). In complex systems, feedback loops interact, and these interactions constitute the structure of the system and determine its behavior. But causation in systems is not wholly obvious and tends not to be direct (Pryor, 2008). Time may pass between an action and its result; such a delay may create a situation where one can easily underreact or overreact, because the full impact of the action cannot yet be assessed correctly.

Some researchers have found strong statistical correlations between systems thinking and project performance (Elm & Goldenson, 2012), and systems thinking has been described as an effective approach in the context of business management (Brown, 2012; Jolly, 2015; Wilson & Van Haperen, 2015). Wells and Keane (2008) demonstrate how Senge's (1994) "laws" of systems thinking may be implemented to develop professional learning communities. Pang and Pisapia (2012) found that for school leaders in Hong Kong, the principal's holistic leadership approach based on systems thinking was the strongest predictor of his or her effectiveness. In general, we can also say that systems thinking is enacted through a willingness to learn from others (integrating multiple sources of info), tolerance for uncertainty (a broad view of possible outcomes), and an ability to integrate a wide range of data (an expanded sense of choices).

Fullan (2005) argues "systems change on an ongoing basis only if you have enough leaders who are system thinkers," and conversely, that charismatic leaders are negatively associated with sustainability (p. 29; Collins, 2001). Ultimately, leaders must become

> *explicitly conscious* that they are engaged in widening people's experiences and identification beyond their normal bailiwicks... the key to changing systems is to produce greater numbers of "system thinkers." If more and more leaders become system thinkers, they will gravitate toward strategies that alter people's system-related experiences; that is, they will alter people's mental awareness of the system as a whole, thereby contributing to altering the system itself. (Fullan, 2005, p. 40)

Kegan and Lahey (2009, 2016) have spent decades conducting research at the intersection of psychological development and organizational leadership. In their work they highlight three predominant meaning systems utilized by adults: the socialized mind, the self-authoring mind, and the self-transforming mind. In general agreement with literally dozens of developmental frameworks that researchers have used to explain universal structures and systems of thinking (Wilber, 2000b), Kegan and Lahey (2016) connect this research to leadership and organizational life, using the following descriptors to flesh out how these perspectives manifest:

- The socialized mind: a team player, a follower; seeks direction; reliant; expresses self in relationships with people or beliefs; says what others want to hear.
- The self-authoring mind: agenda-driving; a leader who learns to lead; follows own compass; independent problem solver; follows personal authority.
- The self-transforming mind: a meta-leader; a leader who leads to learn; uses multiple frames and holds contradictions; problem-finder; interdependent; reflects on limits of own ideology.

They note that "people move through these evolutions at different speeds, and many of us, if not most of us, get stuck in our evolution and do not reach the most complex peaks" (p. 60). They also emphasize that

> experts in organizational culture, organizational behavior, or organizational change often address this subject with a sophisticated sense of how systems impact individual behavior [in the Right Hand quadrants], but with a naive sense of how powerful a factor is the level of mental complexity with which the individual views the culture [in the Left Hand quadrants]. (p. 63)

Reviewing large meta-analyses of research, they found that "the cumulative data supports the proposition that for those at a higher level of mental complexity, a complex world is more manageable" (p. 73). However, the data also suggests that

> the gap is large between what we now expect of people's mental complexity and what our minds are actually like. We expect most workers to be self-authoring, but most are not. We expect most leaders to be more complex than self-authoring, but few are. (p. 77)

Key to the process of facilitating mental growth and complexity is coming to acknowledge the existence of mental models—our own and others. According to Meadows (2008), reflecting on one's own mental models is crucial, because:

> the more you do that, in any form, the clearer your thinking will become, the faster you will admit your uncertainties and correct your mistakes, and the more flexible you will learn to be. Mental flexibility—the willingness to redraw boundaries, to notice that a system has shifted into a new mode, to see how to redesign structure—is a necessity when you live in a world of flexible systems. (p. 172)

This developmental work, which takes place at the intersection of developmental psychology, leadership theory, and systems theory, is a lynchpin for understanding the demands and implications of effective school leadership. I will return to this important area of inquiry, and the attempt to include it within the framework of Integral Theory, in Chapter 5. But first, let's take a close look at how these nuanced, complex, emergent, interdependent aspects and qualities of educational leadership and change manifested in two urban schools.

CHAPTER 3

Jeffrey Jackson School: Repetitive Reform and the Slow Process of Adaptive Change

> The world in which we immediately live, that in which we strive, succeed, and are defeated is preeminently a qualitative world.
> JOHN DEWEY

∴

Jeffrey Jackson School (JJS) is a pre-K through 5th grade school in a large city on the east coast of the USA. The year I began working with JJS the school enrolled just under 300 students: 88% Hispanic, 6% White, and 3% Black. In that year Harold Weatherbee was its third principal in three years, and his transition to JJS occurred on short notice. Yet according to faculty, his transition was smooth, and he was well received by teachers, parents, and students. As one teacher remarked,

> It's been kind of shocking for us [to have three principals in three years, but Weatherbee] has really fared well in the transition.... We always say to each other, "Thank goodness he's not one of those principals that comes in and is rough on the staff."

This statement captures the overall feeling shared by many teachers: there was apprehension about getting another new principal, but overall teachers and parents appreciated the way Weatherbee acclimated himself to the school.

Weatherbee had the impression that he was succeeding a principal with an authoritarian style of leadership, and he intended to shift the JJS leadership dynamics toward a more inclusive, decentralized structure. In his words:

> The principal before me was very effective at leading with a top-down, authoritarian style.... Although results were evident, the leadership method was not in full accordance to my mind-set, skill, and conviction.... During many initial conversations [teachers seemed to] need direction, [help with] decision making, and guidance. I often asked, "How was this

done last year?" The staff consistently echoed, "The principal made all decisions."

From Weatherbee's perspective, his leadership style is "a blend of tight and loose with high expectations," blending teacher accountability with a sense of comfort and ease while focused on student achievement. Overall, Weatherbee sought to shift school culture toward a more collaborative, less hierarchical structure where information flowed easily:

> I have worked a lot on changing the culture and the team atmosphere. One of the things that I learned is that climate and culture can be controlled to some extent.... One of the strands that I really took [from the School Leadership Academy] is that "we are crew, not passengers." That really resonated with me and it is a catalyst of a lot of our conversations here at the school. We have been doing a lot of team building and team communication and have been working on figuring out how to make different decisions as a team.

One central challenge facing JJS was meeting the needs of culturally and linguistically diverse students and their families. The first year of this study was marked by an influx of transfer students, many of whom had recently arrived from non-English-speaking countries. The ratio of Hispanic to non-Hispanic students had increased over the past decade, mirroring a demographic shift taking place in the neighborhoods surrounding the school. Weatherbee, who does not speak Spanish, estimated that over 80% of JJS students speak Spanish at home, many never speaking English prior to entering school.

Teachers at JJS, meanwhile, were anything but transient. Unlike many urban schools, JJS had few inexperienced teachers, and several had been teaching at JJS for more than 15 years. As one of the younger teachers said, "There are many teachers... who could have been my teachers when I was in school—they've been here 15, 20, 25, some almost 30 years." And because JJS is small (two classes per grade), teachers who have been there for many years felt that it was very much a family-like community: the culture of adults at the school is constituted by long-term relationships, a feeling of identity with the school, and a sense that children are known and cared for. One veteran teacher noted, "It is sort of a small school compared to the other schools in [our city]. There's more a sense of family.... [And] the culture of the school has been around for a while." The consensus among teachers is that there is a strong sense of faculty identity at JJS: principals come and go, superintendents come and go, and policies come and go, but the faculty culture at JJS has stood the test of time.

Although faculty liked Weatherbee, being third in line in a rapid succession of school leaders hindered his ability to transmit a sense of urgency to teachers, leaving him in a difficult position. A veteran teacher reflected on the impact of repetitive principal turnover:

> [W]e've had three different principals in the four years I've been here. And each principal has their own missions and their own ideas of what they want the school to become.... [F]or the staff, it's kind of hard to relate to each [principal], not knowing how long they're going to be here or how much time they should put into any new initiative if someone else is going to come in and change it.

This blend of contextual factors—perpetual principal turnover, shifting student demographics toward increased numbers of English language learners, and a strong, cohesive teacher culture—set a complicated stage for a new principal hoping to initiate change. Studies of education reform indicate that leadership effects do not become embedded in the culture of a school until leaders are accepted as insiders, which can take 4–10 years (Hargreaves & Fink, 2006, p. 78). And the established culture of a school has a significant impact on how and to what extent schools change: the "base state" of social relations before the start of reform often foreshadows the depth and success of any change effort (Atteberry & Bryk, 2010, p. 12).

JJS was not a "turnaround" school. Overall, the faculty thought that "things are going fine" and "nothing is really going that poorly." However, there were issues to face, some less subtle than others, and Weatherbee came into his position with a dedication to challenging the status quo and creating positive change. There was therefore a tension between continuity and change, between established faculty and a new principal. As an incoming principal, Weatherbee had to be mindful of and align (to some degree) with the culture of JJS—he had to maintain continuity in order to be accepted and welcomed. Instigating abrupt changes could inhibit faculty buy-in, and undermine his long-term capacity to cultivate positive change. A younger teacher highlighted an aspect of this dynamic, which could be seen as resistance to change, or as pressure for continuity, or as a need for a principal to pay dues when entering an established community:

> [As a new principal] you need to manage the personalities game before anything else happens.... To make [changes] happen there is a toll that has to be paid. Before you get on the good side of these people—who are very, very, very set in their ways—you have to sort of placate them first.

> No matter what your values are, if they're at all different from theirs, you have to placate them. You have to be harmless to them—you have to be harmless and helpful. If you are those two things only then will any of those teachers care at all what you think about anything.

Such advice offered a dire warning for a new school leader, especially one with Weatherbee's history.

JJS was the second school Weatherbee served as principal. He entered education after working in the financial industry. He did not teach long, and took a fast-track toward administration. His first experience as principal, at another urban public school, lasted two years, after which he was transferred to JJS. In Weatherbee's view, at his prior school he tried to implement changes that benefited students, but faculty complained to the district. Afterwards, he was transferred. In his view:

> I went to slowly change [school practices], but my slow was still too fast for them.... I wanted to undo some of the folks who had power [and]... weren't invested in the interest of children. When I started doing that, I got a lot of flak internally.... I felt like, "If I'm going to go down, then I'm going to go down doing what's right for the kids in my eyes and my convictions." I knew that would create a lot of heat. But it had to be done for the sake of the children.

Elaborating on his sense of being constrained by the status quo of district politics, Weatherbee continued, "The district has learned to accept mediocrity.... That was not written but was definitely said to me.... 'Don't upset the teachers too much.' Peace and tranquility are what the district wants."

At JJS Weatherbee cautiously dealt with teachers and acknowledged that he avoided pushing them:

> [C]oming to [JJS], I decided not to change the world; just move what I can.... I felt like, "Okay. I understand. Okay. Don't get teachers upset. I understand.... Try and nudge. Try and lead." ... So my mind-set is different. I'm not trying to change the world. I'm not trying to be the educational Martin Luther King. I take what I can get, and I go from there. And we try to chip away from the [achievement] gap, little by little.

Weatherbee's power and autonomy were further constrained by district policy. A teacher commented on this matter:

> It's pretty hard to [change curriculum and instruction] because a lot of [district guidelines are] already programmed for you.... [T]he math you teach is set. And you have a timetable to go by. And pretty much you try to stay on that. Everybody is giving a test at the same time in the city. For reading, you have the *Reading Street* curriculum. So you're pretty much following that.

District restrictions on hiring, firing, and retaining staff further complicated Weatherbee's leadership. In his first year, Weatherbee hired two Spanish-speaking teachers he wanted to retain—as JJS serves many Spanish-speakers—but due to union seniority guidelines, he could not. On another occasion, the district added a kindergarten classroom and required Weatherbee to interview only internal candidates. There were five applicants, none with kindergarten experience, yet he found "a ton of [qualified] external candidates" who he could not hire.

Both Weatherbee and JJS teachers experienced significant professional turbulence, having to cope with substantial principal turnover (from the faculty perspective) and an imposed job transfer (from Weatherbee's point of view). Driven by his SLA experience, Weatherbee sought to perturb his school system, to disrupt the routine. Teachers, who had already endured the turbulence of principal turnover, were more inclined to preserve the status quo. Although there was reason to believe that some teachers at JJS would resist change, Weatherbee entered his role at JJS in the midst of pressure for reform and improvement, and with a desire to create positive change wherever he works. He did not come to the school to placate teachers and continue the status quo of JJS, whatever it was.

1 Culture, Climate, and Collaboration

Harold Weatherbee came into his first year at Jeffrey Jackson School with a fairly clear conception of how he wanted to approach this new opportunity. The SLA's emphasis on school culture, team building, cultural competency, and distributed leadership resonated with Weatherbee, and were reinforced through an ongoing dialogue with his coach (whose support was provided as part of the SLA program). When asked about the SLA and its influence on him, Weatherbee said that the coursework was "wonderful," and that its theme of teamwork, captured in the idea of being a "crew" as opposed to merely passengers, recurred often in interviews with Weatherbee and his faculty.

A primary means through which the SLA aimed to support Fellows in building their leadership skills was through developing and implementing a "Leadership Growth Project" (LGP). Weatherbee's LGP focused on cultivating a sense of teamwork, or "distributed leadership." As he explained:

> I want teachers to feel that they have voice.... I want them to say that this has been a collaborative experience.... [Ultimately,] the objective goes back to this school being a collaborative and well-organized team.

To be clear, for Weatherbee the aim was not collaboration for the sake of collaboration: "The ultimate end result is that I want students to learn.... We need to get our proficiency levels up." He continued, "One of our theories is that if we increase the level of communication and get parent buy-in, and if we as a team get deeper in our work, we will get a higher proficiency rate."

Weatherbee's primary intention in his first year was to begin creating a culture of shared responsibility and teamwork in service of improving student learning outcomes. Success was envisioned as a collective goal, attainable only through collective action and coordination between administration, faculty, staff, and parents. For while Weatherbee believed that "all of the students need to be at grade level by the end of the year," he also insisted that "my Growth Project will be reflective of the growth that teachers and parents are making [together]." In his view, the success of his LGP, and ultimately the success of the school, was not just up to him, or to teachers, but to the whole school community.

1.1   *Communication: The Key to Cultural Change*

Weatherbee conceived of communication as the primary lever to enact cultural and educational change at JJS. Elaborating on his LGP, he explained:

> The objective goes back to this school being a collaborative and well-organized team. What is driving us is that we need a communication tool for the rest of the school. So I am trying to make sure that if we all have a discussion [that links to our work as a school]... that it also goes through the grade level team. As simple as it sounds, it is difficult to do in terms of organization. That is a driver [for creating a collaborative team].

The communication tool he refers to came to be known as the "communication cycle": every major topic of discussion and decision-making that emerged in a meeting at JJS was addressed explicitly in other meetings of other members so that the different teams, committees, councils, and grade levels were all aware of, sharing, and communicating about the same issues with the same information. In particular, the communication cycle Weatherbee put in place served to bring information and decisions from the school's Instructional Leadership Team (ILT) to every grade level team, and vice-versa. He had meetings with grade level teams every week and met with the ILT roughly once a month. One teacher described the process:

> ILT is a group of 6 teachers, [one] from each grade level, and we meet and talk about the issues at the school, things that need to be changed, important changes that might be happening or structures that need to be set.... All of the information from that meeting is sent out to the entire school within a week, and that's someone's role in the meetings, to take notes and send the information out to everyone. Then we come back for the next meeting and bring our results and feedback from our peers and we take it from there and continue on with the next set of agenda items.... We have been responsible in getting that information out and then also, during grade level meetings once a week, we do talk about the agenda items from that meeting as well.

In addition to closing the communication gap between the ILT and grade level teams, Weatherbee sought to include parents' perspectives in the communication cycle. For instance, he used surveys to get feedback from faculty and parents, a strategy he learned about and was encouraged to enact by a SLA colleague. He said the information he received through the surveys conducted by the SLA "was eye opening for me, [and] it also gave the staff something [to think about]." And beyond the feedback surveys offered, the very process of administering surveys communicated to faculty and parents that he was listening and cared about their perspectives. Such outreach represented one way Weatherbee established his relationship to the community, creating a foundation for transparent communication.

Including parents as informed and active members of the JJS community was central to Weatherbee's overarching goals, as he sensed "a disconnect between what parents say effective communication is and what the staff is willing to do initially." He talked at length about how he improved communication with the parent community by using surveys and utilizing technology:

> We are using parent surveys to help us understand the children more.... Then we realized that everything we did in the agenda book is in English when 80–90% of our families are Latino and Spanish-speaking. So they can't read it. It made us take a step back and to look at how we are

> communicating. What is communication? We started sending letters home in Spanish telling the parents to look at their kids' agenda book as a main source of communication.... The level of response increased drastically based on that letter.... Using that data to inform how we perceive and how we approach things has increased the level of communication [with parents].

The use of surveys, responsiveness to feedback, and the attempt to close gaps in the school's communication cycle all worked to create a culture of improved communication at JJS. Another manifestation of this cultural shift was the use of the notion of "crew" as a consistent theme, ideal, and mantra. According to teachers, Weatherbee persistently verbalized this notion of team membership:

> When he first came to the school, at one of our first professional development meetings, he did mention the School Leadership Academy that he went to and he took a quote from there that he always refers to: "We are crew, not passengers." ... So that's kind of been our mission among the staff and he refers to that often. "We're crew, not passengers." He asked everyone what we thought that meant and how we can implement that as part of our mission as a school.... I'll overhear if someone is complaining about something or "She's doing this, and I'm not doing this," and he'll say, "Remember, we're crew, not passengers." So I think that's just his way of reminding everybody we all have to pitch in even if it's not necessarily in our job description but if it's to benefit the school and the students then we all need to do the best we can to pitch in and do what we can.

Beyond using this language, many faculty testified to how Weatherbee operationalized this ideal—how he walked the walk. It is a truism that actions speak louder than words, and it was through his behavior that Weatherbee was perhaps most effective as a communicator. One way he communicated the message of teamwork was in his willingness to step into many different roles, some of which other principals may not be willing to embrace. Another way he showed his commitment to the "crew" was by making himself available to teachers. One teacher brought both of these characteristics together when she described the work she had seen from him this year:

> He definitely tries to be supportive. I've worked with a lot of principals, and a lot of principals have a closed-door policy.... With him it definitely is [an open door] and sometimes I deal with him and just say, "You know, you make yourself too available sometimes." But he'll step into any role

he needs to. For instance, he's been a lunch mother.... If a lunch mother is absent and we need it, he'll go and cover. He's been a paraprofessional. He's been a classroom teacher. He'll just jump into any role that he needs to, and that's the one thing I really look up to, and look for because I've never really seen a principal do that. They always kind of push it to somebody else but he's out there doing recess duty, he's there being a lunch mother serving food. I think that's really important for a leader because, again, it just goes back to, "We are crew, not passengers," and we have to jump in when needed. So he's setting an example of that when he does those things.

In addition to maintaining the theme of teamwork throughout the year, in speech and in practice, Weatherbee allowed faculty to adjust to new initiatives and structures in ways that felt relevant and meaningful to them. He was responsive and flexible. For instance, one of the younger teachers described how the school's overall vision had shifted over the course of the year from a school-wide lens to a focus on productive grade level teams:

I think that he was pushing the whole team thing. "Team, team, team, we are a team," from the beginning of the year.... And as the year has gone on we've sort of separated into our... grade level teams and so we work as grade levels more than anything else. I think that he went from pushing "We are a school team," to "You are a grade level team," because at the end of the day, as much as he would like to manage the group thing in the school, it's more important that the second grade teachers can work with other second grade teachers. The grade level team meetings are where the work gets done.

The data from teachers suggests that the aim of creating a culture of teamwork and collective identity remained consistent while being enacted in different ways, and that communication, responsiveness, and flexibility were crucial to that process. Weatherbee's effort to bring faculty on-board with his vision and style of leadership was an attempt to establish "cultural universals" at the school—to make one out of many and get everyone on the same page (Sergiovanni, 2005, p. 121). As Davis and Sumara (2006) argue, it is important to understand "the process by which a collection of *I's* becomes a collective of *we*—that is, the transition from a disconnected to a connected structure around a matter of shared concern" (p. 76). In the name of establishing "a collective of we," building trust, and garnering faculty buy in, Weatherbee worked to be flexible and responsive, as opposed to hard-lined and non-negotiable, and adjusted his expectations and plans in several small but not insignificant ways. As a result, this flexibility, which supported the effort to generate trust and shared identity, also produced a form of conservatism in Weatherbee's leadership, because flexibility can easily slide into casual acceptance of the status quo. For example, the move from stressing whole school teamwork to grade level teamwork could be seen as a responsive adaptation or as settling for less in the face of staff resistance. This theme will emerge more fully below.

2   Distributed Leadership: Consistency and Structured Collaboration

For Weatherbee, a focus on school culture and climate meant systems, structures, and norms for transparent communication had to be in place. In his view, he "worked hard to build [a] communication cycle through the whole school.... [A]t the same time, it forces me to not be an authoritarian type of leader. It is a collaborative effort." Weatherbee therefore created new structures of communication—all of which can be understood as networks.

Describing the work of the ILT, one teacher remarked that the committee was a place where "[e]verybody has roles and responsibilities. He is not the facilitator every time... [but] he ensures that... everybody gets to speak." Another teacher shared her view of how Weatherbee supported buy-in and distributed leadership through the ILT:

> Responsibility is delegated in many aspects in the school.... Everybody got to sign up for roles at the beginning of the year for certain school teams, like the Math Leadership Team and the ILT.... We were able to make the decision among our peers [about] who chose what but he made it known that he wanted one person from each grade level on these teams.... At our meetings for the ILT, as far as who leads the meetings, we all got to decide. We set a schedule, we made the decisions about who was going to be leading.... [But] if things got off-track or we got off-track with that, he has taken the role of being responsible.... He steps up when he needs to.

This teacher went on to explain how including teachers in leadership roles involved a balancing act for Weatherbee, and how he was both a leader and a facilitator of more egalitarian structures and roles:

> I absolutely think he gives opportunities for leadership within the school, especially within those kinds of meetings. [Yet at the same time] he has no problem, from what I can see, taking ownership and running the

meetings.... I like it like this because I've been in other schools where it's been different, where the principal runs it and it's [not as good].... [At JJS], I think everyone has a piece of ownership in that meeting and something to be responsible for, and I think it keeps everyone on task.... He allows everyone to have their piece and have their say.... I have appreciated that. It makes you feel valued and that's something that a school needs and I think it is a positive thing.

Weatherbee's "cycle of communication" involved a three-tiered network: an Instructional Leadership Team (ILT) served as the primary faculty decision-making body. The School Site Council (SSC) included parents and teachers and addressed non-instructional, school-wide issues, such as community events and fundraising. And Weatherbee met with each Grade Level Team weekly. In creating these groups Weatherbee aimed to generate productive conversations and ensure that decisions emerging from these networks were embraced school-wide.

However, given his tenuous relationship with faculty, his negative past experience in the district, and his strong desire to ensure positive outcomes, Weatherbee sought to control much of the teamwork that he championed. While speaking profusely and repetitively about being crew and teachers having a voice, and while trying to promote collaboration within teams, he maintained a high degree of control while managing the process of establishing a positive, results-oriented school culture, and put himself at the center of the JJS network.

Ultimately, the creation of a culture of collaboration cannot be measured in the principal's actions or in teachers re-framing work they are required to do (e.g., conduct grade level meetings). Weatherbee's notion of "crew" implied ongoing, consistent, and unforced contributions and leadership from multiple crew members—what the SLA understood as distributed leadership (Hallinger, 2011; Harris, 2008; Heck & Hallinger, 2010). Many teachers gave examples and offered testimony to how they were encouraged to take on leadership roles and contribute to activities and the overall progress of the school. They spoke about what they had done and how Weatherbee encouraged and supported their efforts. But a closer look at how these interconnected teams functioned provides some insight into how Weatherbee encouraged and facilitated teacher involvement and leadership, and what the limits of this approach were.

As Figure 2 portrays, the JJS network was highly centralized, with Weatherbee acting as the driving force of every team. While teachers described the ILT as "faculty-led," and emphasized the inclusive, flexible nature of Weatherbee's attempt to delegate responsibility and involve faculty in processes and decision-making at the school, Weatherbee established group norms, set the agenda, and facilitated each of the six ILT meetings I observed; only when he was absent did a teacher chair a meeting. A similar dynamic pervaded Grade Level Teams and the SSC: Weatherbee directed what happened, and others seemed minimally invested. And even if other teachers took the lead in meetings that I did not observe, the model of distributed leadership that Weatherbee enacted at JJS was definitely more aligned with what Hargreaves and Fink (2006) call "guided distribution," as opposed to "emergent distribution"—the impetus for teachers taking on any form of leadership was being explicitly delegated and requested by Weatherbee. In my time at JJS I did not perceive faculty leadership emerging organically, undetermined by Weatherbee.

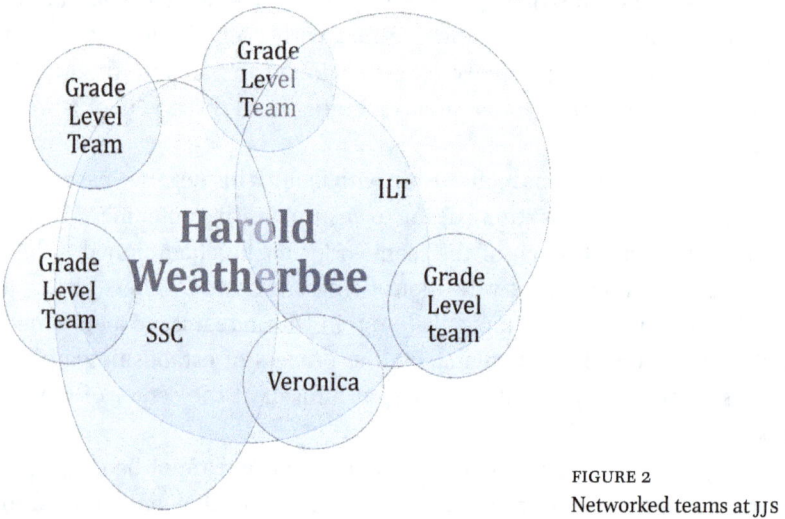

FIGURE 2
Networked teams at JJS

As Hargreaves and Fink argue, emergent and assertive patterns of distribution tend to develop at innovative schools with selective cultures, while more traditional schools tend to need more careful guidance at first (p. 137). My experience at JJS supports the justification of "guided distribution" preceding "emergent distribution" (if the latter is ever achieved), and the designation of JJS as a traditional school feels fair, given the approach to pedagogy (discussed below). Overall, teachers responded positively in interviews to Weatherbee's approach to sharing leadership. But a significant gap remained between the version of distributed leadership that Weatherbee was exposed to by the SLA and the manifestation of distributed leadership at JJS during the period of this study.

One way to understand the context of this tension is as an element of repetitive change syndrome: school cultures that experience perpetual leadership succession and/or reform agendas are less likely to have the necessary trust to establish decentralized networks of power and influence (Hargreaves & Fink, 2006). Decentralization is an "adaptive change" because it requires individuals to alter their ways of thinking and acting, as opposed to merely applying knowledge they already have (Heifetz, 1994; Heifetz & Linsky, 2002), and adaptive change requires relational trust (Daly & Chrispeels, 2008). This contextual understanding of why the initial conditions of Weatherbee's leadership project at JJS did not foster a more emergent or decentralized structure of decision-making allows us to see why the leadership capacity of the school was not more developed. As Lambert (2009) defines it, leadership capacity is "broad-based, skillful participation in the work of leadership," and the teachers at JJS attest to their involvement in leadership roles (p. 122). But similarly to Hargreaves and Fink, Lambert understands leadership capacity to emerge sequentially—from an Instructive phase to a Transitional phase to a High Capacity phase—and at the time of this study JJS appeared to be just initiating an Instructive phase of shared leadership capacity (p. 125).

All of the committees at JJS—the ILT, Grade Level Teams, the School Site Council, and the Parents Council, to name the four major decision making groups—depend on Weatherbee to lead them. As Daly (2010) assures us, "formal structures matter and thus need to be thoughtfully crafted and enacted in a way that supports opportunities for interaction that enhances the social capital of educators to do the work of change" (pp. 261–262). At JJS, the intention was inclusive and Weatherbee's leadership style was appreciated and supportive, but the structures were not yet in place to enable a culture of collective inquiry and emergent, high capacity leadership. The intention was to enact adaptive change, and the demands of Weatherbee's LGP required an adaptive change, but was his approach to distributed leadership evocative of adaptive change, or was it another example of applying a "technical" solution to an adaptive demand (Heifetz & Linsky, 2002)? My two years at JJS led me to believe that it was much more the latter.

2.1 Festivals and Fundraisers: Taking on Big Projects Together

Another avenue for understanding the distribution of leadership at JJS is through the way that Weatherbee was able to successfully put together major projects and initiatives during his first year. Five major school-wide projects warrant mention: a Fall Festival social gathering; the creation of school uniforms and a new school crest; an initiative to increase parent involvement in a district-led Parent University; a long-term project to plant trees and improve the school campus; and a 5K family run/walk fundraising event. While Weatherbee solicited support to get all faculty on board as a team, and many contributed to various projects and took on responsibilities in the school, he relied especially on two team members to take on administrative and leadership duties for school-wide projects: Veronica, an early-childhood paraprofessional, and Mandy, an intern who was doing her practicum for the principalship at JJS. Mandy is fluent in Spanish, and helped translate communications sent to parents. Veronica assumed many responsibilities in addition to her classroom work, especially with school-wide projects.

Veronica's work outside the classroom was crucial to the success of many developments at JJS. Lacking a vice principal to consult, Weatherbee benefited from having not only a part-time administrative intern to rely on but also (and especially) a faculty member fully attuned to the administrative aspects of running a school, someone willing to wear many hats to get things done. One veteran teacher described Veronica's role as being a big change in itself at the school and described the significance of her work, especially with broader, school-wide projects:

> That's a big change [the role of Veronica in the school]. She is doing a ton of stuff. Most of the stuff that she's doing is extremely valuable. I don't even know how she's doing it.... She's definitely done a lot as far as promoting the school's crest and the branding. She has done a huge amount towards that: meeting with people, emailing people, making phone calls. She's done a lot with the 5K and any of our fundraisers—she's pretty much responsible for raffle tickets, cover letters, distributions, collections of proceeds, [among other things].

In her interview, Veronica described the evolution of her role at JJS and the work this involved:

> This year... in addition to [my work in the classroom], I have taken on the role of multiple other things.... I started writing the monthly newsletter. I am a school site council member.... I've planned field trips, [and] our school's parent-university involvement with the [district] Parent University. I design, and order, and distribute all the school uniforms and I run all the fundraising efforts. So, [for example,] the Fall Festival. We've done three or four raffles throughout the year. We did a school-wide movie night. One of our families were victims of a fire back in April, so I headed a fundraising effort for them, getting cash and donations for them. And then most recently the [JJ5K] Fun Run.... Basically now we're at the point where any new initiatives, or projects, or fundraising, or anything that involves the whole school climate, I'm involved in. [Weatherbee and I] hash out the details together and brainstorm together to try to make

it happen.... It's definitely a lot more than I had taken on last year. We started a lot of new stuff this year. It's been challenging, but rewarding at the same time, and he's done a great job at supporting me, and my idea is that I've done vice versa.

As one example, a monumental effort was undertaken to enable parents to go to Parent University, a parent education event sponsored by the school district. Weatherbee and Veronica, along with Mandy and a few teachers, offered free childcare on the Saturday of the event, personally registered parents on school computers during open hours for three weeks leading up to the event, translated all district materials and JJS communications, got a bus to drive parents all together to the event, and gave parents JJS t-shirts that said "parent" on them. Their efforts to put all the pieces together to make this parent event happen speak to their commitment to develop the JJS community. According to Veronica, "that was a huge, huge thing for us. The parents were delighted... [and] we had the second highest [turnout] of any school in the district [27 parents]. That was a huge milestone for us."

For Weatherbee, all of these various initiatives accorded with his overall intention to be a responsive crew leader uniting as many constituencies as possible in the process of school change, especially parents. And his efforts in the process of enacting these initiatives were not lost on teachers or parents. Speaking about the campus improvement project, which involved Weatherbee helping to plant trees, one veteran teacher commented:

> Most principals won't go outside and dig a big hole [but that is what Weatherbee did].... For him to use his muscles to dig a big hole, not just one, but three, and to move gigantic trees into holes and fill them in with dirt with the kids witnessing him working—it wasn't like [he said,] "I'll do it for a little bit." He was actually working in the schoolyard, making sure that the trees were properly placed in the holes.... That's community service. And he is showing us that you are more than being a leader in a building. It's like, "I can help too" in a community.

In many ways, these initiatives embody the way that leadership is distributed at JJS. Weatherbee was deeply involved—he didn't just swoop in at the end for a photo opportunity to plant trees. However, given the demands of the principalship, he was not able to spearhead these major projects by himself; he was too consumed by his daily demands. So in the absence of formal administrative support, and with teachers expecting the administration to be in charge, Veronica stepped forward to lead the project and coordinate other contributors, thus playing a crucial role in turning their ideas into reality. Yet as impressive as it was for a paraprofessional to step into an administrative role successfully, the degree to which Weatherbee and Veronica became a de facto two-person administrative team left some faculty feeling left out, and Veronica's ability to take on so much work let other teachers off the hook to meet the collective demands of such ventures.

It does not seem that anything close to what this team accomplished could have happened had these two leaders—one formal, one informal—not taken the definitive lead. And without the free services of a one-year Spanish speaking intern, much of their parent outreach would have either not happened, not been as effective, or taken much more time and energy from an already over-extended duo. The desire to make things happen—big, culture-building initiatives—led to some short-cuts of sorts. While Weatherbee was attempting to develop teamwork, establish buy-in, and create a new and more collectivist culture at JJS, he simultaneously pushed forward with many decisions and projects that did not come from well-distributed decision making and perhaps reinforced the impression among some faculty that a traditional hierarchy was in place; or worse, that the new principal was playing favorites and allowing some teachers (i.e., Veronica) to wield unearned power.

From Veronica's point of view, it is clear that

> of course there's the handful that don't agree with what we're doing, or there's always going to be pushback from some people—but I think the majority are starting to trust in him, and also the school, and just starting to believe we're really doing what's best for the families and the students.

However, this hopeful, positive, and productive attitude failed to register how Weatherbee and Veronica had enacted change in ways that could hinder the ongoing process of establishing greater buy-in and participation from a wider group of stakeholders at the school. It was an example of thinking that "the ends justify the means," which is not what a conscious approach to complexity would look like, according to Schein (2004):

> In the face of greater complexity, the leader's dependence on others to generate solutions will increase, and we have overwhelming evidence that new solutions are more likely to be adopted if the members of the organization have been involved in the learning process. The *process* of learning must ultimately be made part of the culture, not just the solution to any given problem. (p. 395, emphasis in original)

The significant expenditure of time and energy on these various projects and changes—none of which had any direct impact on teaching or learning—also held significant implications for the impact (or lack thereof) that Weatherbee was able to enact as an instructional leader.

3   Instructional Leadership: Principal Presence in the Classroom

Instructional leadership was a key component of the vision put forward by the School Leadership Academy and was a major part of Weatherbee's work at JJS. To understand how Weatherbee's approach to change and continuity played out in the realm of instructional leadership I describe his efforts to conduct classroom observations, provide teacher support, and increase teacher expectations for students.

To be effective urban school leaders, principals need to be informed about and active in classrooms—they need to be instructional leaders (Bambrick-Santoyo, 2012; Robinson, Lloyd, & Rowe, 2008). Much of that role involves spending time in classrooms. In general, teachers perform better and develop better relationships with administrators when principals observe their instruction frequently (Marshall, 2005), and classroom visits improve both the quality of and satisfaction with teaching (Rowan, 1990). Being present in classrooms was a big part of Weatherbee's role at JJS. His presence was a positive and mostly welcomed shift for faculty. Many teachers commented on his consistent and active role in classrooms. Some acknowledged that he had a positive impact on their teaching practice and that they saw a positive response from students:

> He is a go-getter. He... is very animated in terms of talking to the staff and talking to the kids. He relates very well with the students.... He comes around unexpectedly, which is good.... I would have to say... I do a little bit more in terms of [preparation]... this year.

Another teacher talked about how she thought Weatherbee spent time in classrooms, and noted what a priority it was for him:

> I've never seen a principal in classrooms as much as he is. He spends entire days, at least one day a week, if he has time two days a week, just in classrooms for entire days, just jumping from classroom to classroom with his notebook taking notes.

A veteran teacher who noted that Weatherbee visited her "more than the average principal" went on to say that Weatherbee also used observations as an opportunity to understand what each classroom needed, and he followed up his visits not only with verbal or written feedback but with tangible resources and assistance, based on the needs he perceived from his time in the classroom.

Overall, feedback from teachers about Weatherbee's leadership presence in the classroom was exceedingly positive. But when asked about perceptions of the staff overall, there was more of a mixed response; some teachers felt that *other* teachers may not like having to be "on their toes" quite so much. Perhaps they did not want to admit that they were themselves uncomfortable with the increased transparency of their teaching; or perhaps they assumed that others are less comfortable than they really are. Either way, with increased accountability comes increased pressure, and not every teacher enjoys pressure, whether or not it benefits them and their students. When asked about the general teacher reaction to increased accountability, one teacher said:

> It's probably 50/50. Some people may look at it as [undesirable, but] I look at it as a great thing. I think people need to step up their game a little bit and always be on their A game, whether or not the principal is coming in.... [But] I think other people may think of it as a hindrance. The people who aren't always on their toes and don't always have lesson plans—it may be a hindrance to those people.

The need for principal presence, and making teaching public, is widely agreed upon, in part because "when teaching and learning become public, the loosely coupled system becomes more tightly coupled," and both accountability and transparency are therefore increased (Bower, 2008, p. 129). Yet this increase in transparency and accountability in the classroom can be seen as a source of disequilibrium for faculty—a disruption which they can either utilize for their professional development or not. It is an "opportunity tension" or "disequilibrium condition," in that it is both a chance to change by engaging in a process of professional growth and a potential source of discomfort (Goldstein, Hazy, & Lichtenstein, 2010, p. 83). Yet it is not clear to what extent Weatherbee pushed his faculty to change their classroom practice; as with the push for distributed leadership, it appears that the disequilibrium was not very intense. His presence in the classroom was a change in itself, and a first step toward instructional leadership, but by no means a sufficient one.

The issue of teacher accountability is linked to student expectations: the primary purpose of classroom observations, instructional feedback, and increased accountability is to improve teaching and learning. The push to improve teaching and learning coincides with a push to increase the expectations and standards for students. For Weatherbee, communicating and fostering high expectations for students and teachers was a central aspect of instructional leadership.

3.1 High Expectations and Critical Thinking: Raising the Bar and Closing the Gap

The idea that students, particularly urban students, should be held to consistently high expectations has become a truism in the new orthodoxy of education reform in the USA. In order to ensure ongoing improvement and close the achievement gap, collective responsibility and shared faculty beliefs are crucial (Penuel, Frank, & Krause, 2010, p. 176). At JJS, pressure for raised expectations could be seen as one aspect of the tension between change and continuity: increasing student expectations was at the center of Weatherbee's agenda, yet the effort to increase concomitant teacher expectations could instigate resistance, which may not foster improved teaching and learning. Most faculty appreciated that Weatherbee could generally strike a balance between pressure and support, and between professional accountability and casual conversation, while being grounded in humor and light-hearted interactions with teachers and students. This balance extended into his approach to high expectations: Weatherbee pushed faculty to increase their standards and expectations—of themselves as well as their students—yet tried to avoid being over-bearing.

Teachers did perceive Weatherbee trying to raise standards, including an emphasis on test score gains. A younger teacher conveyed the overall sense for how Weatherbee shifted student expectations at JJS:

> I think that the biggest sort of change that I feel happening is the idea that everyone can do well, and I think... that he's pushing harder on that idea: that everyone can do well, and that everyone can do better. All the students can do better but we as teachers can do better as well. It seems like he's pushing towards that a bit more and he's really into the whole team thing. I feel like that's maybe a shift from last year.

When asked to unpack what it meant to do better, this teacher continued:

> I think that it's a mix of proficiency as measured by all the assessments that we're burdened with, but in addition to that, [the aim is to stimulate]

kids who can think critically. We understand that while the assessments are a necessary evil and the kids need to do well on them, that thinking critically is what's going to help them everywhere—on those tests [and] on every test they're ever going to take. If kids can't think and they pass the test, that would be a failure.... [But] if the teachers don't want to open up their minds to possibilities, I think it's very hard to transfer [critical thinking] to the kids if it doesn't exist in the teachers first. So maybe he's trying to build [a culture of critical thinking] because those things seem important to him.

Overall, the message around expectations and student learning at JJS consistently aligned with the orthodox message of ever-increasing and ever-improving standards, but it was done with a gentle, human touch, and balanced by an emphasis on critical thinking. Weatherbee's overall message was: all children can succeed, teachers should expect and strive for 100% proficiency, and students need to work hard and focus on academic success to make up for what may be (in many cases at least) an academic disadvantage (especially for students learning English-as-a-second-language). Critical thinking was prized as a meaningful aspiration, but the standardized tests that the students are "burdened" with remain the primary means the school used to assess thinking and learning; little if anything was done to assess or encourage critical thinking outside of the state mandated standardized assessments, so it remained unclear what critical thinking meant to Weatherbee or to teachers in that context.

However, the main tension regarding student expectations at JJS resided between Weatherbee's push to achieve academic success for every student and teachers' more tempered aspirations and beliefs. According to some teachers, most of their colleagues *did not* embrace the notion that all students can succeed. According to one teacher, there was "almost unanimous disagreement with that point"—almost all teachers rejected the belief that literally all students can "succeed" (where "succeed" means testing as proficient on standardized tests). This teacher went on to clarify:

> The question is: What is success? ... The general consensus at the school is that everyone can do a little better, but there are some kids who are just never going to be proficient and that's how it is and we have to live with that.

This is a difficult issue, especially for urban schools whose students perform below suburban students and national averages on standardized tests. It is particularly thorny for principals like Weatherbee, sandwiched between the oppositional attitudes of classroom teachers, stakeholders outside the classroom—lawmakers, administrators, the media, and ultimately the public at-large, who demand perpetual improvement in the name of a hoped-for equality of educational outcomes—and his own ethical imperatives for educational outcomes. Weatherbee tried to transcend the reductionist tendencies of test-score accountability and potential blame by focusing on skills like critical thinking, hard work, and study habits. But he kept student progress on state tests front and center in his thinking, as this is how the district administrators ultimately evaluated his performance. Potentially, his orientation toward reform—to focus on school culture and create a collegial, collaborative team—could be undermined by inadequate test scores, even if a decrease in scores resulted from an influx of immigrant students, or was the result of a predictable "implementation dip" (Fullan, 2007).

One teacher spelled out the demands being placed on Weatherbee from a teacher's point of view, and described how Weatherbee had been especially supportive of and sensitive to the pressure on teachers to improve:

> I think that in a situation when you say to a teacher, "I want all of your kids to be proficient," you need to make sure the sentence before that and the sentence after that is, "And I'll do everything I can to help you get there." I think in that situation it puts the ownership on the teachers in a... subtle way. If you're saying, "I want you to do this, I'll help you as much as I can," as a teacher you have to think. You have to say, "Okay, how can he help me do this?" ... Everything he says about doing more is always bracketed with support and some kind of praise. "Things are going great, I'd like them to go better. 70% proficiency is great. You're doing a great job. You're doing everything you can for these kids, but I'd like it to be 100%. I'll do anything I can to help you get there because the kids come first."

In addition to being verbally and emotionally supportive, another way teachers described Weatherbee's support was through his resourcefulness—a trait mentioned by several teachers when describing him. Teachers felt that Weatherbee persistently tried to get them what they needed to be successful, with an aim toward increased learning and performance. One veteran teacher noted how Weatherbee was willing to provide extra help and support staff for small groups of children to be pulled out of class for extra help—both those who are behind and those who are ahead—while another teacher noted how such resourcefulness extended to both academic and school-wide needs. Teachers also commented on how Weatherbee was not only a provider of resources, but also a respectful colleague who listened and responded to teacher expertise:

He's really come to us... and he seems to value our input as to what happens.... That has been a really positive thing.... [And] after every meeting we have he always asks, "Is there any way I can support you?"

However, while many teachers talked positively about what Weatherbee had done to support them, both verbally/emotionally and by being present in the classroom, the embedded culture at JJS did not enable teachers to engage deeply or collaboratively to enact substantive change in their teaching practice during the course of this study; nor did it allow significant growth in the ways that staff interact with each other. The tensions around student success, and the demand for literally all students to test proficiently on state exams, was deep and persistent, and unearthed gaps and shortcomings in the shared culture of achievement that Weatherbee sought to foster.

Staff meetings consistently displayed profound differences between Weatherbee's ideals and staff perspectives. At ILT meetings, curriculum- and instruction-related conversations reliably veered toward patterns of blame, defensiveness, and cynicism. In one meeting, Weatherbee introduced a protocol for literacy instruction—a district initiative—and teachers offered pushback against the protocol and against the fact that the district offered another "new" teaching strategy teachers should embrace. As Weatherbee presented the protocol, teachers grew increasingly vocal. Three experienced faculty commented in succession: "This is the problem of reinventing the wheel!", "What is the true purpose of this?!", "Is this going to be out the door in a couple years?" Weatherbee tried to remain on topic, reaffirming that the initiative aimed "to build [reading] comprehension." The learning specialist joined in to explain the protocol, to no avail. Concluding this agenda item, Weatherbee said he would follow up in grade level meetings.

The conversation then moved to teachers examining data together—a practice Weatherbee hoped to make an ILT norm. Again, teachers resisted. An experienced teacher observed, "We are testing more than teaching some weeks." Another added, "We are not teaching because we're testing. So [students] fall farther behind." Weatherbee said he would try to find support during intensive testing weeks while quickly shifting to press the team to strive for 100% proficiency on upcoming standardized exams:

Weatherbee: I want to lay a new goal out. No failures. Nobody fails. Nobody in red [below proficient].

Teacher 1: Impossible. You're going to need more services. [Others also say, "Impossible," and Teacher 1 talks about the extra services this would require.]

Weatherbee:	Students need interventions but we are not getting to them.
Teacher 2:	What are the actionable principles? I want an idea from you about what are the most actionable ideas that we can get this year. There is no point in talking about more teachers and smaller classes.
Teacher 3:	Students need a step-by-step process. We can't just squeeze their brains to get their scores up.
Weatherbee:	I've tried to get extra resources in rooms but I can't afford it. If we said, "Sixty days until [State exams], that no child fails," what would it take [to ensure all students are proficient]?
Teacher 4:	Saturdays. Five o'clock [school days].
Weatherbee:	Nobody in red [below proficient]. Everybody passes.

The conversation ended with no resolution. Weatherbee responded to a request for actionable suggestions by simply restating that no student should fail on the upcoming exam. The gap between Weatherbee's ideals and the school culture he envisioned—where teachers believed all students can succeed—and teachers' on-the-ground feelings about challenges they faced loomed large, and resurfaced often.

Within this context (which includes limits on Weatherbee's autonomy and problems of district bureaucracy that exceed the scope of this data), and specifically in regard to increasing student expectations, Weatherbee faced significant challenges at JJS. In several interviews, teachers shared appreciation for Weatherbee and conveyed a sense of balance—between challenging them to improve and also supporting them, emotionally and tangibly, to do so. Yet while faculty appreciated Weatherbee's support in the collective effort to increase student achievement and reach the goal of 100% proficiency, that goal was his, not theirs (in the sense that they did not believe it was plausible), and there was little evidence that the "support" they referred to had much to do with helping teachers to change their classroom practice.

As Fullan (2005) notes, successful school cultures are more demanding cultures, which require not just trust but "demanding trust" (p. 60), in part because "adaptive challenges require the deep participation of the people with the problem" (p. 53). Collective responsibility and shared perceptions are necessary in order for teachers to take up the difficult work of change themselves; in the absence of such shared beliefs and goals, the likelihood of attaining such goals is nonexistent, and the status quo becomes a self-fulfilling prophecy.

As Coombs (1968) proclaimed in his "systems analysis," "the conservative nature of the system, by the momentum of its own mass... grinds down even a would-be bold administrative innovator until even he is absorbed into the conservative mass and reflects its conservative behavior" (p. 121). Jackson (2000) also summarizes this conservative predilection in human systems:

> There is often a general fear of change in organizations. Unconscious group processes can favor sticking firmly to bureaucratic routines and avoiding confrontation. The felt "need to belong" can mean that even spontaneous self-organization produces groups favoring cooperation and the status quo. Politics can be covert, rather than openly challenging, and so detract from proper dialogue. The tendency for all these things to occur becomes greater the longer the organization's "dominant schema" has held sway. (p. 194)

At JJS, the verbal support was there, the goals were being articulated from the top, and Weatherbee was both present and working to help meet teachers' needs; but the beliefs were not yet shared, the expectations were not yet being raised in unison, and while Weatherbee was working to establish relational trust in the school, it is not clear how demanding it was (Bryk & Schneider, 2002). The dominant schema that permeated teachers' thinking about their practice and student success had held sway at JJS for a long time, and the conservative impulse to protect that schema stood firm in the face of Weatherbee's proclamations about 100% proficiency. He had already felt that impulse at his previous school, and his attempts to overcome it at JJS were ultimately unconvincing.

If we consider some of the factors involved that influence teacher thinking and behavior, this should not be a surprise. As Cohn and Kottkamp (1993) argue,

> The absence of teachers from the dialogue and decision-making on reform has been a serious omission. It has yielded faulty definitions of the problem, solutions that compound rather than confront the problem, and a demeaned and demoralized teaching force. Efforts to improve education are doomed to failure until teachers become respected partners in the process. If reform is to be successful, their voices and views must be included in any attempts to improve and alter their work. Although their involvement cannot insure success, their absence will guarantee continued failure. (p. xvi)

This is important food for thought for leaders such as Weatherbee, who maintain lofty aspirations and try to convince teachers to buy-in to reforms and changes and yet do not include teachers in the creation of those aims.

4 Reform Is in the Eye of the Beholder

Many things changed at JJS after Weatherbee arrived, but those changes came about mostly outside the classroom. Weatherbee instituted a school uniform policy and created a school crest, both points of pride for the school community. The school hosted its first Fall Festival, a Saturday school-wide gathering with food and games. Parents were recruited to attend the district-sponsored Parent University, for which staff enlisted parents and provided daycare and transportation. There was a 5K family run/walk fundraiser, and throughout the year JJS held "Friday Night at the Movies," where parents and students returned to school to watch a family film. Yet none of these efforts sought to improve teaching and learning. Instead of generating adaptive changes, moving "beyond their comfort zone... to integrate new knowledge or reshape existing perceptions" (Nadler, 1993, p. 59), JJS teachers maintained a familiar equilibrium, especially in the classroom.

Learning organizations, such as schools, are most effective and responsive when control is decentralized to include multiple stakeholders (Davis & Sumara, 2006). Given his rocky past and resistant JJS staff, Weatherbee approached school-wide collaboration cautiously. Though ostensibly sharing power, the network structure he created remained highly centralized. In ILT meetings, no one led but Weatherbee, and when he signaled where he wanted to go—toward ensuring success for all students—few followed him. In grade level meetings, given Weatherbee's presence and persistent facilitation, teachers had no time to collaborate autonomously. Believing that if he controlled communication he could shape school culture and practices to align with his vision, Weatherbee dominated each hub of the emerging JJS network. When work proved substantial, Veronica, not classroom teachers, assumed increased responsibility. Consequently, teachers remained on the periphery of the network Weatherbee created, and changes that took place did not impact teacher practice significantly.

Ultimately, during the time of this study, Weatherbee failed to translate good intentions and high aspirations into an empowered staff culture where teachers take on responsibility for the success of all students. It is in this failure that Weatherbee's leadership demonstrated the interdependence of instructional leadership, distributed leadership, and cultural leadership. His inability to provide teachers with authentic autonomy—or, inversely and perhaps equally true, their inability to take and/or use such autonomy—led to atrophied embodiments of distributed leadership. The tensions that persisted through Weatherbee's top down insistence that all students must be proficient, combined with his insistence on leading all meetings, stunted the growth of a truly "crew"-like culture. And these tensions pushed Weatherbee away from substantive instructional leadership and led him to focus his efforts on tasks and changes that were more easily accomplished without teachers—changes external to the classroom. It would be a mistake to blame Weatherbee for his staff's recalcitrance, but it would also be a mistake to blame teachers for balking in the face of what appear to be unreasonable goals and demands. This is simply one way that the diverse perspectives of actors can play out in a complex adaptive system, where such actors respond and adapt to each other and yet remain influenced by the path dependence of their past interactions. Unsurprisingly, differences persisted not only in staff perspectives of educational goals, but also in regard to assessing Weatherbee, his leadership, and even his ultimate intentions.

The question of balance between pushing and supporting teachers, highlighted above, was a pivotal challenge for Weatherbee in his first years at JJS. The stability of his staff, combined with the relative instability of leadership at JJS in recent years, made for an especially delicate context for change. Having a new principal *was* change; any educational changes that Weatherbee brought to the school would be additional changes that the rest of the school community would have to adapt to. As a new principal, Weatherbee had to balance two potentially contradictory aims. On one hand, as a new principal, he had reason to strive for a smooth transition, one that would enable him to be accepted and to consolidate the community of the school around a new principal. On the other hand, change was the imperative, reform was the goal. In the context of pressure from the district (and society), combined with the mission of school improvement reinforced by the Leadership Academy, Weatherbee's charge was to cohere a community at JJS in service of improvement, not as an end in itself.

Weatherbee appeared to have been keenly aware of some of the complexities of this context from early on in his first year, and he tried to be sensitive and skillful in his approach to change; he tried not to rock the boat too much, at least to the extent that it would be counter-productive and evoke resistance. In some ways it seemed that Weatherbee's personal style of leadership was well suited to this task—his casual, friendly, personable approach to school leadership may have helped to further his educational and organizational aims. A 5th grade student confirmed this balance from her point of view, and said that Weatherbee "likes to joke a lot.... [But] he's strict when it's time for something serious."

Teachers described the practical effects of this leadership style, noting that there was "less protocol" than in previous years, and a "looser style" overall, which they mostly appreciated. Teachers testified to the fact that a principal's leadership style does much to determine the overall culture and feeling of work at a school; the principal sets the tone for how adults in the building relate to each other:

> I feel like as a staff as a whole, the culture is a little bit different [now].... This principal is a little bit more laid back and you can really feel that in the school.... It has changed a lot.

For this teacher, Weatherbee's approach has been positive, and he has been successful in fostering trust. But this increased autonomy and "looser style" also led to some teachers feeling a lack of structure and protocol. It is a difficult balance to maintain. This same teacher went on to say that the looser style "has been beneficial, but I still feel like he needs to do more than he is doing now.... I would like him to be slightly more involved but not overbearing." Several teachers confirmed the tension between autonomy and teacher accountability. As another put it:

> Staff members work extremely hard and he definitely recognizes that. Other staff members do not work quite as hard and seem to be, as some of us call it, "getting away with it." ... It kind of leads to a feeling that some people are really working very hard to make sure they're doing things as best they can and others are not.... I'll speak for myself, and maybe for some of the others: [we] miss some of the protocol.

From another point of view, some teachers felt that Weatherbee was successful precisely because he got out of teachers' way:

> He doesn't come across as overbearing.... He wants to help more than he wants to do anything else and I think that's how you have to start with [teachers]. So, [he is] helpful first. I think that the thing that they respect the most is someone who will just kind of get out of their way. More than anything, that's how [to help them]: get out of their way. And I think that at the end of this year, it was a good year. He was a good principal, but all because he did that.

This diversity of viewpoints is important to note. In a school, as in all systems, balance is key to keeping systems working well (Meadows, 2008). The roles, relations, and responsibilities that make up the JJS system have undergone perpetual recalibration based on input, feedback, and policy changes; there is not a simple linear relationship between Weatherbee's leadership, faculty practices, and student learning—all are factors in a complex and dynamic system, and the internal diversity in this system is significant. And there is no single version of truth that can declare the impact of Weatherbee's leadership. As principal, he has an influence on other actors in the system, and teachers have been forced to adjust to his leadership and the changes he has made, but in this interplay of change, feedback, and reorientation, Weatherbee and his faculty continually sought balance in their work and relationships, and each individual had his or her own interpretation about that process and the degree of balance it achieved. From one point of view, the fact that different teachers emphasized different aspects of the tension between structure and autonomy—with some wanting more structure and others appreciating their newfound autonomy—is a sign of balance. The process of calibrating diverse approaches toward the work of teaching is iterative and ongoing, and the communication structures and leadership style that Weatherbee established with his faculty can be seen as a foundation for ongoing cultural, professional, and instructional progress. It could also be seen as too passive, too conciliatory, and too enabling of the status quo.

So what was the result of Weatherbee's Leadership Growth Project, his participation in the School Leadership Academy, and the first two years of his leadership at JJS? Teacher interviews offered varied perspectives, not only about Weatherbee's leadership, but about whether he sought to change the school. Some teachers emphasized the continuity Weatherbee managed to preserve, felt "nothing major" had changed, and downplayed any notion of reform he may have been attempting:

> I don't think that he actually is trying to change the culture of the building right now because it is his first year. You can't make a whole lot of changes in the first year. So, I have to say no, he is not trying to change the culture of the building right now. I think he's tried to do one thing at a time. Change is kind of hard when you have teachers in the building [who] have been there 17 years or more.

Another teacher emphasized the difficulty any principal would face coming into a school like JJS with plans for change, and agreed that Weatherbee had done well to maintain continuity with what was happening at the school prior to his arrival:

> I think it's difficult for the staff to get on board with some of the stuff because we've had three different principals in the four years I've been there, and each principal has their own missions and their own ideas of what they want the school to become.... That's kind of been the challenge. But for me I think he's been supportive—very supportive—of the

new things that we've wanted to do, and has continued to build upon what was started last year.

Another teacher was even more straightforward in pointing out that cultural change, and accomplishing buy-in from senior faculty, is an up-hill climb:

> What "buy in" looks like for one person is not the same to another person. And I think that once you have an idea about who you are as a teacher and what you have to offer, and what the principal's job is [it is hard to change]. I think that a lot of people have decided the principal does X, Y, and Z, and they decided that fifteen years ago. So whether it's this principal, or whoever, there's only so much they're going to let the principal do.

Many teachers seemed to have a clear sense of the principal's plight coming into JJS, and of the challenges linked to creating change in that context—even if they did not want change, they were aware of the pressure for it. Their judgment of his leadership came not just from what he tried to do, but also from how he responded to that context. Overall, teachers appreciated that whatever Weatherbee did, he did it slowly, respectfully, and inclusively; he did not come into the school and radically alter established modes of operation in the name of reform, *even if that was his ultimate goal*. He showed that first, with those overarching and at times abstract goals in view, one can start by acknowledging, respecting, and even continuing what already exists: his approach to reform acknowledged a need to fully understand the initial conditions of the existing system.

One teacher described this approach as an attempt to "lovingly fracture" faculty norms. In this context, "love" implies patience, respect, and support, while "fracture" denotes the ultimate aim to initiate change and growth:

> When I see him working in meetings [he will] sort of lovingly fracture people's perspectives that aren't openly helpful to the students. He generally asks teachers to push for more for the kids. You know, a little bit more. If their test scores went up a little bit, [push them] a little bit more. [He is] always pushing for a better result and I think that sometimes he's been met with resistance because people say, "We can't do that. Ninety percent of kids can't be proficient. It just doesn't work. It's impossible." And he... lovingly fractures that idea, that nothing else is possible. It has to be gentle, you know? These are people that need to be handled very gently. They're the kind of people who, I think for the most part, they don't believe they need a principal [and so are slow to change].

From this teacher's point of view, Weatherbee's slow and gentle change goes to the heart of instructional and educational change, where what needs to be "fractured" is the notion that not all students can achieve. Elaborating, this teacher outlined Weatherbee's approach to the task:

> I think that he does a good job of trying to approach every issue... [by] creating a kind of firm base of personability.... As a principal, if teachers feel supported, which I think they do, they might not always agree with what he wants to do, but they feel like he supports them.... Before he asks for anything more, he'll always sort of compliment teachers on what they're doing so far. And these [teachers] need that. They really do... they don't want to feel like they're being directly challenged. You know, "a spoonful of sugar."

Ultimately, this teacher viewed the intended changes as substantial, if not radical. What has happened this year is one step in a long-term process:

> I think that he's trying to change every dynamic at the school in almost every way.... He's trying to push on peoples' perspectives and sort of hopefully change as much as [he] can. But you're between a rock and a hard place here, where the kids have needs that need to get met but the teachers have their own [demands] that they need... before they can continue. So it's tough.

Teachers I spoke to appreciated that Weatherbee approached change through a platform of respect and continuity; balancing pressure and support had fostered relational trust (Bryk & Schneider, 2002; Daly & Chrispeels, 2008). Some took this approach as a sign he was not pursuing disruptive change, and appreciated that, since it aligned with the general sense that the school is doing well and does not need a dramatic turnaround. Others saw his approach as a gentle but persistent way to engender lasting change, both cultural and instructional. In interviews, Weatherbee's remarks suggest he leans toward the latter goal and is both consistent and sincere in his beliefs. But the trust and appreciation of teachers who do not see him intending fundamental changes is not necessarily erroneous. While pursuing both change and continuity simultaneously seems paradoxical, there need be no contradiction between the two objectives. As Hargreaves and Shirley (2012) observe, dynamic and effective leadership often requires embracing paradox, and understanding the merits of Weatherbee's approach to change at JJS requires such a paradoxical, both/and view.

Weatherbee tried to instill new beliefs and model desired behaviors, with the theory of action that these efforts will instigate change in the beliefs and actions of teachers. As Kegan and Lahey (2001) explain, "It is very hard to *sustain* significant changes in behavior without significant changes in individuals' underlying meanings that may give rise to their behaviors" (p. 3). The question is how to foster such deep changes while adhering to the "Goldilocks Principle" of disequilibrium: finding the "just right" amount of intensity to both enable real growth and avoid unproductive resistance or regression (Opfer & Pedder, 2011, p. 389).

Because Weatherbee's effort to have a positive impact at JJS was rooted in the somewhat intangible and qualitative focus on culture and climate, the very success of this work depended on establishing healthy relationships with as many stakeholders as possible. Given his ideals, Weatherbee had to generate trust: trust that he was in it for the long haul; trust that he would not raise havoc with radical change and disrespect hard-working, experienced teachers; and trust that he would put the interests of the school community ahead of any professional aspirations or political agenda he may have. In his first years at JJS, Weatherbee demonstrated the three pillars of relational trust—reliability, sincerity, and competence (Bryk & Schneider, 2002). Establishing trust is central to maintaining healthy continuity, which is in turn conducive to fostering sustainable change. In the context of cultural change, conceived as fostering a healthy and collaborative "crew," initiated by a new principal whose credibility begins at zero, change and continuity are two sides of the same coin. And the ultimate "success" of such a program of reform requires us to take a longer view of progress than what may be customary, where year-to-year comparisons of test scores are the accepted norm of judgment. Schools are complex and real change has proven to be slow and difficult (Tyack & Cuban, 1995). Meanwhile, the communicative, collaborative, cultural, and relational qualities that were in flux at JJS were complex, dynamic, and in the early stages of change—and so was the leadership capacity of Weatherbee himself, whose ability to be a highly effective leader may take upwards of 10 years of cumulative development (Fullan, 2005, p. 34).

The staff's acceptance of Weatherbee as a leader could be seen as a successful first step of leadership succession, and therefore an effective step toward positive school change. While the view of leadership success presented here is somewhat tentative, it may be wise to acknowledge, and avoid, the hubris involved in many approaches to school reform that aim for bigger and bolder short-term impact. There is "an upper limit to turbulence if schools are to engage in sustainable change" (Beabout, 2012, p. 26), and "dynamic learning systems cannot be forced or legislated into existence" (Davis, Sumara, & D'Amour, 2012, p. 398). Moreover,

> Even when school reforms attempt to redirect relationships by reconfiguring teachers into small learning communities or other collaborative settings... established relationships persist.... [F]indings show that teachers continue to be much more strongly influenced by the traditional relationships in their schools... [and] any reform that seeks to change attitudes, and subsequently teaching behaviors, has to recognize this reality. (Cole & Weinbaum, 2010, p. 94)

If we are to accept this somewhat limited view of school leadership and reform, informed as it is by an attempt to account for and include the multifaceted, dynamic, and nested nature of school systems, we can do so without abandoning hopes for positive change. We may just need to adjust the horizon of our timelines, and embrace the fact that adaptive change is a slow, challenging process. Weatherbee may not have instigated sufficient disequilibrium to enact significant adaptive change in his school; or he may have been laying an essential foundation of trust, buy-in, and rapport that will enable sustainable progress to emerge over a period of years. What is certain is that the complexity of JJS as a whole would render bold assertions based on short-term data suspect, and that the diversity of perspectives within the school system combined with the difficulty of adjudicating the relative success of leadership and change demands both a framework of interpretation and a time scale that can cope with such complexity. These methodological demands will find fuller resolution in Chapters 5 and 6.

CHAPTER 4

Saint Catherine's School: Collective Urgency at the Edge of Chaos

Helen Matthews was also a member of the first cohort of School Leadership Academy Fellows, and thus a colleague of Harold Weatherbee. However, the many differences of their school contexts, and their positionality within those contexts, along with individual leadership differences, led to different processes and outcomes at each school over the course of this study. I trace these differences below with attention to the characteristics of Helen Matthew's leadership, and the ways in which her promotion of distributed leadership, instructional leadership, and cultural change interacted to promote positive outcomes at Saint Catherine's School.

As noted above, "the project of formal education cannot be understood without considering, all-at-once, the many layers of dynamic, nested activity that are constantly at play" (Davis & Sumara, 2006, p. 28). At SCS, there are several interdependent layers of context that form and inform the complex whole of the school. Below I mention a few of the most relevant aspects of this context: demographics, economics, principal succession, and faculty tenure.

St. Catherine's School is an urban pre-K through 8th grade school in the same city as JJS. Ninety percent of students live in the neighborhood. In 2011–2012, SCS enrolled 358 students: 48% Black, 35% Hispanic, and 10% White. Forty-two percent of students received free or reduced price lunch. There were 31 faculty members; 28 were White and 29 were female. Fifteen had been at the school for more than 10 years, and six more than 20 years. Over the past several years, the student population changed significantly—from a predominantly White population to largely Black and Hispanic. As one veteran teacher remarked,

> The face of the school has changed quite a bit. But it's a reflection of the community as well—that's what's really cool about it.... [But] one of the concerns about that is that the parents are not as fluent [in English]. Many of them are, but a lot of them have a difficult time communicating in English. So I see that as a concern that we have to address.

With a faculty composed almost exclusively of White women, many of whom have sent children to the school and taught at SCS for many years, the demographic changes are both dramatic and personal. The experience of and response to these changes relates to the issue of cultural competence, which is something that Matthews addressed with her staff in professional development sessions. At SCS, the demands of teaching English language learners effectively combined with other social and economic pressures, many of which are being felt by Catholic schools nationwide.

A second contextual factor that impacted change at SCS emerged from the pressure generated by financial, staffing, and enrollment difficulties facing many area Catholic Schools—challenges further complicated by demographic shifts toward public and charter schools, leading to parochial school closures and mergers throughout the country. Many SCS teachers alluded to the precarious position Catholic schools face in a competitive market and credited recent changes Matthews initiated as allowing the school to remain open. An upper-elementary teacher, for instance, alluded to the impact of Matthews's efforts and her links to the SLA:

> I like [the changes that are happening] a lot because the school could not exist the way it had been going. It just couldn't.... I love the changes that are happening because it's forcing everybody to step up their game. So many teachers become complacent and just do what they've done year after year after year.... [But] the ideas that she's bringing back [from the SLA] help us think about how we can do things a little different to reach more kids. So I think, for the survival of the school, it's very important.... We have to offer new things.... We're teaching people to be lifelong learners. We have to be that way ourselves. So that's good and she's forcing us to do that.

In much the same vein, a lower-elementary teacher described recent changes promoted by Matthews as key to sustaining the school:

> I'm not sure under the previous leadership if we'd still be open, if things had been done the way they had always been done. Our demographics have changed over the last 20 years, and the socioeconomics and a lot of other things have changed. And unless we have a competitive edge, then I'm not sure that we're going to be open.

In my research at SCS the threat of decreasing enrollments and concerns about limited funding were consistent themes in interviews and conversations. Yet even more consistently and overtly, I found members of the school community were optimistic about the school's direction and future. The parent of a middle schooler who has been at the school for eight years was quite optimistic, in great part because Matthews was the school's leader:

> The kids are excited to be there. The kids are happy to be there. Teachers are happy to be there.... I am just excited to see what she is going to do in the future because I know she is a part of the Leadership Academy.... I know she is really going to make it one of the best schools around.

Why so much excitement? In my efforts to answer this question I found this optimistic sentiment, while not shared by all, was prevalent, and seemed to reflect a consensus that the school was improving. The excitement was not just about the school, it was about *change,* and the way the culture of the school was perceived by many as changing for the better.

Along with demographic shifts and the pressure and uncertainty that colored the experience of adults at SCS, perhaps the biggest change that occurred from the perspective of teachers and parents is the leadership style Matthews brought to the school. Matthews is an energetic and charismatic woman, and she entered the Academy knowing she wanted to change the structure and style of leadership at SCS:

> [Under the leadership of the] former principal... it was all top down... very strict, very regimented.... [There was] very little freedom for faculty.... [T]hat wasn't me. I wasn't comfortable with that leadership style.... I wanted to learn how to be a principal who could recognize leadership in others and then empower those people with the proper tools and resources.... [My style] is definitely not top-down.... But that's all I was mentored [to do] during my whole formation here... But then I started the [School Leadership Academy] and it was like, "Wow, I don't have to do that! There are other options here!" So for me personally, [the Academy] made me realize what kind of a leader I want to be. And its given me the tools and resources to get there.... [As a result] most of [our teachers] have stepped up to the plate and are sharing things that took large portions of work off my plate.... It's a lot of work. There are a lot of pieces that you have to put together. But they have stepped up and taken off [with it].

Matthews had a long history at SCS. The first year of this study was her fourth as principal, and prior to becoming a principal she was a middle school science teacher for five years and assistant principal for 14 years. However, this continuity of leadership from within the school did not translate into a continuity of leadership style. In fact, Matthews's familiarity with SCS prior to assuming the role of principal enabled her to make significant and meaningful changes right away—she had a sense of what she wanted to accomplish before she had the power to do so. Indeed, shortly after being named principal, Matthews moved quickly to change the faculty composition, removing seven long-term SCS teachers while hiring several new, younger teachers.

This change in faculty had a big impact on the school, and teacher interviews revealed that, in general, teachers' interpretations of and responses to change at SCS, and the challenges that entailed, corresponded to teacher experience—more experienced teachers were seen as having greater difficulty with change. For example, one experienced teacher noted the prevalent attitude of her peers—that the combination of multiple changes and limited time and staff constituted a significant challenge:

> When [Matthews] took over, the vice principal position was lost... and there were a lot of changes very quickly. So it was difficult for a lot of people because they were used to doing things a certain way for a long time and then not having that vice principal there to go to [made it harder].... They feel that they've been doing something for 30 years a certain way and now they're getting ready to wind down. And [they are thinking], "I don't know if I really have it within myself to do this."

Another veteran teacher also described challenges she faced, including the stress generated by changing her teaching (primarily the move toward differentiated instruction, discussed below):

> It's hard to change.... When you've been teaching for a long time and if you were taught to teach in a certain way, it's basically taking everything that you did and kind of throwing it out and asking you to start over. So it's been a lot of changes thrown at us at one time.... I love teaching, but it is more stressful than it used to be.

A middle school teacher identified the same theme, relating experience to difficulty with change, though noting that Matthews and other faculty have supported each other in managing the stress generated by the related disequilibrium:

> I think change can be scary at times, but it needs to be done.... I can't even imagine [what it is like for] some of the teachers who have been here

25–30 years.... It might be a little scary. But I think they feel comfortable, because they see so many other people are willing to help them out. And they're open about it. They'll say: "We're nervous about the change." And I think [Matthews] wants that. [She will say] "Lets try to work together," and "This is where we're going." She's patient with that.

In light of these reflections from teachers, the following points should be kept in mind: many changes happened simultaneously; some SCS faculty had difficulty acclimating to these overlapping changes; and the qualities of Matthews's leadership (e.g., her patience and support for teachers) were appreciated by faculty as they navigated the challenges of school change, i.e., she maintained a balance between challenging and supporting her faculty. It is in this sense that I conceptualize the process of change at SCS as being "on the edge of chaos": the faculty and staff were engaged in a turbulent and ever-changing upheaval of their school—demographically, financially, pedagogically, and structurally (in terms of the structures of relationships and networks that were being established)—and yet they also maintained a palpable continuity and stability in terms of the longevity of adults in the building (Lewin, 1992; Waldrop, 1992). They were neither locked in repetitive iterations of the status quo nor subject to wild fluctuations (Davis & Sumara, 2001). They were enacting change in an open system, which entails "an ongoing process of order-disorder-interaction-organization" and the vigilant attempt to maintain not static equilibrium, not regression or disorder, but dynamic balance (Montuori, 2008, p. xxxiv). The balance between challenge and support was crucial because it enabled this tension to be constructive and growth-oriented, as opposed to overly stressful and chaotic.

Beginning in the 2011–2012 school year Matthews enacted three overarching change strategies—creating a common school culture, promoting distributed leadership, and using both strategies as a means to enhance her instructional leadership. The explicit focus on creating a common culture (symbolized by DREAM BIG, explained below) is seen as a broad and overarching aspect of school change that included other reforms. Distributed and instructional leadership represent overlapping elements within the broader environment of school culture. All of these aspects of change represent behavioral manifestations of school culture: actions and strategies community members might draw upon which align with the institution's prevailing values and beliefs. Acknowledging that there is not a simple cause-and-effect relationship between any of these initiatives—or their combination—and educational outcomes at SCS, we can view these reforms as "triggers for transformation": inputs into the school system that foster emergent and novel developments, aimed at improved teaching and learning (Davis, Sumara, & D'Amour, 2012, p. 396). With this overarching understanding in mind, I will now look at how these strategies, or triggers, were enacted at SCS.

1   DREAM BIG: Creating a Common School Culture

Creating a common school culture was both a central theme of the Leadership Academy and a focus of change at SCS. Throughout its program, the SLA emphasized the value of having Fellows create an institutional culture in which prevailing beliefs and values align with operating norms to promote beneficial outcomes for all students. Sarason's (1971) notion of "principal as culture builder" captures what the SLA sought to instill in Matthews and her cohort:

> Life for everyone in a school is determined by ideas and values, and if these are not under constant discussion and surveillance, the comforts of ritual replace the conflict and excitement involved in growing and changing.... If the principal is not constantly confronting one's self and others... with the world of competing ideas and values shaping life in a school, he or she is an educational administrator and not an educational leader. (p. 177)

In pursuit of this ideal for educational leaders, every SLA Fellow was charged with developing a Leadership Growth Project (LGP), a unique and context-specific action plan that likely would entail aspects of cultural change—created in consultation with their coach, fellow cohort members, and SLA faculty based on the needs of their school.

At SCS, Matthews's LGP became the most visible change she implemented, as it focused on establishing a new conception of school values and beliefs, a new slogan for the school, and the consistent and intentional use of new terminology—e.g., all students are now referred to as "scholars," all scholars are expected to do their work conscientiously, and all scholars are expected to attend college. Collectively, these deliberate and overlapping changes are known as DREAM BIG, which stands for Determination, Respect, Excellence, Accountability, Mastery, and Belief in God. Every time I visited SCS I was greeted with a public invitation posted on the school's billboard, "Become a BIG DREAMER," and found this message reinforced in the hallways and classrooms, a constant reminder to the school community of its underlying collective aspirations: DREAM BIG.

For Matthews, DREAM BIG offered a means to clarify and communicate the school's values, providing "a laser focus on core values and the routinization of culture norms" which "was important [because]... we are all now speaking the same language." From a systemic perspective, DREAM BIG served as a paradigmatic leverage point for change in the SCS cultural system, transforming both the overt use of language and the underlying practices and beliefs it communicates (Meadows, 2008). As Hargreaves and Shirley (2012) point out, such "change is about constantly pulling people toward a certain mode of thought and action, as the key way to create momentum, direction, development, and coherence" (p. 84). And as Hemmings (2012) explained in her extensive exploration of urban schools, "True change rests on shared moral purpose... [and] schools can be remoralized through the construction and institutionalization of an ethically justifiable moral order to which all school actors owe allegiance" (p. 140). At SCS, DREAM BIG was an attempt to instigate such a remoralization.

DREAM BIG was communicated and reinforced in many ways. According to Matthews, it "impacts all communications—visually, orally, the website. It's everywhere. DREAM BIG is everything we do." This description from a lower-elementary teacher provides a sense for how DREAM BIG was communicated to students:

> I introduced each word [from DREAM BIG] and did a mini-lesson on it. I also pick a [student] every week out of my kids, someone who embodies the different words. Once again, I try to emphasize the words in DREAM BIG. I made a little chart [of the words]. They always want to DREAM BIG. That's what they're working towards. I folded it into what I was already doing. They get it, they know it, and hopefully they try to live it.

Teachers also reinforced the DREAM BIG message by having students write on "reflection sheets" when their behavior did not align with school values. Matthews introduced these reflection sheets in concert with DREAM BIG to promote consistency and accountability in school culture, so that now when a student misbehaves he or she is asked to reflect and write about the DREAM BIG values.

Teachers I spoke with found that the DREAM BIG initiative had been helpful—they found the new consistency promoted positive interactions. One lower-elementary teacher explained why this strategy for dealing with inappropriate behavior was significant for her:

> One thing that I definitely see a big change in is the way that consequences and issues are dealt with: it's more consistent. I think because

of DREAM BIG and because of the way that some teachers model that and the way [Matthews] discussed that we should handle that.... I see that consistency start to build from teacher-to-teacher, which is great.... I also notice... more positive interactions between teachers and kids, and between kids, too. I've really noticed dramatic... improvement there.

The use of reflection sheets and the connection of DREAM BIG with consistency and behavioral norms reveals how the values embedded in this overarching ideal were combined with more behavioral, discipline-oriented changes at SCS—the big ideas and concrete protocols were intended to be broadly applicable, a touchstone for many aspects of school life. Other changes that took place as a result of or in connection with DREAM BIG include: enforcing single file lines and no talking in all hallways, changing the dress code, and the institution of a parent contract to ensure accountability around student tardiness and uniforms. According to a middle school teacher, this new contract led to "a huge difference in the amount of kids who are tardy" and noticeable shifts in behavioral norms. So while DREAM BIG values did not necessarily entail such changes, Matthews and the faculty saw these as appropriate manifestations of DREAM BIG ideals and implemented these changes to support cultural change. Students were not just walking quietly in the hallway; their hallway behavior was an example of dreaming big—at least that is how the matter was framed at SCS.

Another aspect of the DREAM BIG initiative was the focused and consistent communication that *all* scholars are intended to go to college. This message made its way to parents effectively, and the parents I talked with valued and appreciated this commitment. One middle school parent felt that "all [teachers at SCS] believe in the same thing.... They're referring to students as scholars, and they really are trying to instill the belief that all students will go to college and [that] they are scholars.... That's a wonderful message."

Middle school teachers I spoke to generally agreed that the college-bound message had been significant for their students. Elementary teachers also felt that the message was important, though perhaps in a more general sense. One elementary teacher explained how DREAM BIG was accessible to her second grade students:

My kids get it. They know what all of those words mean. They know how to exemplify them. I like it because, as educators, it puts us all on the same page, which is really great because it builds consistency for the kids and for us, too.

Echoing this notion that students "get it," the scholars I talked with could explain the DREAM BIG acronym and outline its relevance for them. A 7th grade girl said:

> My personality and my self-esteem and my academics have gotten better [this year]. I think that's good because all students need to have a type of education where they can feel good about themselves and they can come to school and say, "I am ready to learn." ... [E]ven if a kid gives up [the teachers] say, "You can't do that. You have to keep going." ... [Y]ou have determination to go and reach your goal. We have the [DREAM BIG] motto and there's not a day that we forget it. We are reminded that we have to have the determination and respect and excellence and accountability.

Of course not every student embraced this language or these ideas. Written responses from 20 7th graders who were asked to reflect upon the influence of DREAM BIG in their lives revealed some skepticism toward this ideal. More typically, however, the DREAM BIG mantra appeared to resonate with students, and most spoke positively of the changes that took place at SCS since the implementation of DREAM BIG.

Overall, Matthews's Leadership Growth Project, encapsulated in the shared efforts to DREAM BIG, represented a significant change for the SCS school community. It was both a symbolic statement of goals and ideals (e.g., all scholars are college-bound) and a cultural support for concrete and behavior-oriented protocols and rules faculty used to attain greater consistency in student behavior. It appeared in every room and in the hallways. It was spoken, yelled, and reinforced every Monday morning by the entire school at assembly, and it abided in bold letters outside the building, reminding parents why they drop their children off at school every morning. It became a cultural attractor that served to impel actors at the school to align with particular ideas and values (Reigeluth, 2008); it represented a new paradigm to orient the system (Meadows, 2008). And perhaps most importantly, it was only beginning. From the outset, Leadership Growth Projects were conceived as initiations of ongoing growth, generating insights that transcend a single enactment. And Matthews took this conception to heart:

> Now I see this—Dream Big, Culture Matters—as not just a one-time project. This is an evolutionary project. And I see this expanding over the next two and three years as I fine tune it and add more. I just think it's

forever going to be evolving. And… I think that's wonderful. So it's not just a one-stop shop.… This is becoming who we are.

2 Distributed Leadership: Creating Structures for Organizational Learning

The benefits of distributed leadership are well documented. As a system, schools are most responsive when control is appropriately distributed throughout system elements—including faculty, parents, and students. As the Wallace Foundation (2011) observed, "leaders in all walks of life and all kinds of organizations… need to depend on others to accomplish the group's purpose and need to encourage the development of leadership across the organization" (p. 6). In reference to schools, the report asserts that "effective leadership from *all* sources… is associated with better student performance… [and in studies we reviewed] higher-achieving schools provided all stakeholders with greater influence on decisions" (p. 7). Typically, increased collaboration enhances the process of change and helps ensure robust outcomes. One way of thinking about such distribution is in terms of the decentralization of systems, and as noted above, "the evidence in favor of decentralization is overwhelming" (Davis & Sumara, 2006, p. 84).

Building on the notion of distributed leadership promoted by the SLA and in response to the turbulent context that enveloped SCS, Matthews accorded teachers more responsibility and agency in creating change. During her year with the SLA, several committees were formed, and leadership positions were delegated. An Instructional Leadership Team (ILT) addressed school planning and instructional improvement. Teachers led various school-wide projects: aggregating student performance data, curriculum planning, and organizing extracurricular programs. Ultimately, Matthews and faculty created a network of teacher-led groups: the ILT, Student Support Team, Curricular Planning Team, Grade Level Teams, and Academic Teams across grades (See Figure 3). One teacher offered her sense of Matthews's thinking: "Helen's attitude is that she can't do everything, and that we're professionals. And so she gives a lot more responsibility to us, and basically thinks we need to own what we're doing."

Two points are noteworthy here: first, many teachers belonged to more than one team and therefore had multiple opportunities to disrupt old practices and expectations—laying a foundation for relational trust (Moolenaar & Sleegers, 2010). Second, and perhaps most telling, Matthews belonged to only two teams—the ILT and the Student Support Team. She oversaw group work, but established early on that teachers would direct these teams. This represented an adaptive shift for faculty who spent many years following administrative directives rather than creating them. Distributing authority via networks was complemented by an informal emergence of shared leadership; SCS teachers were encouraged to assume increased responsibility, while shared learning and teacher initiative also increased.

At SCS, teachers increasingly assumed leadership roles throughout Matthews's first years as principal, a development directly related to how Matthews supported and encouraged them:

> I think [I encourage leadership] by acknowledging my teachers as teachers and professionals. I constantly thank them for their professionalism.... I give them big projects and they run with it, and they love it.... For example, one of my teachers took over standardized testing. She arranges all of the professional development. She loves it. And that's something that before would never have been allowed. We have another teacher who runs all the enrichment now.... And I think that... treating them as professionals, and giving them the tools and resources they need to do their job as professionals, goes a whole long way in making my job a whole lot easier. That's what I've learned. So I think it's made me realize what my leadership style is, and how to hone it now. Now I'm honing it. Now I'm perfecting it.

In her remarks, Matthews underscored three assumptions that informed her work: (1) encouraging faculty and offering emotional support are crucial aspects of promoting distributed leadership (Weathers, 2011); (2) leadership at SCS became increasingly distributed as a result of her encouragement and teachers' willingness to take on extra work and assume new roles; and (3) the SLA supported Matthews in making distributed leadership central to her overall leadership style.

For teachers, beyond assuming leadership roles on individual projects, leadership was distributed at SCS through the work of committees and peer mentoring. A middle school teacher summarized the work of committees:

> There are a lot more committees this year than last year. I'm on the SST [Student Support Team], but there's also a committee for technology and new curriculum mapping. There's a committee for testing. There's a committee for getting this accreditation program started. As things go

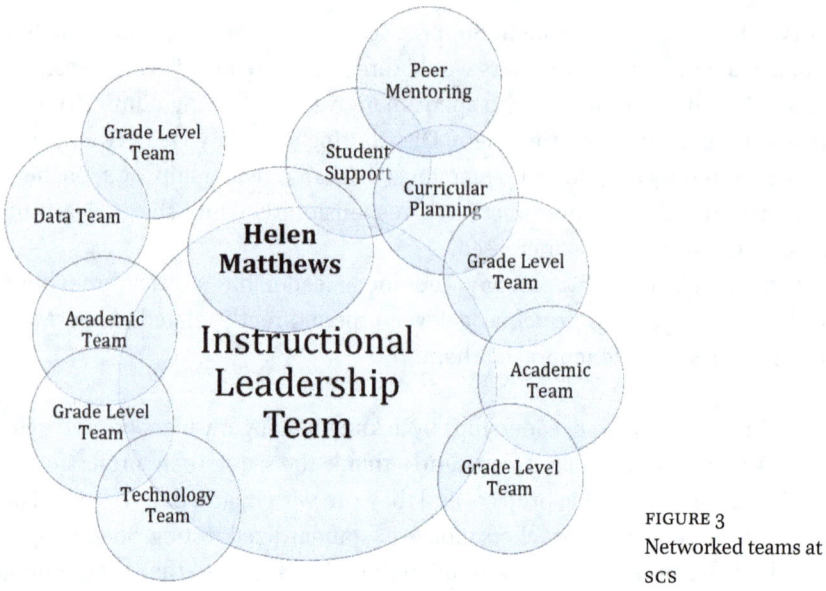

FIGURE 3
Networked teams at SCS

on throughout the year, there are always committees. There are more of them this year than last year.

When asked if Matthews had delegated greater responsibility to faculty this year, this lower-elementary teacher was definitive, and gave several examples of how Matthews fostered and supported teacher leadership:

Absolutely [leadership is distributed]. I think one of her key ways to do that is the ILT [Instructional Leadership Team].... I know she is trying to bring in more people, like with the SST. That's another way to bring the staff in. [And] with the instructional planner this year that we're doing with the online curriculum mapping [a new system of lesson planning and sharing], she's largely been hands-off. And then there are some point people that you can go to for help.... I definitely think that she is delegating in that way.... [Matthews says] "I trust you to do this. I'm going to [help] when I can, but this is what I expect you to do. I've laid the groundwork for differentiated instruction, or DREAM BIG, and it's up to you to follow through."

A veteran teacher also noted that such manifestations of distributed leadership "build more interactions between teachers, which is something that I know [Matthews] has also been trying to do.... [And] that can really help open up lines of communication between classroom teachers."

These teachers portrayed faculty committees as serving not only to identify relevant instructional strategies for specific students, but as fostering teacher communication, community, and collaboration. In this sense Matthews established what Torre and Voyce (2008) call a "relational model," where leaders "provide processes designed to encourage sincere consideration of new thinking and change and means for clear, honest, and meaningful communication and interaction among all constituents" (p. 162). And this decentralization of power fostered by the delegation of authority can be understood as an effort to develop what Lambert (2009) calls leadership capacity: "broad-based, skillful participation in the work of leadership" (p. 122).

The primary committee at SCS is the Instructional Leadership Team—a new administrative committee Matthews created after being inspired by a cohort member from the SLA (just as Weatherbee had been). The ILT meetings I observed at SCS were fast-paced, talkative, and engaging encounters—collegial in the best sense of the word, though not necessarily free of conflict. The overall dynamic suggested a genuine trust between Matthews and the faculty. At one meeting, Matthews began in an informal and playful tone, saying, "I want to pick your brains about the process of looking at test results." To this a teacher replied, "I think it's a waste of time to look at tests during the professional development day." Though this response was potentially oppositional, Matthews responded matter-of-factly, clarifying her intention while acknowledging the merit of the teacher's concern and continuing to pose questions and solicit feedback:

> Teachers should already know the test results prior to the professional development day, so that we can look at them together at the meeting [i.e., we will not be wasting time by just looking at them for the first time]. What is the best grouping to look at the data?

The meeting continued in a professional manner—with no apparent hesitation, self-consciousness, or defensiveness on Matthews's part—though there were instances when teachers responded to Matthews's thinking with starkly different points of view. Most dialogue involved rapid sequences of differing opinions, with no sense that teachers deferred or capitulated to Matthews's authority. Clearly, she was the leader—initiating most topics and consistently responding to others—but a creative tension permeated the meeting, balanced by an egalitarian and respectful sense of collaboration. The following exchange was another typical encounter:

Matthews: I am planning on having us look at the instructional planner in September.

Teacher 1:	We will have a real delay then. You said it should be done by September.
Teacher 2:	I think we need to review it in June, not wait until September.
Matthews:	We need [to present] a PowerPoint to look at [our] test scores. We can do that the morning of June 14th. Then in the afternoon we can look at the instructional planner.
Teacher 1:	We had talked about standards teachers should know.
Teacher 2:	[Teacher 3] has been working hard on standards. [A few teachers thank her.] Teachers should have a Q&A about the instructional planner and set goals for it.
Matthews:	Okay, so set goals for the instructional planner at the meeting.
Teacher 3:	Teachers won't have a lot of questions. We need a set agenda because some teachers will want to leave and others will be discouraged from asking [questions].
Matthews:	Thank you! That is why I need you all to be my eyes and ears! [Laughter]

Here, teachers shared opinions openly, offered contrasting viewpoints (to one another and Matthews), and shaped meeting outcomes, some of which led to increased responsibilities for their colleagues. Matthews not only accepted teacher input but was appreciative of it—which she readily acknowledged, thus modeling trust in faculty. I was told that these interactions differed notably from what had been typical at SCS in prior years.

In the ILT meetings I observed Matthews appeared to intuitively grasp what Ylimaki and Brunner (2011) mean by utilizing "conflict within collaborative decision-making processes" to further the work of the ILT (p. 1278). The dynamic nature of the meetings manifested a tacit knowledge that "if *all* participants were to express their views in a collaborative (shared power) process, opposing or conflicting views would quite naturally emerge. [Yet to] disallow the expression of conflict... would shut down authentic participation" (p. 1278). Matthews's conception of power "not only supported collaboration, but also included authentic participation with embedded conflict" (p. 1278). In other words, knowing that "intelligent group action is dependent on the independent actions of diverse individuals" (Davis & Sumara, 2006, p. 85), Matthews actively encouraged independent thought and the free exchange of ideas at SCS. In the five ILT meetings I observed, Matthews's responses to teacher input, even when in disagreement, encouraged teacher contributions and teacher leadership.

Matthews also encouraged independent action and distributed leadership by establishing teams and networks that she herself did not participate in, such as Grade Level Teams and peer mentoring. A lower-elementary teacher commented on peer mentoring, relating its effectiveness to Matthews's flexibility and responsiveness to teacher diversity and ability:

> If someone is like, "I can't set up these centers. This is really difficult for me." Or, "How are you doing your reading groups?" then we can observe each other and share those ideas. I think that's very important.... One thing that has been successful with those particular teachers is pairing them up, saying, "Okay, this particular thing is stressful for you. So-and-so is very good at that."

The practice of peer mentoring demonstrates how the culture of distributed leadership permeated relationships among staff. Beyond establishing committees and formal positions, the informal support teachers provided colleagues revealed how distributed leadership can be understood as a function of leadership style and school culture, not merely formal structures and roles. As Heifetz (1994) argues, leadership is an action, not a position. Yet the structures of committees and teams help to support a collaborative culture. Teachers working in grade level teams, for instance, met every week to address problems of practice, and several of these teams developed curricula and assessment practices for their grade level—a job many schools assign to administrators or outside specialists. Further, the model of developing curriculum was passed from one Grade Level Team to another: the first grade team learned from the kindergarten team, and then they shared the process of curriculum development with the second grade team. It was an emergent development conceived, shared, and completed by teachers acting in communication with, but significantly autonomous from, Matthews's leadership. In this sense the faculty as a whole was modeling Lambert's vision of leadership:

> Leadership is about learning together, and constructing meaning and knowledge collaboratively. It involves opportunities to surface and mediate perceptions, values, beliefs, information and assumptions through continuing conversations; to inquire about and generate ideas together; to seek to reflect upon and make sense of work in light of shared beliefs and new information; and to create actions that come out of these new understandings. (quoted in Hargreaves & Fink, 2006, pp. 33–34)

By granting teachers autonomy and power over curriculum and assessment, Matthews utilized distributed leadership as an approach to instructional leadership: she supported teachers in their instructional planning and established committees for teachers to focus on and improve their teaching. The characteristics that foster teacher leadership and learning—emotional support, committee work, peer mentoring, practice-based professional development, increased autonomy in curriculum and assessment, and establishing a common school culture of excellence—also promote better teaching (Showers & Joyce, 1996; Smylie, 1995). And while much of this work involved dramatic changes to teachers' work lives—with many more meetings and higher expectations—the trust and support from Matthews and each other allowed the teachers at SCS to stay engaged in intense and stressful processes of change while remaining on this side of "chaos."

3   Instructional Leadership: Challenging and Supporting Teachers

The third strand of school change that emerged at St. Catherine's was focused on instructional leadership. Building on the initiatives to establish a common school culture and encourage distributed leadership, Matthews promoted new approaches to teaching and learning among faculty. The primary instructional initiative at SCS was differentiated instruction. A lower-elementary teacher offered her thoughts on the matter:

> [I think] that [Matthews's] focus on differentiated instruction and assessment is the most prominent [change]. I think that that stretches across every classroom in this school in one way or another. I would say that's number one. I think most teachers are feeling very confident in that. I think teachers understand why that's important and how to make that happen. And like I said, a lot of those resources have been really useful and the professional development has been there. So I think that has been really, really key. And I think that has really changed a lot of instruction, a lot of learning.

Another teacher also maintained that efforts at differentiated instruction impacted the school, shaping not only students' learning but their behavior as well:

> I would say too that… with differentiated instruction… we've had less discipline problems, which is good. There was a time when you could walk through our middle school and see several students in the hallway—which meant they weren't behaving in class and were asked to leave for a while. You rarely see that now.… I believe it's our differentiated instruc-

tion.... We're using different approaches to try and work with each type of learner. There's less opportunity for [misbehavior], because a lot of the discipline comes out of hiding the fact that [students] don't understand what's going on and [they] don't want other people to know that [they] can't do this.... And we all took extensive classes in [differentiated instruction]. There were daylong seminars that we either did over the summer or on Saturdays. So we invested quite a bit in it... and now we're more giving them choices and helping them in different ways.

In promoting instructional leadership, Matthews relied upon directly evaluating teachers on a regular basis, a process teachers believed was shaped by her SLA experience. As one upper-elementary teacher remarked:

[S]ince [Matthews] started that program, there's been a real critique of our lessons. She doesn't [observe] a canned lesson anymore. She'll come into the room and just observe and hone. And if she notices something, she'll let you know. She'll tell you. And that has been so helpful.

Teachers noted that Matthews was "a constant presence in the classroom," making both frequent five-minute visits and regular 20–30 minute observations. They felt that her presence in the classroom "makes us better," that they "enjoy that feedback," and that it "is excellent, that she has a pulse on her school, on every classroom and on every teacher."

For these teachers, classroom observations seemed neither stressful nor burdensome, again affirming the trust that undergirds their relationship with Matthews, and the balance between challenge and support that permeated the social system of the school. Teachers viewed her instructional leadership as personally helpful and important for the school as a whole, as a source of both challenge and support for their teaching. In essence, her commitment to quality teaching generated benefits beyond the practical advice offered teachers—it was a crucial component of a distributed and supportive climate that fostered educational and cultural change. The qualities and characteristics of distributed leadership, noted above, permeated and influenced Matthews's efforts to improve classroom instruction. As Ylimaki and Brunner (2011) argue, "by modeling appropriate instructional leadership behaviors and inviting teachers to share leadership responsibilities, principals build instructional leadership capacity for systemic school change and increase student engagement and learning" (pp. 1264–1265).

Also key to instructional leadership at SCS was the movement toward peer observations and the use of instructional rounds (City, Elmore, Fiarman, &

Teitel, 2009), both of which were in beginning phases at SCS in the spring of 2013. I did not have the opportunity to collect significant data on these two initiatives in the time span of this study, but here the point is that at SCS fostering a common school culture and establishing distributed leadership directly implicated instructional improvement and a focus on learning. In particular, peer leadership was essential to creating a learning organization: principals must not simply distribute leadership—they need to distribute "learning-centered leadership" (Southworth, 2009, p. 108).

All of the above initiatives were aimed at improved teaching and learning. Learning is the goal; establishing a common culture, distributed leadership, and instructional supervision were all "triggers for transformation" (Davis, Sumara, & D'Amour, 2012, p. 396). Overall, the strategies of distributed and instructional leadership intertwined to create a fabric of SCS culture where leadership and authority were distributed among faculty, thereby enriching both their leadership and instructional skills while freeing the principal to actively shape what happened in the classroom. After all, culture is not shaped simply by leaders saying what should happen, although such communication does have a part to play. Rather, "culture changes by them putting in place certain processes and restructuring the school through specific systems. Leaders bring about reculturing by restructuring" (Southworth, 2009, p. 103). At SCS, reculturing and restructuring took place concurrently and through multiple initiatives; the school system was changed at various levels through multiple levers of change. In a complex system such as a school, there is no way to grasp the whole, but each part influences others, and the more aligned the different aspects of change are, the more coherent the resultant change is expected to be.

4   Guiding Emergence through Challenge, Support, and Balance

According to Davies (2009), "[l]eadership is about direction-setting and inspiring others to make the journey to a new and improved state for the school" (p. 2). At St. Catherine's School, Helen Matthews took on this charge at full speed. More than charismatic, she tried to embody what Hargreaves and Fink (2006) call "inspirational leadership," which encourages others to join her in the work of educational change (p. 77). In so doing, she brought much change to SCS during the two years of this study, and with it much disequilibrium for her faculty. In the language of complexity, such disequilibrium "creates a state in which the system is ripe for transformation, which is reorganization on a higher level of complexity" (Reigeluth, 2008, p. 27). But in the absence of balance and support, such disequilibrium can veer toward over-stressed and over-worked teachers—or teachers who simply give up because the challenge is too great. Either way the response is unsustainable. The trick is to stay "on the edge of chaos" without falling off either side.

The faculty at SCS had much to say about how Matthews inspired and stimulated them in their work. An inevitable aspect of this stimulation involved increased workloads, expectations, and time commitments. As noted above, successful schools tend to have "a much more demanding culture" (Fullan, 2005, p. 58). In the attempt to make SCS a more successful school, Matthews intensified demands on teachers. One veteran teacher explained that:

> Personally I've gotten a lot more work. I'm on the ILT team and that involves quite a bit of reading. And then I'm doing work in between the meetings.... I'm also the chairperson for the recertification effort, coordinating that. So things are delegated... and it's all done after hours as well, which is hard.... There's just no time to get everything done. We're just constantly juggling what needs to be done today and what can wait until next week, and sometimes that will flip flop. But I feel [Matthews] is in the same boat.

The change process at SCS was an experience of disequilibrium for many teachers—"an experience... beyond their comfort zone which [motivates] individuals... to integrate new knowledge or reshape existing perceptions" (Nadler, 1993, p. 59)—which is why it was critical that Matthews's leadership balanced challenge and support. Balance is key to educational change because faculty resistance or rejection is always possible; the intensity of reform needs to be flexible and responsive to ongoing feedback from other elements of the system in order for the system as a whole to stay on, and not go over, "the edge" (Opfer & Pedder, 2011, p. 389).

In addition to acknowledging the difficulties of educational change, teachers also highlighted how the way in which Matthews introduced new ideas facilitated broad acceptance of such change. A lower-elementary teacher described the process through which Matthews not only introduced the DREAM BIG initiative, but also led faculty through its implementation, explaining how she both supported and cajoled faculty into embracing this change while maintaining a balance between what teachers know and what they can learn:

> Here's this big thing but she's going to give you something tangible that you can reach first. She is going to show you excitement about it. That's her: She is always excited about whatever new thing she has. Then, [she will] give you something tangible that you can reach, like put this in your

classroom. Then, as the year progresses, she raises the bar for you.... It's like starting you here but then pushing it higher, especially for those that can get there.

This structured, progressive implementation of DREAM BIG seemed consistent with her efforts to balance her authority—being hands-on, decisive and authoritative as well as inclusive, delegating, and responsive. A middle school teacher's remarks also captured this dynamic:

> She's very hands-on. I don't think she has ever just said, "This is what we're doing, go." She's [more likely to say] "This is what we are doing," and then she checks in on you when she comes in, and she makes her presence known and she provides feedback when necessary, but without [belittling you]. I've never felt belittled by her. I've never felt like there was a power struggle. I know she's my boss, and I know she's in charge but... she's able to ask teachers for their advice when she needs it.

For this lower-elementary teacher, this balance was itself contextual and dynamic; she saw Matthews becoming increasingly authoritative when circumstances called for it:

> I would say she has been slightly more authoritative this year, which personally I think is good. I think she has been a little more demanding and a little more critical.... So I would say that she has asked for more... but [has] provided more feedback, or more ideas and a little more thrown on this year. I would say this past year she's been a little bit more in charge.

These remarks paint an interesting contrast: many teachers testified to an increase in distributed leadership and delegation of authority, as well as to the responsiveness and inclusiveness of Matthews's relationship with faculty, yet she was also "more in charge." This may suggest that effective leadership for change is not an either-or phenomenon: top-down, authoritative leadership appropriately balanced with inclusive, democratic processes and supportive relationships can engender substantive change. This view may help us to understand why, from a complexity perspective, a focus on bottom-up versus top-down reform "is a bit of a red herring. In other words, the who of leadership may be less important than the what" (Alsbury, 2008, p. 81). The processes and conditions of the system as a whole are what is important. The key questions to ask are: what is appropriate for this particular context, and how do other elements of the system respond and adapt to system changes?

Acknowledging the balance between distributed and authoritative leadership can help us understand why the ongoing process of change requires continual nurturing and attention, as its very success depends upon maintaining trust and a balance of power.

As Bryk and Schneider (2002) demonstrated in their study of Chicago Public Schools, "where high levels of social trust exist, the cooperative efforts necessary for school improvement should be easier to initiate and sustain" (p. 13). They go on to note that:

> In the context of high relational trust, teachers and parents believe in the good intentions of school leadership. As a result, they are more likely to afford principals a wider zone of discretionary authority.... This organizational feature is also especially significant in times of reform. Given the privacy of classroom practice, successful change efforts depend heavily on the voluntary initiative and goodwill of school staff. The presence of high relational trust increases the likelihood of broad-based, high-quality implementation of new improvement efforts. In this regard, trustworthiness across the organization helps coordinate meaningful collective action. (pp. 33–34)

Matthews's efforts to establish bonds of care and trust and to promote distributed leadership contributed to faculty accepting the changes she introduced, and enabled them to provide her with a "zone of discretionary authority" as the leader of the school. A broad sense of buy-in from faculty enabled the more top-down nature of many of the changes at SCS to not impede or contradict the more distributed, inclusive culture that Matthews was also trying to foster at the school. One of the lower-elementary teachers captured this balance in her remarks:

> She has the perfect mix.... I call it "warm strict." She's tough, but at the end of the day it comes down to the person. She wants the best for you. She's incredibly supportive in that she's reached out to teachers who have been struggling.... I think that she has a good mix of being authoritative, in that you know she's in charge, but at the same time delegating when necessary and making sure that all of her staff feels included and welcome. I think that's very important because you feel confidence in her, and she's in charge and she's the end of the line. At the same time, you know that she's reasonable and understanding and ultimately, she's so caring about people. That's what it comes down to at the end of the day for her.

An upper-elementary teacher touched on the theme of balance as well, while highlighting the sense of trust that underlies effective collaboration:

> She's very enthusiastic... [but] she's very pragmatic too. It's like, "If you can't do it, you can't do it. We'll figure another way around it." If you're having a problem, she wants to know about it upfront. I'm not afraid to go to her and say, "Okay look, this is what's happening." You know I'm not afraid to do that because she can help. She helps figure out a way around it.

Enthusiastic and pragmatic, warm and strict, challenging and supportive, in charge and inclusive—these are some ways that, following parents and teachers, I came to conceptualize the leadership characteristics that enabled constructive change at St. Catherine's. And these characteristics, in turn, are significant both in themselves and in their relation to broader school aims and cultural changes. At SCS, cultural change was adaptive change (Heifetz, 1994; Heifetz & Linsky, 2002), adaptive change was fostered by relational trust (Daly & Chrispeels, 2008), and these elements worked together to engender increased innovation and improved teaching (Moolenaar & Sleegers, 2010). It is the multiplicity of factors involved that makes complexity and systems thinking helpful—if not necessary—analytic frameworks for understanding school change. Within the framework of complexity, we can also note that, as a system on the edge of chaos, the tensions between distributed leadership/decentralization and top-down/centralized control are not resolved. There is an ongoing push-pull dynamic in place at SCS that is itself changing. In a complex adaptive system, "a diversity of agents... interact with each other, mutually affect each other, and in so doing generate novel, emergent, behavior for the system as a whole" (Lewin, 1992, p. 198).

At the end of this study, the overall dynamic and culture of the school was moving toward increased distribution of leadership, but it would be premature to say that the SCS systems manifests what could be called "emergent distribution," which no longer requires the direct instigation of senior leadership (Hargreaves & Fink, 2006, p. 122). Sticking with Hargreaves and Fink's formulation, we could say that SCS faculty are moving out of a phase of "progressive delegation" to a period of "guided distribution" or "firm facilitation," where distribution of leadership is still heavily dependent on the senior leader (p. 122). As they note, more traditional schools like SCS tend to need careful guidance in the transition from centralized to decentralized systems (p. 137). This study confirms that generalization, and supports the notion that leadership can be progressively distributed given appropriate support and challenge.

In addition to the balance involved in guiding a cultural transformation toward decentralization, and potentially toward the emergence of a learning organization (Senge et al., 2000), another key takeaway from this study is the significance of having a "growth mindset" (Dweck, 2007), which is an orientation toward ongoing inquiry and learning. As Wagner and Kegan (2006) argue, the new ideal for school leaders is to be a "leader-learner" (p. 213). Perhaps more than anything else, it is the impulse toward learning, experimentation, and transparency that characterized Matthews's leadership, and which explains the progress she and her faculty made toward collective growth. In her interviews she consistently repeated the intention to enact novelty, try new things, shake things up, and push for change in novel and unexpected ways; not in a haphazard or arbitrary way, but coextensive with a process of reflection and ongoing learning. She modeled for her faculty the characteristics that can foster the development of an open, learning organization, one that is "deliberately looking for information that might threaten its stability, knock it off balance, and open it to growth" (Reigeluth, 2008, p. 30).

At the very least, Matthews's actions disrupted the status quo at St. Catherine's School, changing the interactions among elements in this school system in notable ways. From her perspective, much of this disruption and growth was fostered by her work with the SLA. Speaking to her overall experience with the Academy, Matthews said "I thought it was the best damn professional development I've ever had in my life.... I think it's been invaluable." More could be said about connections between Matthews's work with the SLA and her work at SCS; when we see SCS as an open system we recognize that it would be impossible to completely untangle where the influence of external forces begin and end. Matthews captured something of this influence, and its connection to her orientation as the leader-learner of an open system, when she said:

> What I've noticed is even over the past year with [the SLA], my faculty feels more at ease to come into this office with more ideas. And I'll give them the resources to do it. It may not work! And so they'll say, "Well this was a failure." And I'll say, "So what did we learn? We learned this and this. So now let's do it this way. Let's tweak it!" And so to see that there's no blame.... What I'm trying to get across is that we're all in this together. We're all constantly lifelong learners. We're all constantly learning. So if it doesn't work, we'll fix it.

This attitude of ongoing improvement, which demonstrates sensitivity to the relational impact of words and actions on other system actors, seems appropriate for a leader engaged in the perpetual task of balancing and improving a complex system. As Schein (2004) observes,

> we basically do not know what the world of tomorrow will really be like, except that it will be *different,* more *complex,* more *fast*-paced, and more *culturally diverse.* This means that *organizations and their leaders will have to become perpetual learners.* (p. 393, emphasis in original)

As would be expected, a system that is successful in fostering disequilibrium, distributing control, and balancing system elements (and the tensions between challenge and support) will likely be successful in creating and sustaining positive change. All of these elements were in place at scs, and this systems view of school change therefore helps us to see why and how this overall school progress emerged.

5 Case Study Summary: Contextualizing Processes and Outcomes

The data presented above, while just a small portion of what was collected over a two year period at jjs and scs, portrays two schools in flux, and two leaders managing system change at the intersection of various influences and forces: as members of the School Leadership Academy who were impelled to challenge the status quo, as members of unique school systems, with very different histories and contexts, and as unique agents of change with particular personalities and leadership styles. Harold Weatherbee and Helen Matthews both catalyzed significant changes connected to all three foci of their sla Leadership Growth Projects: cultural leadership, distributed leadership, and instructional leadership. And while responses to their efforts were inevitably diverse, each school provided ample evidence that the majority of stakeholders at each site experienced overall positive change and growth during the course of this study. This was true across all three of the primary subgroups at each school—students, parents, and teachers—and was reinforced by my observations. However, each case study also presented significant differences in leadership, context, process, and outcomes.

At the end of Weatherbee's first year, there was significant test score improvement from the previous year on the statewide standardized examination. The improvement was so substantial that the school moved from a "Level 2" school to a "Level 1" school within the district's four-level ranking system. As with the larger questions of school improvement addressed above, the significance of this test score blip is not determinable through a year of data; I believe it would be a mistake to make too much of it. But jjs's Level 1 status continued, and after four years as principal at JJS the district transferred Weatherbee to another, lower performing school, ostensibly so that he could help that school to improve as he did at JJS.

Standardized assessments are not as readily available for SCS, since they are not included in the public school state testing system. But as of 2018, Helen Matthews is still the principal, and the school continues to proclaim the DREAM BIG vision. They have also become a self-proclaimed STREAM school: combining the popular acronym STEM (Science, Technology, Engineering, Math), with (the also now popular) Arts as well as Religion. They have also added a "Rosetta Stone Language Lab" that offers classes in Latin and Mandarin (through self-guided, computer based programs). Both continuity (in staffing and leadership) and perpetual change (in communications and programs) have continued.

Though embracing similar leadership orientations, the contexts in which Matthews and Weatherbee sought to promote adaptive change differed notably, as did the outcomes. JJS is a district public school. For the most part, teachers have job security. The pressure that was so palpable at St. Catherine's was nowhere to be found at JJS—except in the rhetoric and aspirations of Weatherbee, who like Matthews, was inspired by the SLA to bring a sense of urgency for change to JJS. Clearly, initial conditions were critical to shaping outcomes at both schools, revealing that one cannot separate "the school" from the network of relations in which it is embedded. This interdependence demands "not only that we examine an event itself, but also the contextual and relational environment of that event" (Despres, 2008, p. 249). For Matthews, trust was strong. She had a long history with her school. Her professional integrity was unquestioned. Further, the turbulent economic context of Catholic schools generated a sense of disequilibrium and urgency. Conditions were right to disrupt the status quo, and Matthews did this by allowing for the emergence of a transformed system, creating a decentralized network structure, promoting a constellation of cultural values, and offering faculty multiple opportunities to enact power and authority in a very different institutional context, ultimately "abandon[ing] the need to control and dominate… within the dynamic interactions of daily organizational existence" (Bathurst & Monin, 2010, p. 124).

Weatherbee faced a different context, many conditions of which were established before he arrived and over which he had no control. JJS teachers viewed principals with some mistrust, having seen three come and go in as many years. District policies seemed comparably unreliable. Lacking trust, faculty reacted to Weatherbee's plans as they had toward previous principals: with skepticism and resistance. Ultimately, teachers did assume new responsibilities and embrace their role as "crew," but in the classroom the status quo endured.

These studies also highlight an additional issue: the negative effect of frequent principal succession, which "breeds staff cynicism that subverts principals' credibility and their chances of securing long-term, sustainable improvement" (Hargreaves & Fink, 2006, p. 79). Indeed, as Lewin (1992) wrote, "[R]elationships are the bottom line... creativity, culture and productivity emerge from these interactions" (p. 203). Given the highly relational nature of complex systems such as schools, these studies present further evidence that administrators should not be moved among schools like interchangeable parts, and experienced educators who have garnered respect and credibility should be seen as ideal candidates for school leadership. For Matthews, who worked at SCS for 21 years before becoming principal, interactions flowed smoothly. Even teacher resistance served as a source of insight for school planning. Weatherbee, an inexperienced educator, never generated a comparable dynamic. His interactions with teachers were often strained and counter-productive. Consequently, he and JJS faculty struggled to work together productively to enact positive cultural change.

Decentralized networks generate opportunities for school personnel to experience their colleagues' competence, sincerity, and reliability, thereby enhancing relational trust and the likelihood of risk-taking and innovation (Moolenaar & Sleegers, 2010). At St. Catherine's, Matthews initiated a process of professional collaboration enacted through an interdependent network of teams. Teachers planned collaboratively and helped colleagues who struggled with change. Teachers' work became more collective and transparent. The decentralized structure created regular opportunities for the school community to display professional integrity (Bryk & Schneider, 2002), and faculty came to trust one another. JJS was a different story. Faculty seldom discussed teaching and learning as a community. Wanting to control the conversation, Weatherbee was reticent to trust teachers, so he chaired and directed almost all school meetings. JJS faculty neither saw Weatherbee display trust in them nor had opportunities to promote relational trust with colleagues. They did collaborate and offer verbal support to each other, but largely on matters outside the classroom.

When effective, the sum of a network's actions can exceed that of its individual parts, producing unanticipated outcomes because certain factors prove mutually interdependent: "When individual, social and contextual conditions for learning interact to enhance each other... a synergy is created by their mutual influence" (Hobban, 2002, p. 59). This occurred at SCS. Matthews empowered individual teachers, assigning them new roles and responsibilities. The team structure led teachers to interact in new ways and thereby brought about opportunities to enrich relational trust. Building on this contextual shift, people shared openly, offering opinions and strategies they otherwise would not risk. Over time, without Matthews's direction and with no formal planning time, teachers produced networks around matters of genuine interest to them (Moolenaar & Sleegers, 2010). This required them to identify shared concerns, openly communicate those ideas, and develop plans to address them—all of which emerged organically. Nothing comparably unanticipated happened at JJS.

Through interactions they provoke, networks can reinforce cultural values and socialize new personnel into the prevailing culture, both in how you work and what you work on. By creating decentralized networks, Matthews signaled a commitment to shared authority, professional development, and mutual trust, among other factors. Her actions reflected both goals and processes that aligned with the emerging school culture (Coburn, Choi, & Mata, 2010). At JJS, Weatherbee allowed teachers few opportunities to enact power. Professional networks existed but teachers had little autonomy and engaged in few collaborative actions. The school's collective efforts often reinforced a climate of skepticism and resistance, and teacher leadership never really got off the ground.

Cultural values also impacted what occurred at these schools, serving as an attractor that shaped faculty beliefs and practices (Gilstrap, 2005). For SCS teachers, the ideals embodied in DREAM BIG offered a touchstone against which to judge their professional work while providing Matthews with a lens for assessing whether faculty used power she entrusted in them in productive ways. In decentralized networks, having been accorded power and authority, opportunities for SCS faculty to collectively enact, refine, and reinforce school culture were iterative and redundant (Lemke & Sabelli, 2008). Multiple avenues for consistent communication and reinforcement demonstrated that the more levels of the system a policy affects, the more likely it is the policy will have a sustained impact. The common school culture at SCS clearly impacted multiple levels of the school system, from creating common language and common discipline policies to a parent accountability contract.

Weatherbee also tried to promote a common school culture. He encouraged faculty to see themselves as "crew, not passengers" and to embrace new roles and responsibilities, though he entrusted faculty with limited autonomy and was unsuccessful in his attempt to achieve buy-in to the goal of 100% proficiency. Lacking a common belief system, the teams and communication cycle created to empower teachers proved risk-averse and ineffective in shaping classroom teaching. The school's "collective conceptual orientation" (Bowers & Nickerson, 2001) remained largely unchanged—the principal was in charge and faculty maintained control of classroom autonomy.

We cannot reduce school outcomes to leadership behaviors, but we can seek to describe the relationships between leadership and system behavior. Matthews's brand of "transformational leadership," grounded in collective engagement and common purpose, when contrasted with Weatherbee's reliance on a more "transactional leadership," dependent on a desire for control, goes a long way toward explaining the divergent outcomes of these two schools (Daft & Lengel, 1998). Or rather—and this is a claim that will require further explanation in Chapter 5—*those differences in process are the difference in outcome.* The end is the means. The quality of the process is the goal. The value judgments I am making about these schools are based on their relative alignment with systems-based leadership principles and the ways in which actors in those systems responded to leadership in that context. The school district in which JJS exists reinforces a very different framework of value (based almost exclusively on standardized test scores). In the absence of these studies, and the qualitative data and theoretical framework that forms their interpretation, a very different (and arguably superficial) assessment of these two schools could easily be made based on test scores, perceived demand, and school ranking in which the outcomes and judgments would be completely inverted. SCS continues to struggle in the declining market of parochial schools while JJS remains at Level 1 and is therefore in high demand. In the district's view, JJS's status as a Level 1 school *means* Weatherbee was a successful leader, period. The end is the scores; scores are the goal. But in the systems view, it is the nature and quality of the relationships that constitute the system itself—and the impact of those relationships on different parts of the system—that determine and qualify value, merit, and success.

Building on the centrality of relationships, Fink (quoted in Hobban, 2002) spoke to the possibilities and limitations of utilizing the Complex Adaptive Systems (CAS) heuristic to conceptualize educational change:

> [P]reventing, or at least minimizing, the attrition of change requires attention to a complex interrelationship of many factors that influence purposes, structures, and cultures in schools.... The complexity of... their connections and relationships make it virtually impossible to determine exact pathways of causation, and therefore impossible to *predict* with certainty that attending to this factor or that will ensure a school's continuing growth and development. The best that can be said is that schools that become aware and attend to the factors [identified earlier] will *be more likely* to retain their innovative edge and remain 'moving' schools over time. (p. 38, emphasis in original)

And as Bower (2008) reminds us, "renewal, sustained change, growth, and creativity emerge from within. We cannot create these qualities by fiat or by devising lists of goals and objectives. We can, however, help to create the conditions that allow for these qualities to emerge" (p. 110). What both of these authors point to (though not necessarily overtly or intentionally) is that the systems view itself is a closed system; it is a self-referential constellation of ideas and meanings, constituted by symbols and signifiers, that describe complex systems and therefore enable the evaluation of changes that occur in complex systems according to that description.

I noted above the disconnect between Weatherbee and his staff regarding educational goals and the limits of possible change. The gap between Matthews's perspective and that of her staff was smaller in significant ways, and this contributed to their ability to collaborate productively. There was also a perspectival gap between Weatherbee and Matthews. Even though they espoused the same ideals (as they both seemed to buy into and repeat the ideals and aims they were exposed to by the Academy), they lived and enacted those ideals and intentions very differently. Their espoused theories were almost identical, but their theories in use were quite different (Argyris & Schon, 1974).

There was also another important gap: the gap between these two school leaders and me. The CAS metaphor is mine, not theirs. To what extent could they be good systems leaders when that was not what they were explicitly trying to be? Is it fair to assess leadership using a framework that the leaders themselves do not share and espouse? And if what they espoused mirrored the words and concepts they received from the SLA, to what degree were those concepts and intentions "theirs?" How independent are they as actors, and to what degree do they deserve credit or blame for the manifestations of the school systems they participate in? How aware were they of the economic, political, and social forces that surrounded them, and how did those forces impact them and other stakeholders at their schools? These are some of the questions I was left with as a researcher as I finished the process of data collection, review, and interpretation for these case studies—and the questions that impelled me toward a meta-analysis.

CHAPTER 5

Perpetual Learning in an Integral Ecology

> Big ideas and big theories have the power to transform social systems.... Theories and metatheories of organization and management not only interpret what goes on in the world of commerce and work, they also influence the design and implementation of those systems.
>
> MARK EDWARDS

∴

> A man with one theory is lost. He needs several of them, or lots! … If you are to get on you need to know that there are lots of theories.
>
> BERTOLT BRECHT

∴

The process of understanding never ends. For those of us engaged in the work of researching, interpreting, and seeking understanding of social reality, we must do so knowing that there is no final interpretation, no singular objective truth, and no clear line to distinguish where the context of our study ends and the rest of the world begins. As Puhakka (1995) observes,

> We live in systems within systems, contexts within contexts indefinitely, and the systems are constantly sliding and the contexts shifting. The vision of an open universe unfolding and enfolded upwards and downwards without end effectively removes all bases for certainty and completeness.... The evolution that we are all part of excludes nothing, not even the contexts that bound our understanding and awareness. (p. 11)

Whether seeking to understand school systems, social systems, or ecosystems, we draw our lines of relevance and meaning into a dynamic and interdependent flux and do our best to explain our abstracted portion of reality; there are no lines unless we draw them. In qualitative educational research, as in the study of developmental psychology or ecology, "the analysis begins *in medias res*, in the middle of things. Starting in the middle of things means that people's activities are embodied, contextualized, and socially situated—understood in their ecology" (Fischer & Bidell, 2006, p. 315).

Our ecology is not made of only physical stuff. The ecology of humanity cuts across and through all of the domains we have created to understand our world: physics, biology, chemistry, psychology, sociology, anthropology, theology, philosophy, cosmology, etc. Ours is an Integral ecology (Esbjorn-Hargens & Zimmerman, 2009). We can see this clearly in schools. SCS is not merely the bricks, mortar, and electrical technologies that make up the "school," nor those things in combination with the human bodies that traverse the space of the schoolyard. As we saw above, SCS is constituted as much by ideas like DREAM BIG (and now STREAM) as it is by smart boards (which they could not afford anyway). Schools are constituted by the noosphere as much as by the biosphere; by the mental world as much as by the physical world (Wilber, 1995, 2000b). The culture of a school—and the lived reality of each individual in that school—is indelibly influenced by currents of thought, belief, and ideology that neither begin nor end within the school itself. There are larger forces at play. As Smith (1999) reminds us,

> What makes ideas 'real' is the system of knowledge, the formations of culture, and the relations of power in which these concepts are located. What an individual is—and the implications this has for the way researchers or teachers, therapists or social workers, economists or journalists, might approach their work—is based on centuries of philosophical debate, principles of debate and systems for organizing whole societies predicated on these ideas. These ideas constitute reality. (p. 48)

While I can never fully explicate the living reality of Jeffrey Jackson School or St. Catherine's School, I seek here to unpack more of the explanatory context that permeated and influenced each of these school communities. I am not seeking a full or final truth, but I am seeking to explain more; ultimately I am the one who must draw the line of what is relevant and what is not (e.g., some of the problems of urban public education are indelibly connected and related to the historical influences of colonialism, slavery, racism, and neoliberalism, but connecting the dots to any of those forces would require a separate book). But by addressing the questions noted at the end of Chapter 4, and attempting to surface and elucidate broader and deeper philosophical questions and considerations that surround and inform educational research and theory building, we can move toward disclosing a bigger picture of educational change and leadership—a picture that illuminates and explains not only the field of education, but aspects of the broader social and cultural world in which we live, learn, work, and continually strive for progress and growth.

In this chapter I will re-introduce Integral Theory as a way to frame the parameters of the meta-analysis. I will then highlight the two areas of inquiry that I find to be particularly relevant and important for understanding leadership and change in education: the domains of human development and socio-cultural infrastructure. In Chapter 6 I will offer a summary, recommendations for future inquiries, and a fuller account of my positionality as a researcher, school leader, and theorist.

1 Post-Postmodern Pluralism: Integrating Perspectives on Leadership and Change

> The opposite of complexity is not simplicity, it is reductionism.
> NORA BATESON

The questions that impel what follows are methodological, philosophical, historical, and deeply personal. My initial reflections on these cases stemmed in part from a recognition of the tension between explanation and understanding, and the fact that actions can be explained in ways that undermine or contradict how actors themselves understand them. Ideally, as a researcher, one achieves both an understanding of research participants, in terms they would confirm, and an explanation that transcends that shared understanding. Understanding can be seen as a condition for good explanation (Apel, 1984; Habermas, 1988; Stein, 2016).

As I continued to reflect on this data and my initial interpretations, I became increasingly aware of the critical perspectives I had available to me, which I had largely bracketed throughout the research process as they were not germane to answering my initial research questions. As I will describe more below, my own work as a school leader, my awareness of critical theories of educational discourse, and my exposure to a wide variety of school contexts impelled me to articulate what I felt were important interpretive contexts for these studies; the fact that they were not germane to my initial research questions meant that I needed to develop a second set of (post) research questions and conduct a meta-analysis. Ultimately, I sought a way to be as intellectually honest and authentic as possible, and found that my explanations, grounded in a framework of systems theory, did not adequately encapsulate the understanding I developed of the schools I experienced. So I seek here to make connections to a broader theoretical framework that enables me to contextualize not only my own data and interpretations, but also the philosophical and methodological underpinnings of educational research as a whole.

As noted above, Integral Theory is one way I have found to incorporate a greater depth and span of perspectives into my interpretations. IT operates from the basic proposition that every perspective and every theory has some merit; to seek the "correct" theory is to take a wrong first step on a path of (mis) understanding. As Edwards (2010) notes, "every theory embodies some insight and systematically bringing theories together makes possible the emergence of more humane and efficacious ways of understanding the world we live in" (p. 1). Toward that end, "metatheoretical research is the systematic and deliberative study of theories and their constituent lenses" (p. 2).

Because metatheoretical inquiry includes the study of the lenses and perspectives that co-arise with theories, the researcher is unavoidably implicated. As Esbjorn-Hargens and Zimmerman (2009) explain, "the Integral approach is not just about describing more accurately what is 'out there' but is about changing our own awareness by following a variety of injunctions" (p. 48). Consequently, "the [Integral] model is a 3rd-person map, a postdisciplinary framework for 2nd-person shared language, and a set of 1st-person practices" (p. 56). Integral Theory is a postdisciplinary metatheory that can serve many functions:

> [IT] is *postdisciplinary* in that it can be used successfully in the context of *disciplinary* (e.g., helping to integrate various schools of psychology), *multidisciplinary* (e.g., helping to investigate ecological phenomena from multiple disciplines), *interdisciplinary* (e.g., helping to apply methods from political science to psychological investigation), and *transdisciplinary* (e.g., helping numerous disciplines and their methodologies interface through a content-free framework) approaches. (Esbjorn-Hargens & Zimmerman, 2009, p. 47)

In my work with IT over the years I have found that it is very much like downloading a mental operating system. It is psychoactive in the sense that thinking through the various aspects of the map/framework/matrix increases my subjective awareness of the possible domains of inquiry and limits the likelihood that I will settle for a limited, reductive perspective on whatever subject I explore. I have also found that using IT as a framework or operating system also enables me to find my place in and make sense of the broader historical currents of thought that continue to have an incalculable impact on schooling, academia, and society and culture more broadly. In particular, it has helped me to orient myself within the currents of thought and interpretation that are often referred to as traditional, modern, and postmodern, all of which are alive and well in different forms and subcultures within our society and educational systems.

Very briefly, a *traditional* perspective can be understood as fundamentally conformist, conventional, and ethnocentric, grounded in identification with a pre-established in-group (e.g., family, race, tribe, and/or country), with emphasis on the "one right way" to do things, depending on authoritarian delineations of what is right/wrong and good/bad. *Modernism* expresses the emergence of quasi-universal ideas and identities—notions of the Good, Truth, and Beauty that ostensibly transcend conformity to the standards of any particular group, based on ideals of objectivity, science, and universal human rights. (Though it is still, inevitably, a perspective grounded in the limited assumptions and experiences of particular individuals and groups, e.g., European males, without an adequate account of that positionality.) Modernity can therefore be associated with the search for "theoretical monism" and various manifestations of totalizing, monological, and often materialist and positivistic approaches to science. The development of the modern approach to human inquiry and understanding led to and co-evolved with rapid changes and progress in many fields, and remains the subjective and intersubjective foundation for most of the legal, political, scientific, economic, educational, and cultural norms of international systems and discourse (spread largely through European colonialism) (Diamond, 1999; Gebser, 1991; Harari, 2015; Taylor, 1989, 2007; Wilber, 1995).

Postmodernity—as the title implies—can be seen as a widespread reaction to and rejection of the perceived downsides of modernist developments, though it is also an evolutionary emergent in its own right. From the perspective of postmodernity, traditional and modern social structures and ways of being and knowing can be seen in a very critical light, e.g., Taleb (2014):

> My definition of modernity is humans' large-scale domination of the environment, the systematic smoothing of the world's jaggedness, and the stifling of volatility and stressors. Modernity corresponds to the systematic extraction of humans from their randomness-laden ecology—physical and social, even epistemological. Modernity is not just the postmedieval, postagrarian, and postfeudal historical period as defined in sociology textbooks. It is rather the spirit of an age marked by rationalization (naïve rationalism), the idea that society is understandable, hence must be designed, by humans. With it was born statistical theory, hence the beastly bell curve. So was linear science. So was the notion of "efficiency"—or optimization. Modernity is a Procrustean bed, good or

> bad—a reduction of humans to what appears to be efficient and useful. (p. 108)

The differentiation from, deconstruction of, and problematization of modernist discourse via postmodernity emerged alongside new vistas of perspective regarding interdependence and complexity, as evidenced by the ongoing development of systems and complexity theories, which began as modern discourses and evolved to take on more postmodern perspectives. As Taleb (2014) continues, "at the center of all this [modern reductionism] is the denial of antifragility"—i.e., the disasters of modernity can be traced to a denial (or lack of understanding) of fragility/antifragility related to complex systems (p. 108).

One of the most definitive features of postmodernity is its critical stance toward metatheorizing. As Lyotard (1984) professed in *The Postmodern Condition*, the term postmodern "designates the state of our culture" following the end of the 19th century, while the term modern is used "to designate any science that legitimates itself with reference to a metadiscourse... [that makes] an explicit appeal to some grand narrative" (p. xxiii). For Lyotard, the modern proclivity for grand narrative was so central that it made sense to "define postmodern as incredulity toward metanarratives" (p. xxiv). Thirty years ago this was a key insight into the structural differences in perspective that permeated these broad cultural and intellectual currents. Yet culture has continued to evolve globally, as have the social discourses of various subcultures. Many can now see that postmodernity is not an end point; Fukayama's (1992) "end of history" has not arrived. What has emerged are new vistas of interpretation and understanding, and new possibilities for integrative metatheorizing that transcend yet include the postmodern critiques of modernity. The "postmodern mind" embodies a deeper appreciation of diversity, along with awareness and critique of the limits of traditional and modern perspectives, and is therefore in many ways a positive development (Smith, 1992). But as Edwards (2010) points out, "when diversity is pursued in the absence of integration, factionalism and the compartmentalization of knowledge are the results" (p. 15). And as Forman and Ross (2013) argue,

> Though complexity is a daunting aspect of today's... reality that needs to be taken into account, it is not by itself the issue. What has been missing until now is a unifying theory that relates different existing models to each other, that offers a comprehensive view, and that is simple enough to generate profound and effective means for diagnosis and intervention. What is becoming increasingly apparent is that we need an overarching theory or perspective. (p. 179)

For Edwards (2010), the difference between modern metanarratives, and the kind of metatheory that is emerging in response to postmodernity, "is one between totalising diverse accounts into a single theoretical formulation and integrating diverse accounts into a pluralistic metatheoretical framework" (p. 50). An integral/pluralist approach—which is a decidedly post-postmodern emergence—is analytical and holistic but not totalizing, and certainly not modernist; it aims to build connections between theories rather than unifying them (modern) or deconstructing them (postmodern).

Complexity theory and systems theory have emerged as ways to help theorists explain the increasing complexity and evolution of systems while combining elements of modernity and postmodernity. As noted above in Chapter 2, complexity thinking is often thought of as one manifestation of the New Sciences, which as a whole aligns with the more decentered, post-positivistic, postmodern approach to science. Yet systems and complexity theories, in a hybrid development that spans the discourses of both modernity and postmodernity, have taken on some of the shortcomings of each paradigm, namely materialism and value-neutrality, as noted above (in Chapter 1). They are, as noted with irony, reductive, and yet "complexity theory itself provides few conceptual resources to analyze how and where its own "reduction" occurs, why, or with what consequences" (Fenwick, 2010, p. 58). Integral Theory, on the other hand, is very helpful in explaining how and why complexity and systems theories are reductive, and what would be required to avoid such reduction and embrace more complexity (and therefore understand and explain more of reality).

With regard to organizational theory and leadership, the aim of such an approach is not

> to replace the plurality of approaches with some super-theory of transformation but, rather, to develop a flexible metatheory for considering and situating the diversity of paradigms and theories of organizational transformation within a more encompassing and integrative conceptual landscape. (Edwards, 2010, p. 25)

The emergence of postmodernity as a cultural force in academia is one way of explaining the ubiquitous shift away from grand theory toward mid-range theory. As Edwards explains,

> Given the disastrous outcomes of some of the totalising theories of the nineteenth century, the subsequent focus on ideas of the middle-range is understandable. But middle-range theory will not resolve global problems.

> Global problems of the scale that we currently face require a response that can navigate through theoretical pluralism and not be swallowed up by it.... What is required is a balance between an integrative synthesis and a respect for the pluralism of perspectives. The creation of a more inclusive vision of organizational life will need a nuanced approach, one that values the synthesizing instincts of modernity as well as the pluralising intuitions of the postmodern. (pp. 2, 223)

Of course, the notion that theories of great explanatory power have somehow disappeared or retreated in recent history would be misleading. Perhaps the most dangerous thing about postmodernity is that grand narratives continue to influence thought and behavior, but now do so unconsciously, in the shadows of the psyche. In reality, the impact of social theory and big picture theorizing continues to be deep and ubiquitous (Giddens, 1984; Taylor, 2007).

> Big theories about government, international relations, economics and education have their impact on society and those impacts feed into the everyday activities of the members of those societies. The question is not one of relevance of metatheory but of our awareness of the processes by which certain metatheories already influence social realities. (Edwards, 2010, p. 47)

In very broad terms, IT maintains that the meta-context of all partial contexts is the process of ongoing evolution and development. There is no final truth, objectivity, or perspective because everything is in a process of becoming. Change is the only constant, and we have more than 13 billion years of ever-increasing evidence that change is not linear or random—it is evolutionary in all domains of existence, and is moving in the direction of increasing complexity, via ongoing processes of differentiation and integration (Jantsch, 1976, 1980; Sheldrake, 1981; Stewart, 2000; Wilber, 1995, 2017; Wright, 2000). The increasing complexity of our social world intensifies our need for theories and maps that simplify and explain without over-simplifying or reducing important features of our shared experience. Traditional, modern, and postmodern theories are no longer adequate to the data we have available. New theories, frameworks, maps, and operating systems will continue to evolve along with our access to and perception of continually emergent qualities and quantities of information—and evolutionary development therefore needs to be a constituent element of any adequate framework or system. The idea of multi-domain evolution is pictured in Figure 4.

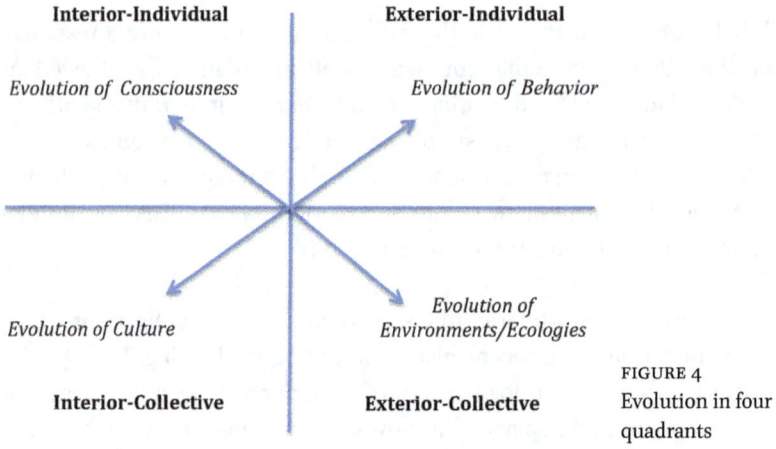

FIGURE 4 Evolution in four quadrants

This four-quadrant development can also be described in terms of the evolution of operating systems (Smith, 2018).

INDIVIDUAL

Consciousness & Philosophy   **Economic Behavior & Currency**

Interior	Exterior
Integration	Transformational/Cryptocurrency
Relativism	Informational/Derivatives
Humanism	Industrialism/Fiat Currency
Empiricism	Mercantilism/Bill of Exchange
Myth	Agrarian/Gold
Magic	Horticulture/Goods
Archaic	Foraging/Archaic
Survival/Protect	Band/Communal
Might/Expel	Tribe/Communal
Order/Sanction	Chiefdom/Chief
Conquest/Power to Reason	Empire/Monarchy
Value/Power to Contract	Nation-State/Democracy
Equality/Power to Convene	World-State/Network
Resilience/Power to Integrate	Trans-State/Panarchy

Organizing Value &   ***COLLECTIVE***   **Society &**
Emergent Power   **Governance**

FIGURE 5 Evolution of operating systems (adapted from Smith, 2018)

The methodological approach of IT is Integral Methodological Pluralism (IMP). The purpose of IMP is to integrate and include as many methods and disciplines as possible that are relevant to any given inquiry, so as to attain and explicate a comprehensive understanding of a given subject. This approach requires that we distinguish and acknowledge multiple perspectives and approaches, without marginalizing or negating any potential avenue to valid information and relative truth. Potentially, such an approach allows us to avoid effacing distinctions and differences, reduction to one methodology or perspective, or retreating into a form of relativism or cynicism. As Esbjorn-Hargens and Zimmerman (2009) illustrate,

> Natural science is not a kind of poetry. Science and poetry involve very different methodologies. Nevertheless, we cannot allow natural scientific truth claims to trump the truths of different methodologies. We can contest objective claims with objective methodologies, and judge subjective claims with subjective methodologies. Within each domain there are claims that are better than others. But you cannot judge a subjective claim with an objective methodology, because the criteria for truth claims are domain dependent. (p. 64)

A framework for including multiple perspectives and methods emerges from two primary distinctions: inside/outside and singular/plural, as illustrated by the four quadrants and the concomitant perspectives we can take on any phenomena.

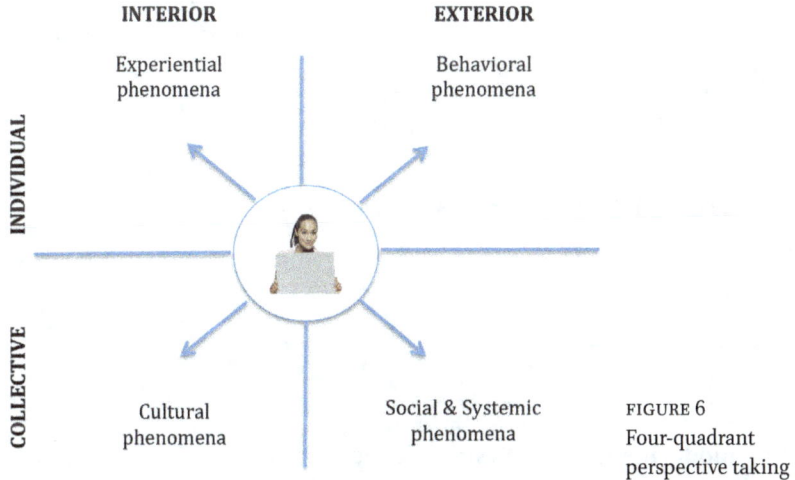

FIGURE 6
Four-quadrant perspective taking

Taking these four domains as irreducibly real, we can see how major schools of thought, science, and inquiry typically restrict themselves to only one domain, effectively bracketing the truth and reality disclosed by other domains. Identifying and delineating multiple domains of reality goes a long way toward explaining many of the historical disagreements and ruptures that emerge in various "paradigm wars"—in education and other fields (Gage, 1989; Howe, 2009; Lagemann, 2000; Smith, 1992). IMP reorients us to a broader field of perspectives and liberates us from having to decide which domain is "really real" and therefore worthy of study, or which paradigm is "correct." This expansion of our conceptual horizon enables us to avoid "quadrant absolutism"—the common yet misguided notion that one domain can explain all of reality. Figure 7 offers examples of well-known theories and theorists and the domains of reality they privilege. Figure 8 illustrates quadrant absolutism.

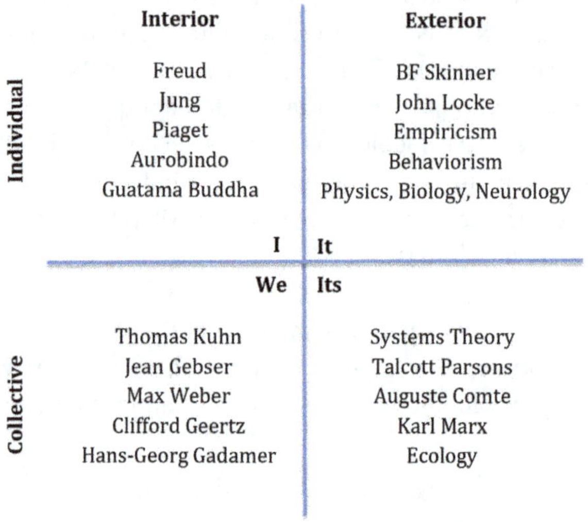

	Interior	Exterior
Individual	Freud Jung Piaget Aurobindo Guatama Buddha	BF Skinner John Locke Empiricism Behaviorism Physics, Biology, Neurology
	I	It
	We	Its
Collective	Thomas Kuhn Jean Gebser Max Weber Clifford Geertz Hans-Georg Gadamer	Systems Theory Talcott Parsons Auguste Comte Karl Marx Ecology

FIGURE 7
Theorists in four quadrants

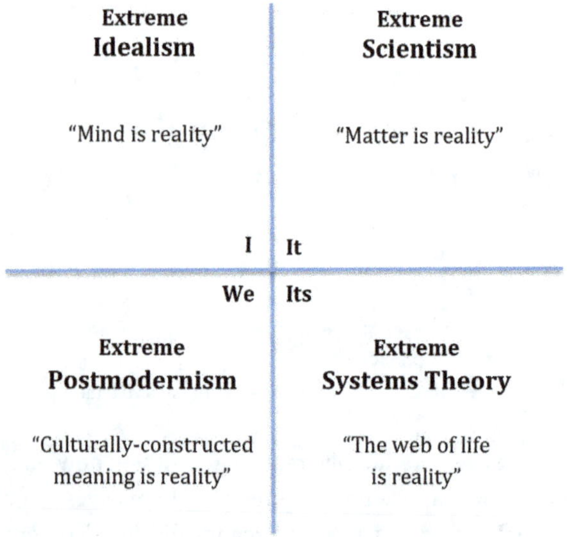

	Extreme **Idealism**	Extreme **Scientism**
	"Mind is reality"	"Matter is reality"
	I	It
	We	Its
	Extreme **Postmodernism**	Extreme **Systems Theory**
	"Culturally-constructed meaning is reality"	"The web of life is reality"

FIGURE 8
Quadrant absolutism

In effect, IMP recognizes that each domain is valid and can be researched in at least two ways: subjectively and objectively, or from within and from without. This leaves us with eight native perspectives, research paradigms, or zones.

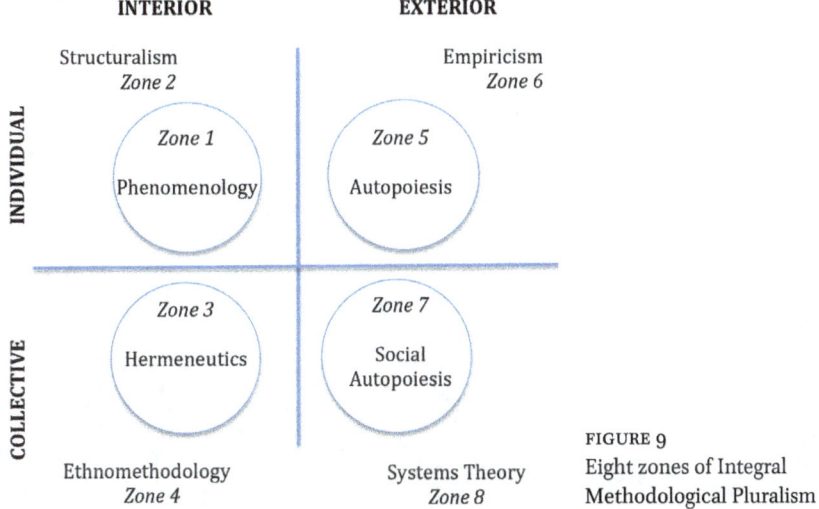

FIGURE 9
Eight zones of Integral Methodological Pluralism

Each zone has real phenomena and is accessed by different methodologies:
- Zone 1: phenomenology, meditation
- Zone 2: developmental structuralism
- Zone 3: hermeneutics, interpretive sociology
- Zone 4: cultural studies/anthropology, semiotics, ethnomethodology, genealogy
- Zone 5: cognitive behaviorism, cognitive science, autopoietic biology
- Zone 6: empiricism, behaviorism, positivism, empirical natural sciences
- Zone 7: game theory, social autopoiesis, social values theory, enactive systems theories
- Zone 8: general system theory, complexity theory, chaos theory, network sciences

The utility of the framework in Figure 10 is readily apparent, as we can see these distinctions in the work of well-known philosophers and scientists, and in the fields of business, medicine, ecology, education, leadership, and systems/complexity (Esbjorn-Hargens, 2010; Wilber, 2000a, 2006d).

As one far-reaching example, we can compare the work of Heidegger and Foucault. Both of these theorists focused much of their attention on the lower left (LL) quadrant, the domain of culture, yet they took different views and focused on different zones: Heidegger was looking primarily from the "inside"

METHODOLOGIES FOR UNDERSTANDING

"I" Subjective realities;
- self and consciousness, states of mind, psychological development, mental models/constructs, emotions, state of self, etc.

"It" Objective realities;
- brain and organism, visible biological features, degree of activation of the various bodily systems, etc.

ZONE 1
(The feel)

Phenomenology: (introspection, meditation, etc.) methodologies for understanding intentions surface structure

ZONE 5

Cognitive Science: (biological phenomenology, autopoiesis, etc.) methodologies for understanding Behaviour surface structure

ZONE 2
(The look)

Structuralism: (developmental structuralism, etc.) methodologies for understanding intentions deep structure

ZONE 6

Empiricism: (behaviourism, positivism, empiricism, etc) methodologies for understanding behaviour deep structure

Intention   Behaviour

ZONE 3

Hermeneutics: (collaborative inquiry, participatory epistemology, etc.:) methodologies for understanding culture surface structure.

Culture   Society & Systems

ZONE 7

Social Autopoiesis: methodologies for understanding Society and Systems surface structure.

ZONE 4

Ethnomethodology: (cultural anthropology, neostructuralism, archaeology, genealogy, etc.) methodologies for understanding culture deep structure.

ZONE 8

Systems Theory: (component systems theory, chaos theory, complexity theory, etc.) methodologies for understanding Society and Systems deep structure.

IntegralMENTORS

"We" Intersubjective realities;
- shared values, world views, webs of culture, communication, relationships, cultural norms and customs, etc.

"Its" Interobjective realities;
-. social systems, environmental systems, visible societal structures, economic systems, political systems, etc.

FIGURE 10   Methodologies in the eight zones (from van Schaik, 2016)

(Zone 3) and Foucault was looking primarily from the "outside" (Zone 4). Dreyfus and Rabinow (1983) summarize this very point:

> although both Heidegger and Foucault attempt to disengage and relate the "factical" principles which structure the space governing the emer-

gence of objects and subjects, Heidegger's method is hermeneutic or internal, whereas Foucault's is archaeological or external. (p. 57)

We also find these distinctions represented in different schools of systems theory. As I introduced in Chapter 1, a shortcoming of systems theory comes from the simple fact that it limits its attention to the domain of social systems and therefore does not adequately account for the reality of individuals or subjectivity (Zones 1 and 2). In addition to this inherent limitation (which is not so much a critique as a resituating contextualization), while systems and complexity theorists agree that the LR quadrant of systems provides the most explanatory purview of reality, the field is essentially split down the middle regarding which view is the best, i.e., which perspective discloses the "truth" about systems—Zone 7 or Zone 8.

As Bausch (2001) describes in *The Emerging Consensus in Social Systems Theory*, many systems theorists hold to the reality of autopoiesis (Zone 7), whereas many others maintain that the more standard dynamic systems theory and/or complexity theory is the way to go (Zone 8). Thus, there are "two grand unifying theories of present-day systems thinking: complexity/bifurcation/components systems and autopoiesis" (Bausch, 2001, p. 15). These two schools represent a systems/rational, objective/outside view and an autopoietic/enactive, cognitive/inside view. Each has merit and validity, but discloses only relative and partial truth—as do data from all the other zones. Therefore, each methodology and perspective, when taken alone to be the only real and true domain of inquiry, can lead to absolutist, reductionist, and sometimes extreme conclusions, almost inevitably. From an autopoietic perspective, "our representations have no reality independent of our minds and languages. They do not re-present an existing reality that is present to us.... We remain bound to self-observation" (Bausch, 2001, p. 374). This is how reality looks from an exclusively Zone 7 view, given the impact of autopoiesis theories—it is a common view in modern systems theories, and yet leaves much to be desired, as it effectively brackets data from other zones. It is but one example of a very common epistemic fallacy—the false idea that there is only the inside/subjective/enactive world. This error is committed often by those who privilege and/or exclusively identify with the methods, injunctions, and perspectives of Zones 1, 3, 5, and/or 7 (Wilber, 2017).

Systems and complexity theorists often commit the opposite fallacy: the ontic or ontological fallacy, which maintains the false idea that there is only an objective, material world, while the enactions of knowing subjects are denied. This is a common fallacy committed by those who privilege and/or exclusively identify with the methods, injunctions, and perspectives of Zones 2, 4, 6, and/

or 8 (Wilber, 2017). Integral Theory, on the other hand, sees both inside and outside views as true but partial. As I argued in less integral terms in Chapter 1, this is the fundamental limitation of systems theory, and the underlying reason I continued to feel that I was leaving out important data and perspectives as I tried to interpret the reality of schools through the systems lens. As Edwards (2010) notes, "the danger of developing invalid lenses that are not generalizable across human and non-human systems is a particular problem when reviewing theories coming out of the systems and new sciences research paradigms" (p. 211). I felt this danger as a researcher, and this meta-analysis is my attempt to account for it.

These same distinctions arise in the fields of leadership and management, as could be expected. The major, general theories of business management (which have been decisively imposed on the field of educational leadership, with mixed results) can be divided into four categories: Theory X, Theory Y, culture management, and systems theory. As Watkins and Wilber (2015) point out, we can see that these broad schools and their proponents fall predictably into the four quadrants:

1. Theory X: managing individual behavior, UR, Zones 5 and 6
   – E.g., *The Competent Manager* (Boyatzis, 1982); *The Managerial Grid* (Blake & Mouton, 1964); *The Human Side of Enterprise* (McGregor, 1960)
2. Theory Y: managing motivation and individual growth, UL, Zones 1 and 2
   – E.g., *Motivation to Work* (Herzberg, Mausner, & Snyderman, 1959); *New Patterns of Management* (Likert, 1961); *Drive* (Pink, 2011)
3. Culture management: managing interiors of groups, LL, Zones 3 and 4
   – E.g., *The Culture Cycle* (Heskett, 2011); *Organizational Culture and Leadership* (Schein, 2004); "Culture eats strategy for breakfast" (Peter Drucker)
4. Systems theory: managing group behavior and relations, LR, Zones 7 and 8
   – E.g., *The Fifth Discipline* (Senge, 1994); *Leadership and the New Science* (Wheatley, 2006); *Systems Thinkers in Action* (Despres, 2008)

Of course, many theories and theorists do not fit neatly into one of the quadrants or zones. Yet when we step back into the pluralist perspective we can discern real patterns and make helpful orienting generalizations to situate ourselves in a given field, make meaningful distinctions between different approaches, and assess shortcomings and oversights, while avoiding "quadrant absolutism."

Much more could be said about each of these approaches—their nuances, elements that cross categories, the historical emergence from Theory X to Theory Y to culture to systems, and other attempts to integrate many of these perspectives. But the aim here is to establish these general categories as prevalent, real, and meaningful, to establish a basis from which to argue for the inclusion and integration of multiple perspectives and methodologies in educational research and the social sciences more broadly. In particular, this framework helps to establish the need to include both subjective and objective methodologies concurrently. The delineation of Theory X and Theory Y can create a false choice. No choice is necessary; integration and skillful means are what is called for. Likewise, the distinctions between culture and systems is important: "Where culture management looks at the interiors of the group and finds interwoven networks of mutual meaning and values, systems theory examines the exteriors of the group, and finds interwoven networks of interrelated systems and structures" (Watkins & Wilber, 2015, p. 66). But that does not mean we have to choose one or the other. It means we should be aware of what lens we inhabit and why, so that we can avoid reduction and seek ever more comprehensive interpretations of our field of study.

Through such integration we can also seek to enact more effective change. As Watkins and Wilber (2015) argue, "there has to be a change in personal consciousness, group culture, individual behavior and institutional systems change" if we are to address the "wicked" problems of our social world (p. 85). This is no easy task, and requires leaders who can see and understand the multidimensional terrain of organizational life. I believe that the attempt to integrate multiple perspectives is crucial for understanding the complexity of the 21st century, and that it is also an essential aspect of leadership that enables individuals to understand and co-operate with others in order to effectively manage systems and culture, self and other. And a good place to begin on this road—as a theorist or as a leader—is with a metatheoretical map that enables one to begin to expand the parameters of sense-making, conceptual integration, and identity. As Forman and Ross (2013) claim:

> The generative leaps we are hoping for in the coming [years] will be made by those leaders who take the next step of reconstructing the four-dimensional map and using it consciously. For leaders to elicit right action in people (Upper Right), they must understand people's interiors (Upper Left), the ways that they talk and make decisions with each other (Lower Left), and the structures of exchange that will facilitate their decisions and actions (Lower Right).... This more Integrally-informed view... allows leadership to make more complete and coherent assessments of complex situations and then to set direction, foster organizational commitment, and coordinate sustainable change more accurately. (p. 12)

Even if this claim is too strong and adherence to IT is not necessary (and I do not think it is), the complexity of perspective that enables a pluralist, multi-perspectival, meta-theoretical vantage point may very well be an absolute necessity for adequate research and leadership moving forward. If this is the case (and I think it is), the question is how to explain, enable, and encourage this perspective-taking. As Wilber (2006a) explains,

> Each of the important methodologies (from empiricism to collaborative inquiry to systems theory) are actually types of practices or injunctions—in all cases, they are not just what humans think, but what humans do—and those practices therefore bring forth, enact, and illumine a particular dimension of one's own being—behavioral, intentional, cultural, or social.... (This is why different forms of praxis yield different theoria.) (p. 70)

There is (from a certain perspective) no ultimate, fundamental separation between perspective and reality; ontology, epistemology, and methodology are interdependent and mutually co-arising. My perspective and the reality that is disclosed to me are two sides of the same coin, two arcs of the same circle. Which is why, as noted above in Chapter 1, the development of perspectives is a crucial area of inquiry in the search for increasingly adequate interpretations of social life. There are levels of understanding, and "at each given level, or worldspace, the epistemology (the knower), the methodology (the "how" of knowing), and the ontology (the "what" that is known) are all mutually interwoven, co-creative, and integrally enactive" (Wilber, 2017, p. 679). "What's visible at a given level or scale depends on what kind of tool or conceptual framework we are using to look at it" (Cunningham, 2014, p. 56).

With this historical and philosophical context now partially surfaced, I will explore two avenues of inquiry more deeply, in order to understand more fully the realities of the two schools we have explored. In an attempt to balance out the systems-oriented interpretation above—which leans heavily toward external descriptions—I will now include some reflections on the individual and collective interiors of my research participants, with an eye toward what methodological approaches would be needed to establish a more comprehensive and valid account of each school. So we turn to the upper left quadrant, Zone 2.

2   Subjective Realities: Understanding the Spectrum of Perspectives

> We are truly beginning to regard adult personality not as a state or form of organization but as a direction of development. We now see adult personality less as a recognizable cross section and more as a multidimensional trend phase of a complex developmental process.
>
> CLARE GRAVES

> The heavens and all below them, Earth and her creatures, all change, and we, part of creation, also must suffer change.
> OVID

The basic claim that we must reckon with the reality and implications of psychological development in relation to leadership is tied to the claim that leaders with more complex and developed perspectives will be better leaders (i.e., more likely to have a positive, desirable impact on the systems they are enmeshed in, where what is desirable is determined in light of a broad consideration of all direct and indirect impacts, in all four quadrants). Researchers in the fields of management and business leadership have supported this claim, and it is important to continue these lines of research (Kegan & Lahey, 2016; Torbert, 2004). The significance of developmental leadership complexity has been applied in other fields as well, from facilitating cross-cultural healing in South Africa (Beck, 2014; Beck & Linscott, 1991) to negotiating ecological and cross-cultural restoration in British Columbia (Martineau, 2007). Based on his work in British Columbia, Riddell (2005) notes:

> When [post-conventional/self-transforming/Integral] capacities emerge, complex issues and diverse perspectives can be more readily integrated into holistic, long-term solutions. Leaders acting from Integral capacities act as cultural empathizers and transformers who operate dynamically across multiple worldviews motivating people with diverse interests toward common ecological, economic, cultural, political, and social goals. Leaders with Integral perspectives can foster healthy ecological worldviews, enabling mutual understanding, and fueling individual and cultural transformations of increasing scope and depth. (p. 73)

Speaking more generally, Wilber (2006c) argues that

> In order to have sustainable economies living in harmony with ecosystems, human beings must have interior levels of development that can hold ecological consciousness: there is no sustainable exterior development without correlative interior development, no exterior landscape that can survive without an interior landscape capable of holding it. (p. 32)

More research is needed in education and leadership to tease out the nuances of how the inner and outer realities of leaders and systems reflect and influence each other, and part of my intent here is to trace the outlines of what that could entail and why it is important. But the working assumption for educational leadership, based on prior work in various fields, is that in order to have sustainable and pro-social educational systems working in harmony with the needs and potentials of human development, the human beings responsible for leading and directing those systems must have interior levels of development that are adequate to that task; no exterior educational landscape can thrive without an interior landscape capable of holding it.

As noted in Chapter 1, in general agreement with dozens of developmental frameworks that researchers have used to explain universal structures and systems of thinking, Kegan and Lahey (2016) connect this research to leadership and organizational life using the following descriptors to flesh out how the most prominent and prevalent perspectives manifest. They simplify the spectrum of perspectives into three broad stages:

– *The socialized mind*: a team player, a follower; seeks direction; reliant; expresses self in relationships with people or beliefs; says what others want to hear.
– *The self-authoring mind*: agenda-driving; a leader who learns to lead; follows own compass; independent problem solver; follows personal authority.
– *The self-transforming mind*: a meta-leader; a leader who leads to learn; uses multiple frames and holds contradictions; problem-finder; interdependent; reflects on limits of own ideology.

The correlations between these three broad stages and the even broader categories of traditional, modern, and postmodern culture should be apparent, though of course not exact. There are clear correlations because the frequency and probability of a given perspective has an influence on the culture that is co-constituted by those perspectives, but one cannot reduce the broad currents and patterns of culture and society to more specific stages that correspond specifically to studies of leadership. Such stages are orienting generalizations based on the integration of specific assessments. They are themselves the product of an integral, metatheoretical perspective. And while such generalizations are useful and valid, it is important to note that their foundation rests on specific, rigorous studies that assess the development of specific skill sets. As Mascolo and Fischer (2010) explain,

> To speak of the development of psychological structures is not the same as speaking of the development of a person. There are no general or "all purpose" psychological structures. Although they undergo massive development over the life span, psychological structures consist of localized skills that are tied to particular situational demands, psychological domains, and social contexts. (p. 155)

The research paradigm of "dynamic structuralism" analyzes "how the constructive activity of human agents leads to new relations among systems of action and thought" (Fischer & Bidell, 2006, p. 315). Systems of relations are necessarily dynamic, but a generalized structure of development "refers to the system of relations by which complex entities such as biological organisms and psychological activities are organized," and the description of such structures elaborates a "model of psychological structure as the dynamic organization of self-constructed, socially embedded skills and activities (actions and thoughts)" (Fischer & Bidell, 2006, p. 314).

Zone 2 methodologies like structuralism have become anathema to postmodern perspectives—being "post" structuralist is a close second to denouncing grand-narratives as a defining feature of the postmodern mind. Unfortunately, the early pioneers of structuralism (e.g., Levi-Strauss, Barthes, early Foucault, Lacan) were able to bring neither the nuance nor the rigor of assessment that later, more "adequate structuralism" was able to develop, and the postmodern reaction to and critique of this early structuralism failed to recognize the ways in which the methodology could (and would) be improved (Wilber, 2006c, p. 23). The notion of "structure" is common in many schools of biology, psychology, and sociology, and generally means "recurring pattern," or "an organized, patterned, relatively stable configuration." As Wilber argues,

> the simplest way to look at these patterns is as a probability space. The 'structure' of an individual agency and/or cultural nexus-agency is simply the probability of finding, in a particular locale of the interior dimensions... the behavior that is described or defined as 'within the structure.' (p. 23)

In other words, structuralism is an exterior description, in third-person terms, of the probability of finding a particular "I," or first-person/subjective behavior, in a particular space-time context. It is "the study of an *interior* as seen from *outside* its own phenomenological boundaries" (Wilber, 2006c, p. 25). This distinguishes it from systems theory, for instance, because while they both utilize third-person language, the terms (or signifiers) of structuralism take as their referent first- and second-person interiors; the terms (signifiers) of systems theory take as their referent third-person exteriors.

> When researchers engage in the social practice of systems theory, they are particularly interested in describing the behavior of observable systems; they are describing the exterior behavior of compound individuals such that their relationships or exterior interactions are internal to a social system or nexus-agency. They might take an 'inside' view of this exterior system (such as Luhmann's social autopoiesis) or a more traditional

'outside' view (such as standard systems theory), but at no point do they attempt to get at the first-person (singular or plural) dimensions.... They look at the inside or outside of exteriors, not at the inside or outside of the interiors.... If all we do is describe the traffic patterns of sentient beings—using ecology, systems theory, chaos and complexity theory—then we have indeed reduced all first-person consciousness to third-person objects, its, and artifacts: we have killed all culture and consciousness. (Wilber, 2006c, pp. 25, 29–30)

On the other hand, if we acknowledge both interiors and exteriors—honoring consciousness and culture, instead of killing/reducing them—we can identify structural patterns and probabilities from the foundation of specific and technical assessments. We can find, with Graves (2005),

> The data [suggest] that one must think of levels of psychological maturity moving on a scale from low complexity to higher complexity. It [indicates] that one must think of a tendency toward organizing, stabilizing around a certain central core, and re-organizing around a different central core, possibly *ad infinitum*. (p. 149)

Many models of and approaches to adult development and leadership development exist. The question is what to make of them. The answer, inescapably, depends on the perspective we ask and answer the question from. It is helpful to be familiar with numerous models, to be able to apply one or more appropriately in a given context, to understand the pros and cons of each, and to identify generalities and principles that hold across contexts and models. Even earlier leadership models that are not explicitly based on developmental theory, such as Argyris and Schon (1974), highlight many salient points that have since been bolstered and strengthened by ongoing developmental studies. They were amongst the first to recognize that "the main task... is to identify the conceptual models that form the basis for people's theories-in-use," and from there that "reeducation has to begin with an attempt to specify the patterns of existing theories-in-use" in order to help people grow from what they called a Model I approach to a Model II approach (Argyris & Schon, 1974, pp. xxiii, xxix). They identified some of the underlying qualities of dynamic structures of thought and action, recognized the underlying unity of being, knowing, and doing ("the behavioral world is an artifact of our theories-in-use" (p. 17)), and even utilized what has a become a frequent analogy in developmental studies, where "theories-in-use tend to be tacit structures whose relation to action is like the relation of grammar-in-use to speech" (p. 29).

More recently, Wilber has made this point about structures and grammar, because it is important to realize that, like rules of grammar, people utilize structures of thought without being aware of them or even being able to explain or describe them when asked. We only explicitly know actual rules of grammar if we study them, just as we only know about structures, patterns, and levels of development if we study them. A structure of consciousness is something you look through, not at (Watkins & Wilber, 2015, p. 89). This is why the appropriate methodology is structuralism (Zone 2) and not phenomenology or meditation (Zone 1). We cannot see structures of consciousness via introspection; structures are how thinking looks when generalized across multiple data points from the outside, not from the inside (and not with a sample size of n = 1).

In light of more recent and sophisticated models, we can ascertain that the patterned dynamics that constituted what Argyris and Schon (1974) thought of as Model I and Model II map fairly well onto what Kegan and Lahey (2016) call "self-authoring" and "self-transforming." An advantage to the latter framework is that the contours of these structures are understood within a broader context of an unfolding spectrum of perspectives and thinking, and a broader awareness of this developmental spectrum enables us to make better sense of the particular stages. An even more fine-grained model, developed by Torbert (2000a, 2000b, 2004), also aligns with these and other models, while addressing interdependently the domains of social science, organizational complexity, and individual complexity.

Torbert (2000b) outlines seven stages of development relevant to organizational leaders, which he calls action-logics—overall strategies that so thoroughly inform our experience that we cannot see them—each with discernable and recurring associations and patterns:

- *Opportunist:* focused on gaining control in and over physical world; uses unilateral power; short time horizon; externalizes blame and avoids responsibility; usually transcended in childhood
- *Diplomat:* focus on performance and self-control; masters routine tasks; conventional; controls performance to meet approval of others; usually transcended in teenage years; avoids conflict, masks true feelings and data; does not seek negative feedback—deflects it to maintain status [Socialized mind]
- *Technician/Expert:* focus on strategic experience and mastering cognitive disciplines; logistical power; 6 month to 1 year timeline; views own judgments

as objective; most adults do not transcend the Expert stage; conventional; empirical positivism
- *Achiever:* focus on planning, performing, and assessing; juggles short time lines and 1–3 year timeline; manages single-loop changes in behavior to achieve results; never fully locked into one frame; represents 40% of highly educated adults; conventional; multi-method eclecticism [Self-authoring]
- *Individualist:* post-conventional and relativistic; aware of conflicting emotions; interested in own and others unique self-expression; seeks independent, creative work; less inclined to judge or evaluate; starts to notice own shadow; possible decision paralysis; postmodern interpretivism
- *Strategist:* "self-awareness in action"; aware of paradox that what one sees depends on one's action-logic; more likely to engage double-loop learning; designs situations where others are origin of causation; more frequent efforts to understand others' frames, inquiring rather than dismissing; more likely to see perceptions as perceptions, not reality, and to discuss difference explicitly; more likely to base actions on principles rather than rules, and use awareness of others' point of view to question and revise own goals; cooperative inquiry [Self-transforming]
- *Alchemist:* very rare; playful and leisurely sometimes, urgent and fierce at others—work and play not easily distinguished; active attention to analogies across individual, group, organizational, and international scales of development; continually exercises own attention, seeking single-, double-, and triple-loop feedback; stands in the tension of opposites and seeks to blend them; developmental action inquiry

As is the case with all dynamic developmental models, each later stage includes the possibilities and potentials of former stages, so "at each later action-logic we have more degrees of freedom about which action-logic we use when" (Torbert, 2004, p. 68). The Opportunist and Diplomat perspectives are "pre-managerial action-logics" because they lack the complexity required in leadership positions, whereas Expert and Achiever action-logics together have been found to describe the dominant perspective of around 80% of managers. At these stages leaders begin to value single-loop feedback (about whether or not a past action was effective), but they do not yet encourage double-loop feedback (regarding the effectiveness of one's overarching strategy or structure of assumptions). Achiever action-logics tend to pay attention to differences between their own and others' point of view, place value on teamwork, welcome personal feedback, and seek mutuality, but will reject feedback if it does not fit within the parameters of their already established scheme of things—they are not prepared to question the validity of the action-logic itself (double-loop feedback). The Diplomat, Expert, and Achiever stages are all conventional action-logics—they "take social categories, norms, and power-structures for granted as constituting the very nature of a stable reality" (p. 92).

As Spiral Dynamics (Beck & Cowan, 2006) and Integral Theory (Wilber, 2000a) emphasize, there are significant, describable thresholds that an individual can cross in adult maturity and perspective taking. Spiral Dynamics and Integral Theory both refer to a transformation from "first tier" to "second tier," which constitutes a "momentous leap" in one's ability to take multiple perspectives, be aware of one's own perspective, and understand other perspectives not as right or wrong but as necessary and constituent building blocks of ever broader, deeper, and more integrated perspectives. In Torbert's (2004) model, a key distinction is made between pre-Individualist stages and post-Individualist stages, which mirrors this first-tier/second-tier separation, where

> the Individualist is a bridge between two worlds. One is the preconstituted, relatively stable and hierarchical understandings we grow into as children, as we learn how to function as members of a preconstituted culture. The other is the emergent, relatively fluid and mutual understandings that highlight the power of responsible adults to lead their children, their subordinates, and their peers in transforming change. (p. 102)

In this conception, prior action-logics "have us," whereas "we have" the later action-logics, in the sense that one is "increasingly self-aware and self-transforming" when functioning at those more integrated levels (p. 68).

The leadership implications of fostering this Strategist/second tier development are significant, because

> persons constructing these post-conventional action-logics increasingly appreciate that they are exercising forms of power with others in each social interaction. They increasingly recognize that they are either reinforcing or transforming existing action-logics and structures of power as they do so. They see not only that new, shared frames *can* be generated in the present situation, but also that shared frames often *must* be generated, if high quality cooperative work is to have any chance of occurring. (Torbert, 2004, p. 94)

The Strategist "becomes increasingly attuned to the developmental process," recognizing that others have developed and that "they need the opportunity to develop autonomously toward integrity, mutuality, and sustainability" (Torbert, 2004, p. 105). Accompanying this recognition is a willingness "to let others... make their own mistakes, but to do so in the context of developing greater alertness and capacity for single-, double-, and triple-loop self-correction" (p. 105). In order to lead and shepherd others effectively in these ways one must be able to see the deeper purpose in life beyond one's own needs, so that the development of others becomes a primary concern. Torbert's data suggest that "the [leader's] support is necessary in order to create a culture in which change can start anywhere within the organization and that only a [leader] at the Strategist action-logic can reliably do so" (p. 115). Leaders operationalizing Strategist and Alchemist action-logics "become highly effective at leading organizational transformation, in part because they are less attached to their own frames and, therefore, more aware of how people, organizations, and societies journey through different frames and action-logics over time" (p. 121).

These various models overlap extensively, and cumulatively lend credence to each other's validity. Together they constitute and reinforce what Graves (2005) called a "hierarchal systems perspective," where the psychology of the adult human being is understood as "an unfolding, ever-emergent process marked by subordination of older behavior systems to newer, higher order systems. The mature person tends to change his psychology continuously as the conditions of his existence change" (p. 29). Or as Stein (2016) puts it, "human development [is] an *epigenetic* process, a process of continual self-transcendence, where the self-system and its beliefs undergo qualitative reorganizations—co-evolving in dynamic relations with the social and physical world" (p. 88, emphasis in original).

Understanding these structures and how they develop is important for us all, for we often settle into what approximates a closed (mental/cognitive/ideational) system, and when our perception and identity are centralized within a given structure, we have only the degrees of behavioral freedom afforded us within that structure. Being able to perceive and objectify these structures—much as we can formally describe rules of grammar if we study them—enables us to consciously engage the process of our own development. It also enables us to understand better the words, beliefs, and actions of others, for "it is not what a person thinks that reveals his or her psychology but it is how a person thinks that provides the central material for understanding a person" (Graves, 2005, p. 68).

Having this background framework also helps us understand better the terrain of leadership (and lack thereof), and the ways in which leaders (and employees and citizens at every level of organizations and society) are not meeting the demands that our increasingly complex 21st century society is placing on them. We are—most of us, individually and collectively—"in over our heads" (Kegan, 2003). As Torbert (2004) notes, around 90% of "well-educated"

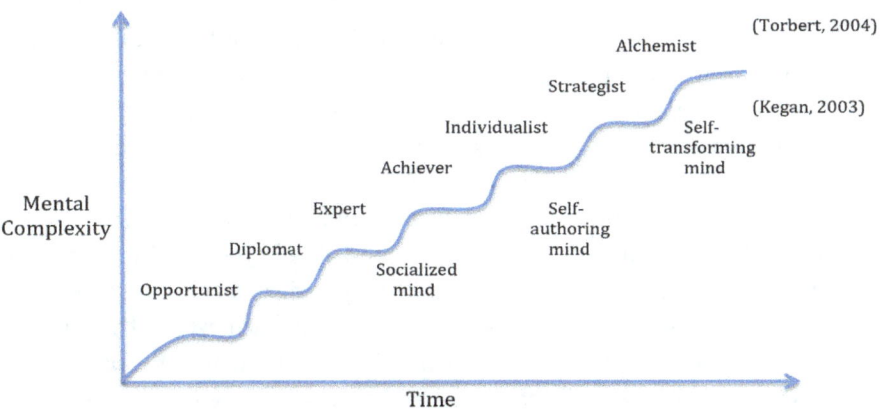

FIGURE 11   Comparison of mental complexity stage models

adults are operating predominately within conventional structures, with only 7% consistently accessing post-conventional action-logics (and 3% at pre-conventional stages).

Because post-conventional leaders have a disproportionate effect on other individuals and organizations, it is all the more crucial that we work to make these frames less implicit and more explicit (which is itself a trait of post-conventional, self-transforming action-logics). Within the framework of Integral Methodological Pluralism, we can ascertain that the appropriate methodologies to surface and develop these frames and potentials lie in Zone 1 and Zone 2, via subjective/interior approaches and objective/exterior approaches to individual subjectivity (e.g., phenomenology, meditation, awareness of awareness practices, triple-loop feedback (Zone 1) and dynamic developmental structuralism (Zone 2)). Developmentalists like Kegan, Torbert, Graves, and Wilber all work in both ways: to describe objectively dynamic structures and to share and foster practices that encourage development across the spectrum of action-logics.

The point of this metatheoretical reflection is that an understanding of this developmental terrain—as one of many interdependent domains of inquiry, represented by the 4 Quadrants and 8 Zones—is relevant and helpful for understanding the present case studies of educational leadership (and schools in general). I believe this is so in at least two ways: as a way to increase awareness of the methodological and interpretive limitations of educational research, and as a way to gain insight into educational leadership. However, in these cases, the former limits the latter: acknowledging the absence of Zone 1 and Zone 2 methods and data increases our awareness of what is missing (potentially increasing our understanding of the terrain of the overall context of the case), and yet what is missing is the data that would enable a fuller account of the leadership profiles and capabilities of Weatherbee and Matthews. That said, it appears that there are real and meaningful benefits to making connections between the terrain of individual perspective taking and development and the data that we have from these two schools.

1.1   Taking a Closer Look: Meta-Reflections on School Leadership

The general contours of both Matthews and Weatherbee's thinking can be tentatively ascertained by looking at how they navigated and understood two central questions at their schools: how to define and achieve student success, and how and why to distribute leadership? For both principals, the parameters of success were fairly straightforward and clear, and were largely defined by forces and judgments external to them and their school communities. Both relied on standardized tests to determine the relative success of student learning, and both were enmeshed in systems of accountability that established a direct and ostensibly causal line between student test scores and leadership effectiveness. Neither principal used their words or actions to directly challenge or question this system of accountability or the definitions of learning and success (for students, teachers, or themselves) that came along with it. Both principals focused their words, actions, and energy toward achieving success within the paradigm as it was.

For Weatherbee, this adoption of conventional, pre-defined (i.e., other-defined) notions of student success led to overt tensions with staff, and to the establishment of what amounted to irrational and even absurd demands. As Weatherbee stated, "the ultimate end result is that... we need to get our proficiency levels up." At no point in my time at JJS did it seem to occur to Weatherbee that those who work at the school should determine the goals and aims of the school. Nor did the question ever arise as to whether or not those aims could be questioned, or that there could exist any other ultimate goal. The goal was pre-established, and Weatherbee saw it as his job to compel teachers to buy into and achieve that goal. All of the other efforts and ends were ultimately subordinate or tangential to those quantifiable outcomes. As he stated: "One of our theories is that if we increase the level of communication and get parent buy-in, and if we as a team get deeper in our work, we will get a higher proficiency rate." And that higher proficiency rate had a very clear, objective, static benchmark: "all of the students need to be at grade level by the end of the year." Or as he said in the ILT meeting transcribed above: "no one in red."

The externality of this aim—the way in which the end of education was for Weatherbee something that he did not generate from his own or his staff's reflection, judgment, and consideration—also led to some confusing and contradictory manifestations of leadership. As noted above, Weatherbee was in some ways tempered and cynical in his aspirations and expectations of teachers. His impact on teaching practice and demands for change were minimal and notably gentle. And yet at the same time he was prone to verbalize somewhat extreme ultimatums: 100% student proficiency was an absolute and unquestionable goal, and any doubt of that on the part of teachers was met with the simple reassertion of the demand: "no one in red." Many teachers saw standardized tests as a "necessary evil," but Weatherbee never disclosed such open questioning of the standards by which he and the school would be judged. Rather, he seemed to oscillate between trying to muster the conviction to convince teachers that 100% proficiency was possible, and being resigned to the fact that there was only so much he could do to get teachers to change their beliefs and practices.

From these observations, it appears fair to conclude that Weatherbee's action-logic in relation to his work and the task of education and leadership was clearly not self-transforming, and perhaps not even self-authoring. What I observed were characteristics that ranged from Diplomat to Expert to Achiever, with a clearly conventional or traditional approach to role fulfillment; there was evidence of single-loop learning, but not double- or triple-loop learning. In respect to the notion that all students can and should achieve proficiency on standardized tests, a post-conventional reflection on this goal would likely lead to the realization that such a goal is literally impossible and therefore nonsensical—the system of testing is designed to require a certain degree of failure. The goal of 100% proficiency is a farce (Ravitch, 2013; Stein, 2016). (This does not mean that teachers who questioned the tests are necessarily operating at a more complex or postconventional perspective; not all who question standardized tests are postconventional, but anyone operating from a postconventional perspective would likely come to question the system of standardized testing as it currently exists.)

Similar evidence and conclusions hold for Matthews. Both principals were greatly influenced by their experience with the School Leadership Academy, and took on their Leadership Growth Projects with full abandon. I did not find any evidence of critical reflection on the aims, processes, ideals, or assumptions of the SLA (nor of the business-school influenced foundation and orientation of the program). At SCS, Matthews's buy-in to educational change as it was defined by the SLA also meant that, while not subject to the same public school test-based ranking system as JJS, the success of leadership would be determined primarily by quantifiable student outcomes (and student enrollment, which is assumed to be directly impacted by those standardized outcomes). And at SCS, this orientation led to what could be seen—if examined from a more critical, postmodern, postconventional lens—as Draconian and authoritarian changes: DREAM BIG meant not just believing in God and working hard, but walking in silent lines in the hallway, signing a behavior contract, and strict dress code enforcement. Teachers described success largely in accordance with the degree to which students were quiet and under control (as opposed to the degree to which they were learning and growing toward their own complexity, maturity, and self-authoring). At SCS both the ends and the means were conventional expressions of "change" within a range of norms that were never overtly questioned. As at JJS, the ends were determined by forces (and perspectives) external to the school, and the principal determined the means to those ends. At no point did staff at SCS discuss or question either. As with Weatherbee, the limits of perspective-taking and action-logic for Matthews seemed to be in the Achiever range, with a focus on planning, performing, and assessing in order to manage single-loop feedback aimed at achieving success within a pre-established framework.

The limits of leadership perspective were also evident in and help to explain how leadership was distributed at each school. As noted in the cases, both schools distributed leadership on the lower ends of what could be considered a spectrum of distribution complexity—what Lambert (2009) calls Instructive as opposed to High Capacity. For Weatherbee in particular, the unwillingness and/or inability to grant teachers significant autonomy stifled the emergence of teacher leadership. (Matthews enacted a significantly different leadership paradigm, and showed more signs of self-authoring and post-conventionality, discussed below). As also noted above, this difference was related to a concomitant difference between the version of distributed leadership that Weatherbee was exposed to by the SLA and the manifestation of distribution at JJS during the period of this study. This difference can be understood as a difference in complexity of perspective. The SLA was drawing from some extent on systems and complexity theory to frame its approach to leadership, but that is not a perspective that Weatherbee (or Matthews) necessarily shared.

Another purpose of exploring these differences of perspective is to understand better what is involved in actually shifting or growing one's overall range of action-logic; it cannot be accomplished by mere exposure to the language or ideas of distributed leadership. Exposure to the SLA led to buy-in about being "crew" and not passengers, and changing school culture to DREAM BIG, but it did not lead to the emergence of any of the "second tier" qualities that would inspire and foster complex distributed leadership in an organic and more effective way (e.g., showing an interest in one's own and others' self-expression; engagement in double-loop learning; designing situations where others are the origin of causation; ability to see perceptions as perceptions and to discuss difference explicitly; use of awareness of others' point of view to question and revise one's own goals).

This brief review of themes from the cases in light of the spectrum of human development and perspective-taking highlights the importance of the question: how do we encourage and facilitate the adaptive change of developmental transformation? As Kegan and Lahey (2016) remind us, "adaptive challenges require changes not only in skill sets but also in mind-sets: changes at the level of the operating system itself, precisely what we mean by development" (Kegan & Lahey, 2016, p. 200). It is this understanding of adaptive change that is crucial for leadership—but this is not the view that dominates leadership discourse.

A key connection and potential bridge between human development and educational leadership lies in the popular idea that many problems in business, education, and leadership are "adaptive problems": challenges for which system actors have not yet developed an adequate response (Heifetz, 1994). The pressures and challenges of educational reform and success, especially in urban schools, as noted at the outset, demand more than merely "technical" solutions; teachers and principals are going to have to change significantly in order to meet these ever-increasing demands. "Adaptive problems resist [technical] solutions because they require individuals throughout the organization to alter their ways; as the people themselves are the problem, the solution lies with them" (Heifetz & Linsky, 2002, pp. 5–6).

However, references to adaptive work do not often capture or explain the kind of vertical transformation that adult development research points to. In addition to describing the now well-known differences between technical and adaptive problems and solutions, it is helpful to clarify what is meant by the kind of transformations of consciousness that developmental psychology refers to. A developmental view highlights the difference between horizontal growth and vertical growth (Cook-Greuter, 2004). The former happens through many channels and takes many forms, but the latter is much more difficult to achieve. Adaptive challenges require learning, innovation, and the development of novel solutions, but do not necessarily entail or require the kind of vertical growth or transformation described by research on adult development. Heifetz (1994) and others talk about adaptive problems or challenges, and adequate responses to such challenges may be conceived as adaptive change or learning, but in their efforts to establish a "prescriptive concept of leadership" that is "practical" and "socially useful," an in-depth explanation of leadership *growth* is not generated (p. 19). It is for this reason that Forman and Ross (2013) refer to *translative* vs *transformative* change. Translative change occurs within an existing set of mental models, organizational structures and cultural systems, while "transformative changes are directed at the mental models, organizational structures, and cultural systems themselves. These systems and the assumptions behind them are changed" (p. 167).

This understanding of transformation goes beyond what is conveyed by the notion of adaptive change, and is more grounded in empirical research that documents substantive, reproducible, stable, cross-cultural shifts in individual perspectives and meaning-making. The integration and embrace of this body of empirical data and developmental theory could constitute a substantive advance in our efforts to understand different lived experiences of leadership.

The metaphor of a building may be helpful. If technical solutions were likened to rearranging furniture on a floor according to set floor plans, adaptive solutions could be understood as finding novel and previously unthought-of ways of organizing space—for instance, a breakthrough "aha" moment when someone realizes the potential advances made possible by an open, network-friendly environment, or by a study of feng shui. This is keeping with the tendency to define adaptive problems as those whose answers are not known—they require adaptive learning that evokes novelty and ingenuity, yet they do not necessarily entail the transformation of mental or cultural structures. In this example, each of these changes would be translative. Actual vertical development—a transformational change—is something else entirely.

Keeping with our metaphor, transformational change could be seen as moving up to a different floor, with an altogether different perspective on the building and all the problems that arise within it. What is more, in the building structure of human development, the floors are made of glass, allowing higher views to see and understand the meanings of lower perspectives to some degree, while the ceilings are more like opaque mirrors, limiting interpretations of higher developmental levels to various kinds of projection and misrepresentation (Smith, 1992; Wilber, 2000b, 2017). The fundamental change is constituted by moving to a higher floor, not by novel behavior. "The real shift is not in technique but in perspective" (Forman & Ross, 2013, p. 147).

Unfortunately, vertical growth in adulthood does not happen automatically or easily, and many forces militate against it. As Marris (1974) emphasizes, the established perspectives of adults are generally rigid and firm, and therefore adult development is tremendously difficult to achieve (p. 9). Evans (1996) captures a similar notion through his discussion of the ways in which our "ways of thinking, feeling, and acting... are firmly established by early adulthood," and by middle age are "firmly entrenched" (p. 101). In regard to personal change, he makes an important distinction between "content" and "structure," where it is much easier to change what we think (content) than it is to change how we think (structure) (p. 102). In other words, change does not equal growth, and vertical growth or transformation—even more than adaptive change—is hard work.

Kegan and Lahey (2001, 2009) provide evidence that meeting a transformative challenge requires developing new forms of meaning-making (dynamic systems of meaning-making that are comprised of various lines of development, and therefore retain developmental characteristics). They also convey that the difficulty of such vertical growth is not a problem of will, but the expression of a legitimate gap between desire and ability. Leaders faced with the myriad challenges of pedagogical, relational, and structural change in school systems cannot hope to manage complexity through single-loop learning and horizontal growth—they must actually grow more complex. Therefore, fostering adult development is a crucial process that must be engaged within the larger processes of educational and organizational change. According to Helsing et al. (2008), who refer to the *vertical growth* possible in adaptive work,

> Those who can successfully do adaptive work are likely to have certain personality characteristics as well as training. Yet none of these skills and dispositions is sufficient because the demands of adaptive work cannot be reduced to a set of externally identified behaviors, skills, or knowledge. Rather, they necessitate an increased complexity of consciousness and an ability to construct one's own internal belief system, standard, or personal filter that enables one to make meaning of oneself and one's work in new ways.... Since many educational leaders (like leaders in other sectors) do not come to their jobs with these capacities, they need opportunities that are specifically designed to foster such growth or 'transformation.' (pp. 438–439)

It would be difficult to exaggerate the implications of these findings for educational leadership and professional development. Without the specifics of developmental stages to flesh out what is meant by adaptive "change," we will be limited in our ability to encourage "the more complex abilities available at higher levels [that] allow greater freedom to see and choose what is appropriate to specific circumstances because the person is able to adopt more perspectives" (Forman & Ross, 2013, p. 72). Suggestions for how to foster developmental growth will be explored further below, as recommendations for future research.

• • •

Another line of inquiry that is crucial for understanding these two schools lies at the nexus of overlapping cultural, social, economic, and political forces. At each school, culture was understood as the domain of shared beliefs, norms, and values that existed within the community (the Lower Left quadrant). However, this realm of school culture constitutes just one piece of a much larger puzzle, and we can see that these schools were greatly influenced by external forces. Schools are not closed systems; they are manifestations of an interdependent and holarchic system of nested sub-systems (wholes that are parts of other wholes) (Esbjorn-Hargens & Zimmerman, 2009; Wilber, 1995). The ideas, ideals, aims, and intentions of individuals within a school do not emerge in a vacuum, causa sui; they are largely contingent, and that contingency forms and is formed by the cultural background or cultural inheritance of individuals and social groups.

> When Bourdieu writes about a culture's habitus; when Heidegger described a culture's interpretation of Being nestled in historicity; when Gebser outlines major frames of interpretation (magic, mythic, mental, integral) inherited in various cultures over time; when Gadamer details the inescapable significance of *solidarity* in establishing mutual understanding—in all of those cases, they are describing *cultural inheritance*.... (Wilber, 2006a, p. 13, emphasis in original)

At the conclusion of my initial data-review for these cases I was left with questions about the importance of individual development and perspective-taking (the UL quadrant) as well as about how I could account more fully for the ways in which these school cultures were products of other systems of cultural and social influence and inheritance. This cultural inheritance has a tremendous constitutive influence on schools and schooling, and these cases are not complete without an attempt to understand some of the characteristics of that influence. As just one example noted above, it is important to see the dynamics between Weatherbee and JJS teachers not just as manifestations of those individual personalities, or even as functions of the school culture. There were larger forces at play, such as "repetitive change syndrome," which speak to the mutual influence between individual behavior and sense-making and cultural patterns of behavior and ideology. Therefore, in addition to offering a tentative exploration of the UL quadrant, I wish to offer a similarly tentative reflection on the concentric circles of ideology and economics/politics that are pertinent to these cases, namely, the hegemonic forces of education reform. As Schein (2004) observed, the

> ability to perceive the limitations of one's own culture and to evolve the culture adaptively is the essence and ultimate challenge of leadership... [and] the bottom line for leaders is that if they do not become conscious of the cultures in which they are embedded, those cultures will manage them. (pp. 2, 23)

3 Social Realities: Surfacing System Infrastructures and Ideological Influences

> The world is a complex, interconnected, finite, ecological–social–psychological–economic system. We treat it as if it were not, as if it were divisible, separable, simple, and infinite. Our persistent, intractable global problems arise directly from this mismatch.
> DONELLA MEADOWS

> If you want a description of our age, here is one: The civilization of means without ends.
> RICHARD LIVINGSTONE

While the inherent diversity of distinct contexts and cultures ensures that children's experience of school will never be uniform, even within a single state or city, a particular approach to education policy is gaining momentum around the world, and is having a significant impact on the day-to-day practice of many schools. The ideas and policies that constitute this overarching program of reform—while far from new—have become increasingly prevalent in the 21st century, and can be collectively identified as the Global Education Reform Movement (GERM) (Sahlberg, 2011). The policies that impel this movement have established a new educational orthodoxy in and beyond the United States, and they are being promoted through a global network of governments, international development agencies and private organizations (Ravitch, 2011; Spring, 2012). The influence of GERM manifests in different ways, but its underlying logic is discernible in state and federal laws, in district policies, and in the norms, beliefs, and behaviors of educators in schools. At the level of education policy, the influence of GERM can be seen in the prevalence of five common features: (1) *standardization*, (2) *a focus on core subjects*, (3) *the search for low-risk ways to reach learning goals*, (4) *use of corporate management models*, and (5) *test-based accountability policies* (Sahlberg, 2011).

As many have explained, students are impacted by both the overt and hidden curriculums of their school, as well as by the influence of forces beyond the schools' control, such as education laws, economic and social policies, and their corresponding ideologies (Apple, 1979, 2006; Bowles & Gintis, 1976; Giroux & Purpel, 1983). Much has been said about how macro-level systems, political and economic ideologies, and imbalances of power impact schools and schooling (Anyon, 1980, 1981; Gutmann, 1999; Howe & Meens, 2012; Sleeter, 2008; Westheimer, 2007). The Integral framework includes and recontextualizes this critical perspective on educational change and practice. IT helps us to see that, because everything is connected, these forces must inevitably have an impact on individuals in schools, and any account of education reform that does not account for influences in and from all four quadrants is going to be inadequate.

The current educational reform movement has coincided and cross-fertilized with trends in economic and social policies that have taken shape over the last 30 years. Market-based and neoliberal thinking has dominated public policy for decades, constituting a fundamental shift in the relationship between government and citizens since the Reagan Era (Harvey, 2007; Katz, 2008). To say that this development has had unfortunate consequences would be a dramatic understatement (Klein, 2007; Picketty, 2014; Reich, 2007, 2011; Stiglitz, 2007; Wolin, 2010).

As Katz (2008) explains in his seminal work on American public policy: "While the tension between capitalism and equality remains as powerful as ever, today it is social justice that is subordinate to market price" (p. 1). In education as well as in the larger arena of economic and social policy, the ideological foundation of the predominant discourse is neoliberalism, which can be understood as a political ideology that promotes individual choice, privatization, competition, free trade, and the reduction of government regulation and spending. Harvey (2007) summarizes the prevalence and impact of neoliberalism in the US:

> There has everywhere been an emphatic turn towards neoliberalism in political-economic practices and thinking since the 1970s…. The process of neoliberalization has, however, entailed much 'creative destruction,' not only of prior institutional frameworks and powers… but also of divisions of labor, social relations, welfare provisions, technological mixes, ways of life and thought, reproductive activities, attachments to the land and habits of the heart. (pp. 2–3)

In the realm of education, the dominance of neoliberalism has accelerated in the 21st century. In the US, No Child Left Behind (NCLB) and Race to the Top (RTTT) have ensured that education policy is kept within the restrictive and narrow parameters of top-down pressure and punishment, competitive systems of resource allocation, and standardized curriculum, instruction, and assessment. The basic logic of these reforms is that schools are in competition with each other to raise their students' standardized test scores, and that only schools whose students' scores improve perpetually are deemed successful. This approach to reform has resulted in tremendous pressure on educators to focus on student test performance, leading to a narrowed curriculum, increased time on test preparation, incentives to cheat, and educational privatization (Meier & Wood, 2004; Ravitch, 2013). The troubling outcomes of this approach surround us: cheating in Atlanta, mass for-profit privatization in Michigan and New Orleans, authoritarian centralization and budgetary bloodletting in Detroit and Philadelphia, and public protest in response to the push for school closures in Chicago (Kumashiro, 2012; Samuels, 2011; Simon, Gold, & Cucchiara, 2011). There has been a significant amount of public dissatisfaction with these trends (Brown, 2013; Davey, 2012), but the underlying assumptions, implications, and causes of their presence are rarely explicated or challenged outside of academic circles. A paradox of our time is that despite a rejection of its outcomes on several fronts, neoliberalism has become "the common sense of an emerging international consensus" in and beyond education, and continues to impact every realm of social life in the 21st century (Apple, 2006, p. 15).

An ideology can be understood as "a system of meaning that couples assertions and theories about the nature of social life with values and norms relevant to promoting or resisting social change"; in this sense it is fundamentally "a cluster of values about what is right and wrong as well as norms about what to do" (Oliver & Johnston, 2000, p. 43). Ideologies act as meta-narratives that give meaning and direction to behavior and experience. An underlying assumption in this meta-analysis is that understanding neoliberalism as a widely assumed system of meaning and values—as opposed to merely a label for certain policies—is crucial in the effort to understand what is happening in individual schools. It is also crucial in the effort to challenge those policies, because without identifying the underlying ideology it is difficult to point toward better alternatives. As Anyon (2005) reminds us, "as in any attempt to resolve complex issues, workable solutions can only be generated by an understanding of underlying causes" (p. 66).

In order to understand the ways in which neoliberalism impacts schooling in the US, it is helpful to note the ostensibly "progressive" values and rhetoric of many neoliberal policies and programs. While some neoliberal economic and social policies are rightly associated with political conservatism (whether instituted by Republicans or Democrats), arguably the most powerful paradigm in teaching and teacher education today has been dubbed "progressive neoliberalism," because it shares the logic and pro-business strategies of broader neoliberal influences and yet retains and reappropriates the socially progressive mission of educators and activists who seek equity and social justice in schools and society (Lahann & Reagan, 2011).

Following Apple (2001, 2006), Lahann and Reagan (2011) argue that "the conservative modernization of education [which GERM embodies] owes its success to the mutually beneficial, but sometimes strained relationship between a diverse set of actors with distinct political beliefs: neoliberalism, neoconservatism... authoritarian populism... and managerialism" (p. 12). The ideological profiles of organizations like Teach for America (TFA) and charter school programs like KIPP, ASPIRE, and MATCH demonstrate that "elements of managerialism and neoliberalism are not necessarily antithetical to the assumptions of social reconstruction in education" (p. 13). And while progressive neoliberalism goes beyond the market-based assumptions of economic neoliberalism in its belief that public education is an arena for social activism, policies like NCLB, programs like TFA, and the movements for increasing vouchers and charter schools are manifestations of "neoliberal strategy in pursuit of progressive goals" (p. 15). This peculiar and prevalent blend of neoliberal ideology, disciplinarian pedagogy, business-friendly policy, managerial leadership, and progressive social rhetoric is captured well in the beliefs and practices of "no excuses schools," which both of the schools in this study sought to embody (Goodman, 2013; Merseth, 2009; Peyser, 2011; Whitman, 2008).

Like Lahann and Reagan (2011), I agree with the critiques of neoliberalism and affirm that "neoliberal education reform, despite its rhetoric of equity, falls well short" of its purported aims in at least three ways: it sustains and promotes capitalism's reproduction of power, it contradicts the civic ideals of democracy by promoting self-interest and individualism, and it "lacks the explicitly political focus that a social justice agenda requires of education policy" (p. 11). As an educator and educational researcher, I believe these critiques are important, and the need for such critiques to be heard is urgent. They are also broad and inevitably abstract when removed from the school contexts they are meant to protect and defend. It is important to make direct connections between these critiques and the experiences of people in schools like JJS and SCS. As my work at these schools progressed, I began to perceive the presence of an unstated yet consistent ideology that informed the assumptions and practices of administration and teaching at each of these schools. Over time I came to see this influence, and the problems that I perceived in conjunction with it, as manifestations of GERM, interpreted largely through the words and deeds of school leaders who embody progressive neoliberalism. Like others, I came to experience these "no excuses" environments as unsettling, unhealthy, and even anti-educational (Smith, 2013). The tacit influence of these overlapping policies and ideologies at JJS and SCS became impossible for me to ignore, and emerged as another impetus for this meta-analysis.

The exchange from JJS noted in Chapter 3, Section 3.1 provides one example of how a professed commitment to shared leadership and student learning can be evacuated in the interest of implementing the GERM-influenced focus on standardized testing. Another ILT meeting similarly captured the tense tone and tenor of the group, and of the school culture overall. The meeting began with Weatherbee reviewing the norms, noting that he is the facilitator, and that "the principal makes the final decision." The group began discussing an upcoming family event:

Teacher 1:	[Asking about the role of family events at the school]: How does this all connect to improved test scores? We should be looking at data about the meaning of these events. That would be more in line with the district's focus.
Teacher 2:	Everything is not test scores. My job is to take care of the whole child.
Teacher 3:	But the problem is that everything is test scores. We are going to have [a new system for tracking data] next year, which means that teachers are going to be staying after school many days next year.
Teacher 2:	Well we need to remember that we need to put kids in the seats. Coming from someone who was at a school that closed, we don't want to be in that situation. My last school did not do enough to connect with parents.
Weatherbee:	Right now we are under-enrolled because two [No Excuses] charter schools came in and took our top students away. Right now, it looks like a lot of 4th graders are coming back. We need to do things to keep families involved. But we need to make sure we are not doing things just to fill up a schedule.
Teacher 3:	There is less and less teaching time. And there will be less teaching time next year [because of testing].
Teacher 4:	[The state tests] will be right around the corner so we should do something with non-fiction. [Under her breath she says]: God there is just so much [to do].

Weatherbee ended this meeting by saying: "This is a lot of good energy.... Thanks for being positive." This comment seemed to be awkward sarcasm, though it was not clear whether he meant it sarcastically or as a naïve attempt to model positivity. Across meetings, in response to distress and complaint from teachers, Weatherbee often feigned humor, quipping at one point that "No Child Left Behind means No Teacher Left Standing." His comment evoked some laughter, but the irony of persisting in his push for compliance with what teachers see as unreasonable demands while decrying the larger context of pressure and stress on those same teachers seemed to be lost on him.

We can also see educational change at SCS as a manifestation of GERM. The process for rolling out DREAM BIG exemplified top-down decision making. As one of the more experienced teachers put it: "We were just told.... I haven't heard anything negative [about it]. But it was not a collective [decision]." DREAM BIG was both a symbolic statement of goals and ideals and a cultural support for concrete, behavior-oriented protocols and rules that faculty use to attain greater consistency in student behavior. Similar to JJS, many of the changes taking place at SCS have been influenced—directly or indirectly—by popular "no excuses" charter schools, which have themselves been influenced by GERM and progressive neoliberalism. Matthews and Weatherbee both went with the SLA to see "exemplary" charter schools (schools that had achieved test score gains), and brought back many of their ideas. They were repeatedly coached to "steal" ideas and practices from these schools, and they did. The focus on discipline, uniformity of behavior, high-energy assemblies with chants, college as an all-important end goal (with classrooms named after colleges), and reference to students as "scholars" are all directly imported from the model of "no excuses" charter schools—the same schools they complain are taking their students from them in the competitive economic marketplace of school choice. And just as at JJS, this shift in cultural practices and norms at SCS led to increased pressure and stress on students and teachers.

From Matthews's point of view, she worked very intentionally to build trust amongst her staff, and this is what enabled her to enact such big changes with minimal pushback. For her, the most important thing "is to solidify the trust... and I think that was so good over the first three years, building up that trust." Being that "schools are networks of sustained relationships," the fact that SCS had not experienced perpetual principal turnover—as was the case at JJS—allowed there to be less disruptive disequilibrium and less resistance from faculty (Bryk & Schneider, 2002, p. xiv). Broad scale change was initiated amidst relationships of trust and support, and the character of those relationships appeared crucial to the collective acceptance of the change process.

Another significant difference between Matthews and Weatherbee is that she did speak out against the pressures and demands of high-stakes standardized testing and the "accountability regime" that has had an impact on so many schools. While continually trying to innovate and adapt to the competitive educational landscape, Matthews challenged the pressure on educators to focus their efforts on standardized test scores. Her attempts to balance the systemic pressures for quantitative data against her own philosophy and beliefs as an educator led her to embrace the challenge of competing in a neoliberal educational marketplace while rejecting standardized tests as the primary tool of judgment. As she stated toward the end of our work together:

> I am quickly coming to the opinion that standardized testing is useless to me. It's done at the end of the year. There is no time for any on-the-spot remediation or quick fix with these kids. You have to wait a whole summer before you can put an improvement plan in. And it really doesn't give me the data I need.

She went on to speak about her transformation into a leader who is willing and able to question and criticize the increasing dominance of test-based accountability:

> I learned not so much to be data driven as opposed to data informed, and I think there is a difference.... [Recognizing the problems of testing] comes from what can happen to schools in a school system when you place such high stakes and emphasis on one standardized test, and it made me a little nervous as to where the Catholic schools are going given all we know and how dangerous that path can be... [because] if you place such high stakes on it you might feel inclined to not be authentic with the results.

Matthews communicated her shift in perspective as a result of seeing unethical responses to the "no excuses" culture, and acknowledged that while she was helped to clarify her views by other educators and researchers, the movement toward test-based accountability was gaining momentum in the Catholic school sector:

> The Catholic schools office is developing new accountability scale indicators. Each school will have to reach benchmarks. I have a big problem with... that [because it is] solely using standardized testing as a measurement of rigor. I don't think it's a measurement of rigor at all.... They asked for input at the principal's meeting.... Let's just say that I was the only one who spoke [out against it].

Even with this strong stance against one of the tenets of GERM and progressive neoliberalism—that test scores are primary tools to measure and judge educational success—Matthews accepts many of the impacts and demands that the neoliberal context places on her. For instance, the notion that her school needs to be marketed and sold in a competitive marketplace of schools, and that the structure and aims of education should conform to and align with the dictates of corporate rhetoric about the job market. One of the results of her being convinced that SCS should try to "win" the race to secure jobs for students was the decision to place new emphasis on STEM (and then STEAM, and then STREAM) subjects (science, technology, engineering, and math):

> It's almost like marketing. We needed to create a niche here in this school to make SCS... an academically superior school that people will want to

> pay the money to come to.... And that was our decision to go STEM and STEAM.... It's coming from a lot of your major corporations and engineering and colleges, that the kids are coming out of elementary school with old skills.... That was good for the jobs that were necessary at that time [but not anymore].... So unless we bend and teach these kids what's going to make them successful, and what the high schools and the colleges—but more importantly the corporations—are looking for [then they won't be successful]. That's what we're responding to.

This acceptance of the pressurized and competitive context of schooling, where the ultimate arbiter of success is test scores, has led to a tenuous and in some ways inconsistent approach, where tests are both vilified and used to determine school policy, such as who is admitted to the school:

> 50th percentile on standardized testing was our goal. We knew scholar-wise, we needed to clean house. What do I mean by that? ... Most Catholic schools would take any child that walks through the door. What does that do to you? What that does to you is that you wind up accepting kids that you morally can't service. Or, you don't have the remediation to help them or move them to achieve, but they're there to give you a number in the enrollment, and yet they're pulling everything down as well. Because you can't remediate, and you can't really help them move along. But they're bringing down all of your achievement—and your data.

This felt need to "clean house" by removing students with special needs may seem to go against the social justice intentions of progressive neoliberalism—where the focus on closing the achievement gap between students of different ethnic and economic backgrounds is framed as a demand for the success of *all students*. But this temptation to push aside students who threaten the test score data of the school should be seen as a logical consequence of the very environment that is fostered by such an ideology, and should serve to expose how progressive neoliberalism superficially leverages social justice discourse to justify fundamentally unjust policies. If there is "no excuse" for low test scores, yet they persist due to factors beyond the school's control, then those students who fail to be "proficient" represent an irresolvable dilemma for school leaders. What is fascinating—and instructive—about Matthews's leadership at SCS is that even a school leader who tries to oppose the dominant discourse and policy pressures of standardized accountability ends up capitulating to those pressures to the degree that she feels it is necessary to ensure the viability of her school and her job. The context of schooling for SCS is such that the stakes are too high to ignore. And while Matthews is fighting to change the approach to testing within her network of Catholic schools, systemic support is minimal, and she remains enmeshed in a system of high-stakes competition. Her response thus far has been valiant, yet limited, and principled, yet exasperated—and sometimes contradictory. In her words:

> I'm competing against schools that somehow showed a 30–50% increase [in test scores] in one year. How does that happen? And we know, there was a slight scandal. There were schools that literally taught to the test, flashcards included.... Have I seen growth in standardized testing? Yes. Have I made the standardized testing the be-all-and-end-all? No. Will I ever? No. And even less now that I know about standardized testing. The more I learn and the more experience I get working with data, the more I'm turned off to standardized tests.

Matthews's conceptualization of this dilemma is distinct from Weatherbee's, as she was able to articulate some of the problems of her predicament and was willing to resist them. She acknowledged that her questioning and criticism of testing was a recent development and avenue of growth for her, and that ability to step outside of the given norms of accountability, and to speak out as an individual in the context of her Catholic school consortium could be seen as a manifestation of an emergent, self-authoring and/or Individualist action-logic. But just like her peers, there is no way for her to extract herself from a network of schools where very few are challenging the new orthodoxy of educational reform.

Overall, my experience at JJS and SCS illustrates some of the ways that overlapping influences from broader social, economic, political, and ideological forces impact school leaders, teachers, and students, and supports the claim that there is significant overlap in the policies, practices, and problems of schools across different sectors (district, charter, and parochial). Many of the cultural norms, educational beliefs, and disciplinarian policies of increasingly popular "no excuses" charter schools are spreading to district and parochial schools like JJS and SCS (Carter, 2001; Merseth, 2009; Whitman, 2008). Standardization is making its mark at various levels of our educational system: from national policy to state curriculum to school norms to classroom instruction. The shared experiences of these two schools serves to document some of what GERM embodies at the school level: unstable leadership succession; high-stakes testing that fails to offer teachers instructionally helpful and formative assessments of students; disciplinarian and authoritarian cultural norms and behavior policies; and environments constituted more by stress and pressure than joy and inquiry.

This is another instance in which an Integral framework can be helpful—as we orient ourselves to this data from an Integral view, we withhold from making overly simplistic judgments, and instead can attend to understanding how these dynamics are interpreted by different stakeholders, and why. Most if not all of these observations and descriptions are open to differences of interpretation. Anyone who believes that the school cultures described above are positive and/or necessary enactments of high quality education, and that the test score gains that these schools have demonstrated are a testament to that, may interpret much of what is discussed here positively. I believe there are clear correlations between perspectives on education reform (e.g., Rhee, 2013; Apple, 2006), structures of identity and meaning-making (Beck & Cowan, 2006; Wilber, 2000b), and dynamic developmental action-logics (Torbert, 2004). However, without being able to fully unpack those associations and their related exceptions and disclaimers, as we adjudicate the practices and cultural changes described above it is important to at least acknowledge that these disciplinarian and test-centered approaches to education do not align with research on human development or learning (Fischer, 2009; Healy, 2004; Hursh, 2008; McCombs, 2001; Sacks, 1999; Stein, Dawson, & Fischer, 2010; Toch, 2006). The justifications for their emergence and dominance are not research- or evidence-based, they are ideological.

Given what we know about the experience of students and teachers in schools, we should be concerned about how our test-oriented school systems are shaping the ways in which students understand learning, and themselves. As Stein (2013) explains:

> The claim that contemporary testing infrastructures have led to systematically distorted forms of self-understanding is supported by the fact that the history of testing has very little to do with the history of psychology and educational theory.... The testing infrastructure [has] changed primarily in response to advances in technology and the needs of bureaucrats—*not* in response to advances from the learning sciences that were progressively revealing the nature of how educational processes *ought* to be structured. (pp. 14–15, emphasis in original)

What critical theories of education bring to light are some of the ways that these and other concerns are connected to broad and historical events, patterns, and trends—trends that are crucial for understanding the reasons why individual school leaders and individual schools enact specific practices. Ideally, critical theories that surface and enable reflection upon such patterns and trends would be included as part of a broader integral framework of interpretation, because while such critiques are grounded in empirical fact, they only emerge as recognizable from particular perspectives or worldviews, and exist simultaneously with data that is accessible from other perspectives and methodologies.

Seen in this light, a reflective critique of standardized testing and the current "accountability regime" can be understood as a recent and particular manifestation of a broader trend: the social and ideological dominance of modern scientific, social, and cultural materialism—what Habermas (1984b) calls the "colonization of the lifeworld" and Wilber (1995) refers to as the "dominance of the descenders." As Young (1990) explains, our educational crisis can be seen as a manifestation of an underlying crisis of modernity—for which there can be no traditional or modern answer. Therefore, fundamentally modern (i.e., Achiever/Self-authoring) solutions like increased testing and technology only exasperate the problem. The only way forward is developmental, into postmodern and post-conventional maturity, individually and collectively. In Young's words, educators need to develop a "critical meta-awareness," and an immanent critique of rationality that can address the "crisis of educational rationality," because "the problem can only be solved by a shift to a new learning level" (pp. 17, 23). Ultimately, "only developmental change can turn existing hierarchies of power into hierarchies of democratic co-ordination" (p. 155).

A crucial first step toward enabling this development across our educational systems is the identification, objectification, critique, and reflection upon these practices in their historical and evolutionary context. Our current infrastructures of measurement are both systems of knowledge and systems for guiding action and administering conduct, and they exert tremendous influence on our lives—individually and collectively, internally and externally (Habermas, 1996). They constitute what Rawls (1996) called the "basic structure" of society: "the institutions of the basic structure have deep and long term social effects and in fundamental ways shape citizens' character and aims, the kinds of persons they are and aspire to be" (p. 68). Porter (1995) expands on this idea:

> Measures succeed to the degree they become 'technologies of the soul.' They provide legitimacy for administrative actions, in large part because they provide standards against which people judge themselves.... Measures succeed by giving direction to the very activities that are being measured. In this way individuals are made governable.... [Measures] create and can be compared with norms, which are the gentlest and yet most pervasive forms of power in modern democracies. (p. 45)

The norms of our educational institutions have become so pervasive and influential that the basic neoliberal premises on which they rest have become a bi-partisan status quo that is difficult even to see. But when seen and objectified through postmodern, post-conventional perspectives, we can begin to appreciate how reductive they are, and to what extent "modern educational systems are dominated by testing infrastructures that neglect the true complexity of social reality" (Stein, 2016, p. 33). It is only from a post-conventional perspective that we can accurately perceive and assess the kinds of materialism and reductionism that have led to the "crisis of educational rationality,"

> in which a system of categories built for purposes of instrumental rationality and control has become the dominant system of categories used in schools to guide the construction of students' academic self-understandings. There is perhaps no greater insight into the detrimental effects of education during the past century than this: efficiency-oriented testing practices have come to provide the categories and terms in which students (and teachers and school communities) understand themselves. (Stein, 2016, p. 34)

Underneath the values, aims, and assumptions of our dominant educational norms lurk the stunted growth of emotional, cognitive, and egoic perspectives that have now become systemically maladaptive and evolutionarily anachronistic. The testing movement that "swept the nation as an educational crusade" in the name of justice and efficiency in early 20th century has failed to adapt to the emergent needs of 21st century society (Tyack, 1974, p. 207). Our conventional conceptions about school, learning, knowledge, and education all developed within what Foucault (1994) called a modernist episteme—the body of ideas that shaped the perception of knowledge in our recent historical period—characterized by ideals of objectivity and autonomous, independent subjects. This modern episteme—or prevalent structure of thought, i.e., predominant action-logic—rests on "pretensions of objectivity" that led to a vision of test-based meritocracy and thus a sorting machine for human capital (Stein, 2016, p. 32). This view supports what Stein refers to as "the education commodity proposition"—the idea that education can be treated like any other commodity (just as the "labor commodity proposition" treats labor like any other commodity that should be sought as cheaply as possible and utilized with maximal efficiency (Bowles & Gintis, 1986)). This way of thinking leads to an extreme form of reductionism, which reasons that in order to know the value of educational investments, one must be able to monetize and therefore quantify educational progress. Eventually, as we've seen, it leads to positions like progressive neoliberalism, where questions of justice are reduced to questions of efficiency. However, as Stein (2016) points out,

> education is not simply reducible to the terms of market exchange because it is *inalienable* from the individual being educated. Individuals are not given an education in the same way they are given a TV or some cash. Individuals *become* educated. We are shaped by the total experience of whatever educational process we participate in.... Just as believing that the value of labour can be reduced to its cost allows the relations of employment to be governed by what the market will bear, so believing that the value of education can be reduced to standardized test scores... allows the relations of teaching and learning to be governed by the demands of economic efficiencies. (p. 106, emphasis in original)

Stein continues, importantly, to maintain that teaching is also inalienable from teachers: "teachers often come to understand their own work according to the measurement categories used to determine its value, which can distort educational processes in profound ways... [and lead them to] adapt their teaching to the measures used to quantify it" (pp. 109, 110). I could see this influence and logic in effect at SCS and JJS, as well as the impact on principals, for whom the terms of the educational commodity proposition came to dominate decision procedures, in part "because school leaders are radically vulnerable to criticism if they base crucial decisions on other ostensibly 'subjective' criteria" (p. 113).

These connections—between the experience and ideology formation of students and teachers, the limits of decision-making experienced by school leaders, and the epistemological confines of modernist objectivity—are informative for our understanding of the network of causality that we are enmeshed in when we analyze leadership and school change. The prevailing "drive toward accountability as a form of mechanical objectivity enabling the quantification of value for bureaucratic purposes" establishes test-mediated relationships that blur the distinction between the students' learning needs and the bureaucratic needs of school leaders and teachers (Stein, 2016, pp. 113–114). These testing-intensive determinations of educational value tend to create situations in which strategic relationships take precedence over communicative and collaborative ones (Habermas, 1984a), and these relationships are influenced and restrained by the parameters of the modern episteme that continues to permeate educational discourse. Our education system is a complex reality in which there is a co-evolutionary dynamic between schooling and testing, and this can be seen as an expression of a larger co-evolution between culture and social structure (or the LL and LR quadrants).

If we can see the "crisis of educational rationality" as a manifestation of the "crisis of modernity," and can further see the reductionism of standardized testing as part and parcel of a broader dominance of neoliberalism, which itself is buffeted by the modern episteme and its attendant crises, we can begin to see what it means to understand a complex system via all four quadrants—and why it is necessary to try to do so. We are living out the effects of a psychological, behavioral, cultural, and social paradigm that emerged with modernity and has grown increasingly maladapted to human life—the "colonization of the lifeworld"—while postmodern alternatives have emerged in segments of society and yet have failed to fundamentally reconstitute our educational structures. It is long past time to take heed to Habermas's (1994) description of the

> gaze that objectifies and examines, that takes things apart analytically, that monitors and penetrates everything, [and] gains a power that is structurally formative for these [modern] institutions. It is the gaze of the rational subject who has lost all merely intuitive bonds with his environment and torn down all the bridges built up of intersubjective agreement, and for whom in his monological isolation, other subjects are accessible only as the objects of nonparticipant observation. (p. 55)

Meanwhile, evidence continues to mount concerning the detrimental effects of psychologically naive testing practices, from their stigmatizing and disempowering impact on students to their tendency to truncate pedagogical and curricular options (RAND, 2010). Until we make connections and seek holistic, all-quadrant responses to improving the health and developmental functioning of our educational systems, attempts to remediate and reform through traditional methods of instruction and technological infrastructures of assessment and accountability will continue to foster iatrogenic effects on students, teachers, principals, and the social worlds they perpetuate (negative outcomes caused by a treatment that is worse than the initial problem it seeks to cure) (Taleb, 2014). The potentially good intentions of progressive neoliberals do not make the damage they cause any less harmful. As Taleb (2014) puts it, "this is the tragedy of modernity: as with neurotically overprotective parents, those trying to help are often hurting the most"—and this is precisely because they are embedded in complex systems, "full of interdependencies—hard to detect—and nonlinear responses" (pp. 5, 7). The lack of self-transforming, post-Individualist, complex systems thinking in our political, economic, and education systems ultimately leads to "naïve interventionism" and "iatrogenics in high places" (p. 114).

Cunningham (2014) offers a good example of how systems thinking can capture some of this critical terrain, precisely because it aligns with concerns regarding our shared external realities. In *Systems Theory for Pragmatic Schooling,* he summarizes several authors who critique our industrial model of "factory schooling," and argues that our dominant educational reform policies legitimate fixes through a discourse of crisis and global economic competition. A systems lens is utilized to emphasize how schooling, political economy, and ideology all impact each other (Tozer, Senese, & Violas, 2013), and he explains why we have to consider larger political agendas operating in society and the larger purposes we serve (Bowers, 2012). Again, IT and the inclusion of multiple perspectives and methods does not displace or demean systems thinking; it seeks to integrate and enlarge the domain of discourse via a process of inclusion. It is neither modern nor postmodern, but decidedly post-postmodern.

Schools are enmeshed in a global economic system that is profoundly inequitable, where the gap between rich and poor continues to increase (Picketty, 2014). And upon inspection, we can see that major legislation and reform movements have been influenced by economic incentives, that having a single standardized system enables the quantification and monetization of educational value (Apple, 2001), and that the perpetual failure of schools in response to the Common Core standards and Race to the Top legislation was predicted and planned to facilitate increased market activity (Ravitch, 2013). The field of education would benefit from further exploration of what is required to nurture and develop the necessary psychological and cultural developments that can discern and deconstruct these anti-evolutionary incentives and develop new, more adaptive systems of exchange, relationship, and valuation. It is, fundamentally, a systems problem: we must close the feedback loops between value and impact, discontinue the externalization of costs, and dis-incentivize for-profit motives that are not aligned with human well-being (Schmachtenberger, 2017). But it is an all-quadrant systems problem, replete with implications for human thinking and valuing, individually and collectively, so the systems theories that dominate academic discourse, which focus on the LR quadrant, will not suffice. A good first step, I believe, is acknowledging the contours and characteristics of the structures of thought that continue to influence our lives, and opening our eyes to the ways in which different action-logics co-emerge with different material realities, because "the characteristics of the shared behavioral world must be changed, and they will change only as we envisage a different theory-in-use and begin to act on it" (Argyris & Schon, 1974, p. 161).

In my experience, the realization that we have a vantage point that we may choose to step away from can open a powerful avenue for learning, and one of the first steps we can take to enlarge our capacity to see our own perspective is to reflect upon the work we have done, the perspectives we have engaged, the methods we have enacted, and the many ways that truths from different disciplines and perspectives co-arise and interpenetrate.

CHAPTER 6

Methodological Hindsight: Reflections on Systems Thinking, Integral Theory, and Educational Research

> It seems plain and self-evident, yet it needs to be said: the isolated knowledge obtained by a group of specialists in a narrow field has in itself no value whatsoever, but only in its synthesis with all the rest of knowledge and only inasmuch as it really contributes in this synthesis toward answering the demand, "Who are we?"
>
> ERWIN SCHRODINGER

∴

The "reality" of K-12 education in the United States is both context- and perspective-dependent. What we see when we look at schools and schooling depends on both the context in which we observe and the lens through which we discern and interpret that context. How we interpret and judge schooling depends on where the school is, what kind of school it is, what people are doing there, and what views we hold about what schools *should* be. Therefore, an inquiry into and interpretation of any educational context will be valid and useful to the degree that it accounts for and explains the school context, the behavior and perspectives of those that constitute the school, and the behavior and perspective of the researcher. This study began with the intention to understand educational leadership and change through the means of qualitative research methods and complex systems thinking. It ends with a self-assessment of how and why the reality disclosed by those means were both true and partial. The intention of this problematizing reflection is to provide avenues of potential exploration for myself and others to improve research and ourselves—as leaders, practitioners, and researchers.

The ability to perceive schools—and the social and cultural networks that influence them—as complex adaptive systems is helpful and arguably necessary for understanding the interdependence of leadership, policy, and reform. Complexity and systems theories, and the leadership theories associated with them, proved valuable heuristics for the two cases in this study for thinking about how Weatherbee and Matthews distributed leadership and impacted culture and how others responded. This study provided reinforcing evidence for the following principles and conclusions:

- The history of a social group establishes a path-dependence for that social system, and is not easily changed or transformed. Therefore, sustainable, limited, and pro-social approaches to disequilibrium and system turbulence are preferable.
- Cultural alignment serves as a strange attractor for system transformation, and the absence of such alignment/attraction can impede intended changes from manifesting.
- Top-down leadership can have a significant impact on a social system, but truly decentralized, emergent forms of shared leadership are inhibited by lack of social cohesion, shared history, and trust, and by significant and/or repeated disequilibrium/turbulence.
- When social cohesion, shared history, and/or cultural alignment are present, the distinction between top-down or bottom-up leadership may be less important, since buy-in to top-down initiatives and the emergence of bottom-up initiatives are both more likely to be successful when the system culture is cohesive, aligned, and "well-attracted."

The two principals in this study intended to foster real change in the overarching culture and climate of their schools, with the belief that such a cultural shift was necessary to improve teaching and learning. In each case these principals initiated new ways of distributing leadership, and attempted to approach instructional leadership both directly (e.g., by spending time in classrooms) and indirectly (e.g., helping grade level teams work together). Each principal also worked to establish new norms and beliefs about student expectations and success by clarifying and consistently reiterating the goals and values of their collective work as a school. In each school, distributed leadership, instructional leadership, and school culture formed an interdependent nexus of working relationships, behaviors, values, and communication. In working to understand the nature and effects of leadership at these schools, I documented what each principal did, how others responded, and how leadership was distributed. I tried to understand both the intentions and actions of the principals as well as how they fostered and enabled the leadership of others. In order to do this well I needed some understanding of who all of these persons were, as well as a sense of what forces and factors influenced them, because their actions, thoughts, beliefs, intentions, and social context are all interdependent and co-emergent. Substantive interpretation required a substantive context.

Fleshing out those contexts in a way that seemed fair and adequate was a challenge. There is no clear line to demarcate where the relevant context ends, and a theoretical framework adequate to the task of interpreting many facets of leadership and educational change can threaten to become too complicated in itself to be useful or understandable. To paraphrase Einstein, a theory should be as simple as possible, but no simpler. In my work to understand leadership and educational change I wanted to avoid oversimplifications and reductions that distort or misapprehend the qualities and characteristics embedded in the social actions of students, teachers, parents, and administrators that I interacted with. Assuming that Integral Theory is correct in its assumption that all perspectives are true but partial (which does *not* mean equally true), the conclusions of Chapter 4 (summarized in the list above) encapsulate some of the partial truths of complexity thinking germane to educational leadership and reform. However, from my perspective as a researcher I concluded that the partiality of these insights, as true as they may be, were too partial to stand alone. They were fair, and valid, but not adequate. By contrasting complex systems thinking with IT, I was able to articulate a frame for conceptualizing how partial the truths of systems theory are when applied to schools. There are ways in which complex systems thinking, while far-reaching, valid, and insightful, does not answer some of the key questions that such inquiry begs answers for, e.g., how to adjudicate differences in leadership perspectives, and how to understand the relationships between individuals and collectives in a way that accounts for those differences. It also tends to leave out more critical social views—and the qualitative judgments they rely on—which are especially pertinent for these school contexts, as noted above.

As helpful and descriptively valid as systems frameworks are, it is important to clarify and restate their limits to explain why a broader meta-theory such as IT is called for. First, there is simply more to what these principals were doing—and certainly more to who they *are* as leaders—than was captured by the complex systems lens. There is, ironically, a "complexity reduction" involved in taking the complexity view itself (Biesta, 2010). While attention to relationships, networks, and the school as a complex system reveals qualities of the change and leadership process that are important, it is also clear that each of the principals in this study were in fact a primary force for change in their school, and any account of what is happening that does not include a substantive explanation of not only *what* they do and *how* they do it but also *who* they are and *why* they lead as they do is going to be unfortunately partial. When Capra and Luisi (2014) state systems thinking "means a shift of perception from material objects and structures to... nonmaterial processes and patterns of organization" they are right, and yet that begs the question of how to delineate, qualify, and describe both those nonmaterial (i.e., subjective and intersubjective) processes and the required shift of perception (p. 79). When Senge (1994) says "systems thinking is a discipline for seeing wholes... a framework for seeing interrelationships rather than things... [and] a sensibility—for the subtle interconnectedness that gives living systems their unique character," he points to a crucial subjective capacity and yet fails to account for how and why it develops (pp. 68–69). When Cunningham (2014) argues "thinking about complex problems requires a more sophisticated understanding of the nature of reality," he implies yet does not account for the spectrum of sophistication he refers to (p. 12). And when Heifetz (1994) argues that leadership is an action and not a position, he is only half right; it is both—and one's position is located within a complex, dynamic, and multilayered matrix of human development.

If we want to understand the important and relevant qualities that constitute effective leadership, we must acknowledge the qualities and characteristics of formal leaders in formal leadership positions. That this needs to be said at all may demonstrate the extreme partiality of strictly "complex" views. Yes, we can understand both learning and leadership as collective and relational (Davis, Sumara, & D'Amour, 2012; Spillane, 2005), but we can and must also understand leadership and learning in terms of individuals, and this entails understanding people both objectively (in regard to their behavior) and subjectively (in regard to their thoughts, ideologies, and structures of interpretation). By taking a complex systems view of distributed leadership, the *individual* characteristics of the leader are often neglected—in fact they are proudly jettisoned by some complexity theorists (Davis & Sumara, 2001). Unfortunately, to lose sight of the influential qualities of the central actor in a system is to lose touch with a significant portion of reality, and of any hope for explanatory power in explaining that reality. A failure to take a both/and view in this respect is unacceptably simple, and constitutes an unfortunate and unnecessary complexity reduction, because "both individuals and collectives are fundamental, irreducible aspects of reality. When individuals create social holons, emergent collective properties form but individuals retain their unique consciousness, characteristics, and qualities. At the non-quantum level, individuality is not lost in relational holism" (Fuhs, 2008, p. 151). We must therefore account for the complexity of *individuals* in a deep and meaningful way if we are to understand the systems those individuals co-create.

While the data for this study includes many elements of change taking place at each school, it was also difficult within a complex system lens to register the *quality* of the changes taking place. It is much easier to document *change* than it is to register and define positive *transformation*. Changes in beliefs can be documented via changes in language and professed ideas. Culture can be documented through those beliefs as well as descriptions of changed behavior patterns and ways of interacting. Shifts in instructional approaches can be documented and interpreted in accordance with professed intentions, such as differentiated instruction. Test scores can be gathered, and quantitative changes can be assessed on scales of student proficiency and improvement. But any notion of increased quality, or the *goodness* of these changes presupposes a framework of value and meaning that must be used to interpret the quality of these changes, and descriptive or relational theories of distributed leadership and complex systems are ultimately devoid of such qualitative assertions. As Hargreaves and Fink (2006) observe, "advanced systems thinking is as useful in tobacco industries as it is in pollution control systems and as valuable for a totalitarian government as for a truly democratic one. It has no inherent moral purpose" (p. 18). This is not to say that complex thinkers do not have a strong moral foundation or purpose—I would argue quite the opposite (Cilliers, 1998, 2010; Davis, Sumara, & D'Amour, 2012; Morin, 2001, 2008). But taking these thinkers together, in all their good intentions, it appears that something is lacking in complex systems frameworks; they do not adequately present a context for adjudicating quality, depth, or goodness, other than the obvious notion of "fit" within the system.

The point is that relational, complex, and systems interpretations share both a great strength and a significant weakness. The perspectives of complexity and systems are both profoundly important and significantly lacking. A complex systems view is helpful but not sufficient to understand leadership. The reality of leadership and adaptive change is more complex than complex systems thinking alone can register or communicate. By looking at leadership through these lenses I am able to acknowledge and incorporate meaningful inputs and aspects of educational change that are easily and perpetually missed by more individualistic, behaviorist, policy-based, curriculum-based, and/or quantitative approaches to educational research. But what is transcended is not easily included, and there is more to include and acknowledge than what is gained from reductionist paradigms; combining a systems view with more quantitative data will not get at the qualitative aspects of leadership that both complexity and quantification fundamentally miss. As a researcher I want to *understand* leadership, and the cultural/adaptive changes that leaders can foster, and that requires a deeper qualitative and theoretical analysis. Attention to relational distribution and complex systems constitutes a *descriptive* approach to leadership and change—and a description that is focused on the objective and interobjective domains of reality (the "right-hand" quadrants in IT). In order to get at a more *normative* approach—which is necessary if we are to promote and foster transformational and beneficial pathways for leadership and reform—we need to surface and interpret the other side of the leadership/change coin: the interior, subjective, and intersubjective domains (the "left-hand" quadrants of IT).

It is also important to understand that this implied, tacit demand for understanding the inner development of leaders is not accomplished by any particular or partial descriptor. There are myriad examples of leadership qualities that one can recommend, from emotional leadership (Beatty, 2005) to ethical leadership (Sergiovanni, 2005; Starratt, 2009) to inspirational leadership (Olivier, 2002) to primal leadership (Goleman, 2004) and adaptive leadership (Heifetz, Grashow, & Linsky, 2009). Each of these adjectives highlights an important quality and/or approach to educational leadership, and each one is, of course, a less than complete signifier for any leader. As a researcher, I could try to choose which lens to use based on what I think is the best "fit" for assessing a particular leader or leadership milieu. In my initial work on these case studies I erred on the side of accentuating the lens of distributed leadership, for instance. But two points are crucial: (1) No single quality, and no aggregation of positive (or negative) qualities, adds up to the lived presence or embodied reality of a leader. Leaders are also complex systems: the whole is greater than the sum of its parts. (2) An aggregation of qualities or attributes does not explain qualitative differences between attributes, nor does it provide an avenue to understand how or if one can integrate or develop attributes in an effective way.

As Hargreaves and Harris (2011) observe from their study of high-performing organizations in multiple fields, no list of descriptive labels could "entirely or accurately represent or capture the form, nature and type of leadership within organizations that perform beyond expectations. Rather, [leaders of] organizations that perform beyond expectations exhibit 'leadership fusion'" (p. 7). Developing this notion of leadership fusion, originally articulated by Daft and Lengel (1998), Hargreaves (2011) states that

> Fusion leadership is more than a repertoire or array of multiple skills... it is the psychological integration of a personality and a community combined with the knowledge, empathy and strategic capability to know what parts of one's own and one's colleagues' leadership are the right ones, for the right time and for the challenges at that moment. (p. 239)

In a sense, this notion of fusion leadership implies the enactment of an exceptional meta-quality: the ability to integrate other positive qualities in a timely, appropriate, and effective manner. For Daft and Lengel (1998), it involves the integration of the inner qualities or "subtle forces" of mindfulness, vision, heart, communication, courage, and integrity—qualities that can enable the emergence of effective and transformational collective growth. These qualities, similarly to those listed by Hargreaves and Harris (2011), can all be seen as conducive if not necessary to enable the emergence of any form of effective leadership. Each distinct quality or skillset represents a normative ideal, fostered by the enactment of various positive qualities that each of us would do well to develop.

Enacting fusion leadership implies being a "whole person," and being a whole person involves developing something like what Maslow (1968) described as "a psychology of being," because "to be a whole person and to make use of all one's capacity requires physical, mental, emotional, and spiritual development" (Daft & Lengel, 1998, p. 20). Fusion leaders are developed leaders who are able to integrate multiple skills and capacities, and thus fusion leadership could also be called integrated leadership. Such conceptions of exceptional leadership involve the ability to register, understand, and align one's thought, speech, and action with not only one's own values, goals, and plans but with those of others: it is a "psychological integration of a personality and a community" (Hargreaves, 2011, p. 239). And yet, we are still left with yet another framework that, while normative, and potentially relevant to the field of leadership, does not offer an overarching view of how its relative truth co-exists with the relative truths of the numberless other potential leadership schemes. It relies on development, implies development, and describes an aspect of development, but eschews theoretical and methodological responsibility for delineating what the contours, structures, and implications of that development are. What does psychological integration mean? How do we transcend separateness? How may an individual leader develop such a capacity, not only to be "whole" in themselves but in relationship with others? It is one thing to describe integrated leadership; it is quite another to actually develop and enact it; and it is yet another task altogether to *explain* how to develop this meta-quality, and how to understand it within a coherent interpretive framework.

This realization is one of the factors that led me to see that we must find a way to integrate and explain the *developmental complexity of the leader* in the *context of systems* if we are to understand educational leadership and related change. To understand the requirements of actually realizing fusion leadership—or any form of effective, mature leadership—we need to understand the contours of human development, and the distinctions between qualitatively different structures of perception and interpretation available to mature adults. Integrating multiple theories of leadership into a coherent framework by aligning them with relevant developmental theory allows us to place these concepts of leadership, which fundamentally presuppose a very developed capacity on the part of leaders, in a coherent explanatory context. Surfacing the developmental aspect of leadership capacity also offers the added benefit of pointing us more concretely toward specific practices that can enable such development.

Integrative frameworks such as IT are helpful at both the descriptive and normative levels: they allow us to make sense of the dynamic complexity of the many qualities and attributes of leaders and schools, and they describe an ideal to aim for and judge leadership against. Both of these functions are important. Without some clarity about what our aims and ideals are, there is little point in describing what is happening. Yet without a framework to help us understand what constitutes leadership development and how to foster such development, idealized leadership descriptions do not fulfill their practical aim—"these approaches are, in effect, presenting a wonderful goal with no way to reach it; a noble vision with no path to attain it" (Wilber, 2006c, p. 35).

To argue that an integrating framework is helpful is not to discredit or deconstruct the place and importance of systems theory or any particular leadership theory. That would be a postmodern move. The perception of complex systems, and the ability to thrive in them, entails complex systems thinking and a fusion of positive leadership qualities. The fact that theories associated with complex systems and leadership fusion fail to account for the leadership development that is necessary to enact their ideals can be explained, in large part, by the broader cultural forces of modernity, and the subsequent postmodern allergies to meta-narrative and structuralism described above (which is why it is important to understand those cultural, philosophical, and historical terrains). The integration of complex systems thinking, normative leadership ideals, and developmental research allows us to place partial theories of leadership into a coherent, research-based context. A developmental context of interpretation enables us to understand what constitutes a good leader. A practical program of guidance enables us to foster and enact good leadership. Integral Theory, which encompasses not only the four quadrants and levels, but also lines, states, and types of human experience, is uniquely situated to serve as both a developmental interpretive framework and a guiding operating system for leaders (Brown, 2011, 2012; Esbjorn-Hargens, 2010; Forman & Ross, 2013; Fuhs, 2008; Hamilton, 2012). As Forman and Ross state,

> The limiting factor of the multitude of approaches and models now available to organizations may not be in the sheer complexity of organization and the seeming contradictions that these approaches can present, but rather, it may be in the lack of a perspective with sufficient depth and breadth to allow a more elegant navigation through the complexity that is genuinely present. (p. 2)

This summarizes the accomplishments and shortcomings of the complex systems view as applied to these cases, the limited role that mid-range leadership theories can play in explaining leaders and leadership, and the reasons that led me to seek a more expansive framework for understanding those shortcomings as well as some of the broader currents and forces that influence the overlapping fields of discourse in which I work. I continue this methodological reflection below with an exploration of recommendations for future research.

1   Fostering and Assessing Development in Complex Systems

This comparative case study was grounded in methods of qualitative research. As I reflected on my research process and conclusions, I found many parallels between the partial truths of my theoretical framework (complex systems theory) and the partial truths disclosed through my data collection (observations, interviews, student work, and assessment data). As noted, the domains that I found lacking in my original analysis—most notably the domain of the individual interiors of my research participants (the UL quadrant)—were absent because they were not disclosed as data by the methods I was using.

I explained this methodological shortcoming by presenting a framework for understanding the interdependent relationships between ontology, methodology, and epistemology, and presenting the eight zones of inquiry as delineated in Integral Theory. The tentative interpretations I offered regarding how Weatherbee and Matthews thought and acted in the context of their schools were insufficient because they lacked formal data collection methods that focused on the UL quadrant—primarily Zone 2. This is not to say that my tentative conclusions were meaningless. Precisely because of the interdependence of thinking, doing, and being, valid connections can certainly be made between one's behavior and one's structures of thought, belief, and valuation. That said, if I were to approach these school contexts with research questions related to the thinking and doing embodied by these principals, I would include a wider array of methods; namely, I would seek to supplement my qualitative observational and interview data with Zone 2 assessments that enabled me to gather data to assess the structural characteristics of each leader's thinking, and to make correlations between data from multiple domains. To illustrate what I mean I will briefly highlight three examples of how this kind of work is already being done, as a guide for future projects in educational research (and elsewhere).

1.1   *Deliberately Developmental Organizations*

Kegan, Lahey, and their associates (Kegan & Lahey, 2001, 2009, 2016; Helsing, Howell, Kegan, & Lahey, 2008; Wagner & Kegan, 2006) have been working to address what I call "the development gap" in leadership by facilitating professional development structures explicitly aimed at enabling vertical and transformational growth. Most professional development aims to help practitioners develop skills or capacities to cope "within the worlds of our assumptive designs," while these underlying assumptions, or "action-logics" are never in question (Kegan & Lahey, 2001, p. 71). In stark contrast to the translative norms of most professional development, this group has developed an "Immunities to Change framework" that "aims to help participants change both behaviors and mental frameworks by making explicit the contradictions between their intended goals and their actual behaviors, thus uncovering an individual's hidden assumptions that give rise to those contradictions" (Helsing et al., p. 459).

Their most recent work has involved extensive case studies of exceptionally successful companies with cultures that foster and in some ways demand the personal development of all employees—what they call Deliberately Developmental Organizations (DDOs) (Kegan & Lahey, 2016). By bringing together the methodologies of qualitative case studies (extensive observations and interviews) with their background in developmental assessment, their characterizations of DDOs shed new light on what it looks, feels, and sounds like to establish a crucible for adult development and organizational thriving. They emphasize that most people spend energy covering up their weaknesses and managing impressions, which impede growth, and at the same time many professionals burn out from their work because they do not experience the rejuvenating effects of personal development. They also stress that personal fulfillment and organizational success are mutually reinforcing and dialectical, not mutually exclusive, and the most effective contributors to organizations are those who experience personal happiness through their own flourishing—embodying what the ancient Greeks called eudaemonia.

In regard to development, Kegan and Lahey (2016) explain that the way humans construct reality can become more expansive, less distorted, less egocentric, and less reactive over time, and the basic patterns of this maturation hold up across genders, cultures, and social classes. "When an evolution occurs from one level of complexity to another, adults take greater responsibility for their thinking and feeling, can retain more layers of information, and can think further into the future" (p. 60). They also explain how this developmental unfolding holds the key to so many organizational questions and yet continues to be ignored by other organizational researchers.

> There is no denying that the descriptions suggest a value proposition for mental complexity.... Each new level transcends and includes the prior level.... The implication is that people having a higher level of mental complexity outperform those at a lower level in real life.... There are now a number of studies that correlate measures of mental complexity with independent assessments of work competence or performance.... Taken together, the cumulative data supports the proposition that for those at a higher level of mental complexity, a complex world is more manageable. (pp. 71, 73)

Perhaps the main takeaway from their work with DDOs is the key competencies that emerge via self-transforming structures of thought are those that are needed to manage the complexity and perpetual change of 21st century organizational life. Quoting Branden at length:

> In the past two or three decades, extraordinary developments have occurred in the American and global economies. The United States has shifted from a manufacturing society to an information society. We have witnessed the transition from physical labor to mind work as the dominant employee activity. We now live in a global economy characterized by rapid change, accelerating scientific and technological breakthroughs, and an unprecedented level of competitiveness. These developments create demand for higher levels of education and training than were required of previous generations. Everyone acquainted with business culture knows this. What is not understood is that these developments also create new demands on our psychological resources. Specifically, these developments ask for a greater capacity for innovation, self-management, personal responsibility, and self-direction. This is not just asked at the top, it is asked at every level of a business enterprise... Today, organizations need not only an unprecedentedly higher level of knowledge and skill among all those who participate but also a higher level of independence, self-reliance, self-trust, and the capacity to exercise initiative. (pp. 73-74)

A "socialized mind" was appropriate for yesterday's demands, but not today's. "A self-transforming mind is aware that it lives in time and the world is in motion. It is aware that what might make sense today may not make as much sense tomorrow" (p. 69). Therefore, a "safe, dependable, collectively-ascribed-to container for interior work" is crucial, because "focusing on behavior without also focusing on the mind-sets that drive behavior is not likely to succeed" (pp. 276, 248). These truths and this approach are at least as relevant in education as they are in business. The next step is for researchers to explore the contours of Deliberately Developmental Schools.

1.2 Lectical Assessments

Any movement toward including developmental frameworks and theories in educational research depends upon the continued improvement and sophistication of developmental assessments. Lectica is an organization that has been researching and designing dynamic developmental assessments for both children and adults based largely on the developmental theory of Kurt Fischer (Fischer, 1980, 2009; Fischer & Bidell, 2006). Their work is intended to address both ends of our educational crisis—the developmentally inappropriate and counter-productive standardization of testing (the accountability regime of the modern episteme), and the dearth of leaders who are able to navigate successfully the demands of 21st century complexity and organizational leadership (the development gap). Therefore, their research and applications could prove very helpful at every level of education, from transforming student assessment to align with human development to providing teachers and administrators with formative feedback that encourages their continued growth and the development of increasingly complex and multi-faceted perspective-taking (Dawson & Stein, 2011a, 2011b; Stein, Dawson, & Fischer, 2010).

This research-based organization is astutely aware and critical of the problems and pathologies of our current educational testing milieu and the context of the Global Education Reform Movement (Sahlberg, 2011), and is working to develop truly formative and developmental assessments that act as scaffolds for vertical growth for the students and leaders who engage them (Stein, 2013, 2016). Using such leadership assessments offers both a promising avenue of research on leadership development and a pragmatic tool for leaders to assess and stimulate their own growth and improvement (Stein, Dawson, Van Rossum, Hill, & Rothaizer, 2014). These assessments, while focused on individual growth in the upper left quadrant, are also explicitly aligned with a developmental view of the four quadrants, and can be used in conjunction with other approaches that address growth in other quadrants (Stein & Heikkinen, 2008, 2009).

Educational case studies would benefit tremendously from the integration of lectical assessments. The inclusion of data from a Zone 2 methodology would make tentative correlations between the speech, behavior, and thinking of school leaders such as Matthews and Weatherbee more robust and valid. In addition, the process of including a Zone 2 methodology such as a lectical assessment could open new possibilities for reflection and dialogue regarding human development and the assessment of learning for children and adults, and this could instigate a meaningful inquiry and learning opportunity for any school community. Both the student-centered and leader-oriented assessments are designed to be actionable and formative—they provide specific next steps for individuals to pursue to increase the complexity of their perspective-taking. These next-generation developmental assessments represent a step-change difference from current tests, such as PISA, GRE, SAT, ACT, and Common Core-based standardized tests. As Lectica co-founder Theo Dawson (2018b) states, "we can not only tell people what their scores mean, but also what they're most likely to benefit from learning next," and that feedback is based on an extensive, "careful, painstaking study of how students construct meanings over time" (para. 15).

In addition to their growing profile of assessments for schools and leaders, Lectica has also recently begun sharing analysis of the cognitive complexity of public leaders' use of language, in an effort to advance public discourse about and awareness of the importance of complex thought for leadership—especially within the context of high-stakes 21st century politics. Interested readers and researchers can pursue that line of research in a series of essays (Dawson, 2017a, 2018a). As I noted above in reference to Kegan (2003), we are almost all "in over our heads," and the gap between the complexity of our social world and the complexity of our current thinking is what I refer to as "the development gap." Dawson (2017b) calls it "the complexity gap":

> This pattern is pervasive—we see it everywhere we look—and it reflects a hard truth. None of us is capable of meeting the task demands of the most complex situations we're likely to face in today's world. I've come to believe that our best hope for meeting these demands is to (1) recognize our human limitations, (2) work strategically on the development of our own skills and knowledge, (3) learn to work closely with others who represent a wide range of perspectives and areas of expertise, and (4) use the best tools available to scaffold our thinking. (para. 4)

Lectical assessments are perhaps the best scaffolds available to us right now, and I strongly recommend that other educational researchers explore them as a Zone 2 methodology. (And I offer an even stronger recommendation for schools to use them with students as a way to transcend and transform standardization, and for school leaders to use them as part of their professional development).

1.3 *Action Inquiry*

Another approach to fostering vertical growth is illustrated by action inquiry, developed by Bill Torbert (2004). Action inquiry is an attempt to both practice and develop higher capacities and perspectives in leadership and mutuality. In this approach the path and the goal are one and the same. It is "a way of simultaneously conducting action and inquiry as a disciplined leadership practice that increases the wider effectiveness of our actions… [and] a way of learning anew, in the vividness of each moment, how best to act now" by interweaving research and practice in the present (pp. 1–2). Torbert's approach to action inquiry is very much aligned with Ross and Forman's (2013) notion of integral leadership, which they describe as "a process of continued exploration of where and how to apply tested and proven approaches, but also a practice of reframing the very foundation of the perspectives we use to explore" (p. 3).

Like the Immunity to Change framework, action inquiry begins with an experience of the gap between what we would like to do and what we are able to do. Unlike professional development aimed at identifying and transcending immunities to change, action inquiry seeks to establish ways of reflecting and acting that facilitate vertical growth "on the ground" and in real time, in the midst of professional relationships. By engaging in action inquiry, leaders attempt to engage in triple-loop learning that includes single-loop feedback (about whether past action has been effective), double-loop feedback (regarding the effectiveness of one's overarching strategy or structure of assumptions), and triple-loop feedback (regarding the relationship between one's actions, strategy, and quality of attention).

The adaptive challenges to this work are great, as "most of us treat our current structure, strategy, or action-logic as our very identity. To accept double-loop feedback can feel equivalent to losing our very identity" (Torbert, 2004, p. 18). Triple-loop learning, which involves conscious awareness of one's own awareness, is perhaps less threatening than double-loop learning, but even more rare in practice. From this view, the secret of "timely leadership" is the practice of triple-loop learning on an ongoing basis (p. 41). Similarly to addressing immunities to change, one begins by recognizing how limited one's ordinary attention is, because there is much that escapes our ordinary awareness. And as with Kegan and Lahey (2001), much attention is given to the use of language, and how leaders can change the way they think and act by attending more carefully to the words they use and the way they use them.

In the context of education this approach would be well suited to any educator who wanted to take on a professional development project that went beyond a self-study and/or taking an "inquiry stance" on their own practice (Cochran-Smith & Lytle, 2009). Action inquiry includes the basic methodology and intention of self-studies and action research, and transcends them in the sense that one's intention is not just to improve practice (single-loop learning), but to improve both one's thinking/action-logic (double-loop learning) as well as to improve, strengthen, and deepen the quality of one's moment-to-moment attention or presence (triple-loop learning) (Senge, Scharmer, Jaworski, & Flowers, 2004). Importantly, the cultivation of presence, or the quality of one's awareness/consciousness, is the most reliable and proven means for fostering structural/developmental transformation (Goleman, 1988; Kegan, 2001; Wilber, 2000b).

2   Plea for a Post-Postmodern Paradigm of Practice

These three approaches have much in common, and provide promising starting points for any leader or researcher who seeks to explore the theoretical and practical benefits of integrating developmental frameworks and practices under the umbrella of a post-postmodern or integral approach to research and practice. These approaches rest on four inter-related, research-based claims:
- Development is a specific, describable, and detectable phenomenon
- Development has a robust scientific foundation
- Development can be encouraged and fostered through specific practices
- Development has organizational/practical/actionable value

Unfortunately, the knowledge base for these claims has been widely avoided and rejected by many academic subcultures, systems, and structures that continue to operate under the influences and assumptions of modern and/or postmodern epistemes, ideologies, and frameworks. As of 2020, the partiality of postmodern truths is becoming increasingly apparent, and the time is ripe for broader, bolder, and more inclusive explications of reality to manifest. It is important for leaders and scholars of education and leadership to be aware of and attend to the developmental demands of contemporary leadership, and an inquiry into any or all of these approaches would be a good start on that path. Each approach provides detailed protocols and exercises for ongoing practice, in order to stimulate the process of vertical growth that is so necessary to meet the demands of contemporary school leadership.

It is also important that we strive to understand better the territory in which our own development emerges, and to interpret and represent it in ways that enable others to recognize the importance of self-development, for it is only by consciously engaging the process of growth that adults will continue along the path of increased skillfulness and awareness. In this regard, we must do better than popular approaches to systems, complexity, and collective learning have thus far done. Torbert (2004) notes that "self-transformation toward fully and regularly enacting the values of integrity, mutuality, and sustainability is a long, lifetime path that most of us follow as we grow toward adulthood, but that very few continue travelling intentionally once we become adults" (p. 65). It does not happen on its own; we must practice. Cook-Greuter (2004) reminds us: "Because acquisition of knowledge is part of horizontal growth, learning about developmental theories is not sufficient to help people to transform. Only specific long-term practices... [have] been shown to be effective [for transformation]" (p. 277).

The overarching point that developmental considerations should be taken into account when attending to the demands and competencies of leadership would be difficult to exaggerate. It is a crucial part of what needs to be addressed if we want to foster exceptional and sustainable leaders, and it is therefore a crucial component of an integral approach to educational research. Yet it is only when we recognize that the different action-logics that people hold are among the main causes of problems and conflict, inside and outside of schools, that we will care enough about the development of ourselves and others to engage in some form of this work.

Taken together, we can see that these and other approaches (e.g., action inquiry, Immunity to Change, lectical assessment, and IT/IMP) have the potential to constitute a new paradigm—namely, a post-postmodern one. As Wilber points out (following Kuhn (1970)—and not the many misinterpretations of Kuhn), a paradigm is not just a theory or an ideology: "'Paradigm' refers to the methodologies of enacting new phenomena, not merely to the theories that attempt to explain them" (Wilber, 2006b, p. 2).

> A paradigm is a mode of phenomena production or generation, a social practice that enacts or brings forth a phenomenological world, and theories are after-the-fact frameworks that attempt to explain or elucidate the newly-disclosed worlds. Put simply, a theory is a map of a territory, while a paradigm is a practice that brings forth a territory in the first place.... The point is that knowledge revolutions are generally combinations of new paradigm-practices that bring forth a new phenomenological territory plus new theories and maps that attempt to offer some sort of abstract or contoured guidance to the new territories thus disclosed and brought forth. But a new theory without a new practice is simply a new map with no real territory, or what is generally called 'ideology.' A scientific revolution is the result of new paradigms and new theories coming into accord with each other, both of which are anchored, not in abstractions but in social practices. (Wilber, 2006b, pp. 3–4)

The next scientific revolution will not emerge from the exponential advance of technological progress that presently dominates our lifeworld, in an apparent march toward the singularity (Bostrom, 2014; Kurzweil, 2005). If a true revolution in paradigm is to come, it will be constituted by a qualitative shift in practice, theory, and worldview, and will emerge from practices that disclose new vistas of knowledge and perspectives of reality, what Wilber calls "new phenomenological territory." I would like to suggest that the new territory, which is and will continue to be discovered by small groups of fringe practitioners before it is acknowledged by a critical mass (as has been the case with every major paradigm shift), will not be constituted by material, physical stuff. Rather, it will be a more integral, holistic disclosure that enables greater understanding of the interior, subjective, and intersubjective domains of our shared experience.

For those of us attuned to the challenges of public education, the need for a change in paradigm is clear. And for those of us working directly with or as leaders in schools, the need for vertical growth to orchestrate the demands of complex learning organizations is palpable. The paradigms of science, education, and economics that have come to dominate our lifeworld and schools are no longer adequate, and we are in desperate need of a revolution if we are to avoid the catastrophe and collapse that looms on the horizon. To paraphrase a well-worn cliché, the journey toward the next paradigm shift begins with a single step—in this case, a step along the path of meta-cognition, self-reflection, self-disclosure, and positionality.

3   Positionality as a Kosmic Address

Coming to terms with one's positionality is... complex. It may seem as though an author in my position (pun intended) should surface and account for his/her positionality prior to the final section of a book. But in the context of post-postmodern pluralism and Integral Theory, the concept evokes and indicates new layers of meaning and implication that cannot be explained adequately prior to an excavation of the basic terms of that context and theoretical framework. Now that I have covered the data and interpretation of two case studies, and completed a review of my interpretation and process in that qualitative research inquiry, I will end with a reflection on my positionality (and positionality in general).

The term positionality typically signifies an attempt in academic discourse to account for oneself in terms of one's unique relationship to various social and cultural categories, such as race, class, ethnicity, and gender. It is an attempt to convey how one understands oneself in relation to relevant and prevalent discourses and the multiple, relational processes that mutually interact to constitute one's personhood and perspective. This autobiographical exposure is also preferably enacted with an awareness of one's social position regarding power and privilege, while also acknowledging that the constellation of attributes that combine to establish this positionality are not self-created, self-sufficient, or manifest ex nihilo, but rather that I am positioned by others, by discourses, and by historical and social structures and systems, and that these external forces have an irrevocable impact on my persona, my ideology, and even more fundamentally, my epistemology—i.e., the very ways that I am able to think about and understand the world (and, ipso facto, how I am able to comprehend the concept of positionality).

All of this is fine and good, and embodies the beautiful self-reflexive grasp of the postmodern mind coming to terms with itself. The very intention of disclosing positionality, and its appearance as relevant, are clear reflections of the qualitative jump from the modern to the postmodern episteme. The catch is, even if confining myself to the categories of postmodern discourses that acknowledge and value the concept of positionality (e.g., race, class, power, etc.), a thorough self-accounting would require a full autobiography (and even that would be inevitably partial). An added catch, from the post-postmodern/integral perspective, is that those accepted categories are extremely partial, since they exclude the entire landscape of interiority and subjectivity that actually constitutes one's epistemology (however interdependent that constitution may be in relation to external forces). In the terms of Integral Theory, one's positionality emerges in relation to reality in all four quadrants. The fact that one's interiority (the Upper Left) co-emerges with the other quadrants is precisely the reason it must be accounted for, not a reason to dismiss or efface it. And accounting for interiority would entail a disclosure of not only one's general or average frequency or structure of consciousness—the probability of locating oneself in a particular pattern or structure of interior experience—but also a sharing of one's constitution in terms of states, personality type, and lines of development, at minimum (Wilber, 2000a, 2000b, 2006d).

To engage a discussion about the relative reality, primacy, or significance of these distinct domains (the postmodern emphasis on the LL and LR quadrants, and the integral inclusion of the UL quadrant) is to return to discourses regarding the history and evolution of philosophy, the interdependence of epistemology, ontology, and methodology, and the ontic and epistemic fallacies noted above. In sum, the dominant postmodern approach to positionality insightfully includes yet ultimately exaggerates the causal influence of society and the domains it seeks to explain, and by undervaluing and largely disavowing the reality of subjectivity and the symbiotic mutuality of epistemology and ontology, commits an ontic fallacy (Wilber, 2017). This overall dynamic is a manifestation of a widespread "taboo of subjectivity" that, again, can be traced to the modern and postmodern dominance of materialist views of reality (Smith, 1992; Wallace, 2000; Wilber, 1995).

The postmodern approach to positionality is also just one small step away from an unproductive and unnecessary relativism, and this is one of the downsides of postmodern development that we should seek to understand, correct, and transcend as we continue to grow individually and collectively. Part of the postmodern ethos that emerges from an increased awareness of the social construction of reality and the relationships between epistemology and social influence is an intentionality to de-center narratives, and to dismantle and discredit any implied "view from nowhere" that judges others while assuming a privilege of perspective that is somehow representative of objective "truth" (Nagel, 1989; Smith, 1992). This is best understood as a widespread and well-intentioned reaction to the many power-driven and inequality-reproducing hierarchies and justifications that we have seen throughout history. In an effort to reduce the likelihood of reproducing such hierarchy and inequality, we aim to account for positionality so as to acknowledge the absence of all-knowing authority, and thus to contextualize and relativize whatever our view happens to be.

Again, this is well and good as a cognitive and cultural development away from the naïve proclamations of those of us who have not yet come to terms with the contextualization of our perspective, and the related "naïve interventionism" that characterizes so much of modernity (Taleb, 2014). However, it is difficult to maintain a view where that de-centering/contextualization is true *and* a broader framework of qualitative distinctions between relative truths is also true and knowable. Holding such a both/and view is a challenging developmental accomplishment along the path of cognitive and perspectival maturation, and a key component of what many of the theorists I have drawn from above have been getting at in their distinctions between different worldviews. To move away from a naïve view from nowhere (the postmodern move), without taking further steps toward developing more comprehensive frameworks of understanding that can accommodate the plurality of perspectives and relative truths (the post-postmodern move), while flattening the ideological/mental space in which some perspectives are truer than others, is to fall prey to what plagues much of our current academic and popular culture of relativism, narcissism, and social fragility (Lasch, 1991; Smith, 1992; Taleb, 2014).

The view of positionality I would like to develop is fundamentally different because it locates one's position in a broader context. Wilber (1995) makes a big picture distinction between the context of the cosmos and the context of the Kosmos. Harkening back to the ancient Greeks, and pre-modern notions of a world that includes both material/objective and immaterial/subjective realities (prior to the "colonization of the lifeworld" in modernity), the term Kosmos designates Universe in its totality, not as a lifeless, pointless, physical collision of atoms reduced to the realm of physics, but as a living, conscious process that is known (partially, but truly) through an integration of all disciplines of human knowing, from physics and astronomy to biology, chemistry, psychology, sociology, phenomenology, and philosophy. It is a view that is not unique to Integral Theory—IT is a recent expression of a longstanding non-reductive/non-materialist worldview that has been partially articulated by many others, both pre- and post-modernity, and it is a lineage and literature that continues to grow (Aurobindo, 1955; Bergson, 1907/2005; Bhaskar, 2012; de Chardin, 1965; Freinacht, 2017; Garrison, 2000; Gebser, 1991; Jantsch, 1976, 1980; Neumann, 1973; Swimme & Berry, 1992; Whitehead, 1979; Wright, 2000). A post-postmodern account of positionality within the context of the Kosmos means describing one's position amidst a web of relationships at every level and dimension—who one is and how one thinks and acts in relation to physical, social, psychological, and cultural domains of an evolving reality. It is a "Kosmic address." This accounting can never be done in toto—we cannot ever fully describe anything, because whatever it is it remains hitched to everything else—but hopefully the general idea is clear.

Given that this study traverses discourses of educational theory, policy, leadership, social justice, and personal development, I will highlight some aspects of my positionality in connection to those arenas. I grew up as a White male in a predominantly Black neighborhood and public school system. The experience of being a racial minority in my own school and neighborhood from age 0–18, and then marrying a person of color and raising a bi-racial daughter has certainly influenced my sensitivity to racial, economic, and social justice. As a young adult I became deeply interested in life's biggest questions—what Tillich (1958) called matters of "ultimate concern." This led me to a study of world philosophies and religions, a BA in philosophy, an MA in philosophy of religions, and a PhD in education. More important than my institutional training, it led me to a life of meditation and independent study. By my mid-thirties I had read hundreds of non-fiction books across the subjects of psychology, history, sociology, philosophy, physics, religion, and education, in addition to the texts I read as part my BA, MA, and PhD programs, including over 10,000 pages of text related specifically to Integral Theory. I have also studied and practiced with Buddhist teachers in various lineages (primarily Zen, Vipassana, Mahamudra, and Dzogchen), and have participated in many long meditation retreats. In the past 20 years I have sat in meditation for more than 10,000 hours (and over time, the distinction between sitting meditation and non-meditation has faded, so meditation is no longer something that can be easily quantified).

Given the predominantly conservative and conventional nature of institutionalized education systems, the autodidacticism of my path is especially relevant. As Walsh (2018) argues, "most of the planet has institutionalized an underestimation of human nature and possibilities. What we take to be 'normality' is actually a form of collective developmental arrest" (para. 1). In general agreement with that statement, I would argue that self-directed learning is a crucial component of post-postmodern education, and a key to fostering the emergence of human potential beyond the current norms that tend to arrest development in schools. The practice of meditation is also essential, since meditation actually recapitulates and encourages the process of perspective-development on a moment-to-moment basis. The process of structural psychological development can be summarized as: the subject of one stage becomes the object of the subject of the next stage (Kegan, 2001; Wilber, 2000b). In meditation, one can practice taking one's current subjectivity as an object of awareness, thus facilitating the perpetual broadening, opening, and deepening of one's awareness to include more subjective experience. This ever-broadening, –deepening, and -opening of the aperture of awareness fosters the expansion and development of subjectivity itself. My self-directed pursuit of transdisciplinary study and Zone 1 practices of phenomenological disclosure enabled me to have first-person knowledge of the perspectives and structures that adequate structuralism describes. Without that direct experience, I could not have approached this study in the way that I did, as the dimensions I included in my meta-analysis would not have been apparent to me.

Regarding my work in schools, I taught PreK, K, and 5th grade in independent schools in California for five years, and later worked as a school leader in public schools in Boston for the four years that followed my data collection for this study, first as a primary school director, then as a PreK-8th grade principal (and I continue to work as a school leader, now in North Carolina, at the time of this writing). During the course of research for this book, in a strange twist of fate, I became a colleague and peer of Weatherbee and Matthews, as a school leader in the same city, immediately following my time working in their schools as a researcher (though the school I served as principal was less racially diverse than SCS or JJS; it was comprised of almost all Black families, almost all of whom were categorized as low income—such is the educational segregation in urban America). This transition from educational researcher to school leader afforded me the opportunity to be principal at a school that was already being studied, just as SCS and JJS were, because the former principal had also been a member of the SLA (a very unlikely coincidence!).

As a result of this, a university researcher, who was in the same shoes that I was a few years prior, asked if she could interview me about leadership and educational change at my school. I did not connect this interview with my own study at the time, but I was able to get a copy of the transcript of my interview, and I offer an extended quotation below, as an example of how I conceptualized matters somewhat differently than Matthews and Weatherbee, and in ways that relate to some of the topics I covered in my work with them. In this interview, the researcher asked me to share how I had come to the school, how it was working out, what changes I made and would like to make, what the top priorities of the school were, and what connections I made to complexity theory as a school leader:

> The institutional, structural impediments that come along with being in a public school, even at a charter school instead of a district, are still very intense, and to me feel overly inhibitive and confining, and I feel like the range within which I can create change in the direction that I would want to go, which is in one way or another the direction of more progressive schools—I was able to sense pretty early on that that range was going to be pretty limited, and actually this school right now is under intense pressure to increase standardized test scores.... So for me, this year has been an interesting process of coming to terms with understanding the school from a really intimate inside perspective and how that's lived every day, and how that aligns with who I am as a person and as a professional and my ideas and values, and then also trying to understand my place in the larger educational landscape, and going through an existential reflection around [questions such as]: where should I be? Is this actually the school that I should be at? ... How can I serve the educational project at large? ... And the cognitive dissonance for me between how I really want things to look and feel versus not only how things are here, but even the way people want things to be—it's just not really in alignment. Like what does a good classroom look like? The version of what a good classroom looks like here [is such that] I think there are too many people who are still too traditional for me. And there is also another layer of complexity regarding the fact that it's a charter school, and the questions that are raised by the very existence of charter schools are complicated.... [For instance] teacher turnover is a huge problem here. [There is] this really widespread

feeling that the work is not sustainable, and the turnover rate is really substantial, and I think that those issues are not easily solved, and I don't feel like they're solvable at my level of operation.... I just feel like what's really necessary is a backwards step and really thinking about how we have constructed school, and what this school looks like, and what's the student-teacher ratio, and how many learning specialists do we have? Is our curriculum ultimately going to be focused on academics or can we take a broader approach to why we're all here? ... [Because I think ultimately] a more therapeutic model is what's needed.... You have to either go one way or the other. You have to accept the status quo and find a way to justify helping students who are not being served well to go to other schools, so that you can maintain your norms. Or, you expand the scope of what your norms are and your programming so that you can serve a wider diversity of students. But you can't just want it to be different than it is because that's not good enough.... There are bigger questions I think that need to be asked, and the work that I've been doing and the work that we're doing as a school is all within the range of the parameters that are already set. It's not questioning the parameters themselves, and that's the struggle of being at a public school is this feeling that no matter how outside the box you want to think, you can only get so far outside the box. There are just so many constraints.... At the last school I worked at, we had this phrase where people just said "Love the struggle." It's a struggle, but this is the work we want to do, and we're here for a reason, and we're working with children for a reason, and we can feel good about that. But I think one of the key factors that enables that to happen is having a core group of committed folks who do that throughout a number of years. Perhaps in the high school here, they had that and have had that to some extent, but with their expansion, they've expanded rapidly, adding ten extra grades K1 through 8, and they expanded rapidly in the sense that they didn't just start in K1 and build up. They started adding fifth graders every year, which has now become the fifth through eighth grade, and that student body has really posed intense challenges for the school over the past three years. The staff turnover that's working with those students has been extreme every year [and we lost nine teachers during the school year this year], so they haven't been able to establish a real sense of stability and consistency during the expansion, and having that sort of institutional buy-in where people can feel good about the work that they're doing and feel sustained in the work that they're doing, it just hasn't been well established.

A full case study would not be able to explain all that we did and tried to do, the challenges we faced, and the perspectives of others I worked with, but the above quote does give a sense of how I thought about and responded to some of the interdependent and multi-layered complexity that arose while serving as principal in an environment that was in some ways well beyond the "edge of chaos." I came in with a fairly clear sense of what my educational values and priorities were, and was not oriented toward meeting the criteria of success that was provided by external sources. The questions that arose for me emerged from my inquiry into the relationships and congruence between my vision and the culture I was apart of. The professional and the personal/existential could not be separated; my need and purpose was to transform the school in a direction that I intuited to be positive and good, and my assessment of the context involved ongoing deliberation about the extent to which I could fulfill that purpose, and the extent to which the context was ripe for that work to be done.

One cannot do everything, and every social system has a range within which it can transform in a given period of time, and particular conditions that must be in place for that transformation to occur. As a school leader I was playing with double-loop and triple-loop reflections on my positionality within the school in real time. I knew that the work to transform the school would take coordinated effort in all domains, and that it would take years for me to instigate that kind of change, for which I would need institutional support that I did not have. I had learned enough to know

> change will only stick if it... [grows] out of the organic background of the group or culture itself and [is] not imposed from the outside. With few exceptions, the 'layer cake' of a culture needs to be organically grown layer by layer by layer—in all four quadrants—in order to take root at all. (Watkins & Wilber, 2015, p. 87)

In this particular context, I came to the realization that the school in which I worked was not going to transform in the direction that I desired, due to many factors: the limits of my role (as a principal working under a head of school and board, with another upper school principal, and within the expectations and accountability structures of the district), the institutional commitment to conventional definitions of success, and the lack of support for my vision of what was possible.

My time as a public school principal brought new meaning to Heifetz's (1994) quip that "people who lead frequently bear scars from their efforts to bring about adaptive change. Often they are silenced. On occasion, they are killed" (p. 235). My life was not in danger, but neither was the status quo. As Forman and Ross (2013) convey, integral thinkers can appear arrogant, aloof, or indecisive to people who are orientated toward linear, conventional, "achievement"-based approaches to work and success. "Earlier levels of meaning-making can easily feel threatened by the actions of later levels, and if they are pushed beyond their ability to tolerate the inevitable anxiety of change, they will react in an effort to restore their world to "the way it should be" as seen from their perspective" (p. 134). It was interesting for me to note the wide range of responses I received to my insistent attempts to ask big questions, challenge prevailing operations, and suggest new frames for our educational work. I was told more than a few times that the school "wasn't ready" for what I was trying to do. I received positive feedback and encouragement from many teachers and staff, but some who were higher on the organizational chart did not appreciate me rocking the boat, and at the same time may have experienced my relaxed, non-rushed, non-authoritarian, decentralized, and long-range approach to leadership as "aloof," or as not "driven" enough (toward linear goals), as Forman and Ross predicted.

It has also been telling to witness a radical difference in response in a different context. At the time of this writing I am a school leader at an independent Quaker school, where the mission, vision, and culture of the community is explicitly post-conventional. In my conversations with staff and parents, I consistently explore the themes of love-based and research-based education, where the goal is not success within the world as it is but simply and ultimately to make the world a better place. The aspiration of our school is to raise children who are deeply loving, always learning, and motivated to improve and transform society. It is a school that operates under different assumptions and a different paradigm than most schools, where the elders understand that children need and deserve to be listened to, that what happens in schools should emerge organically from the relationships between people of all ages, and that this requires patience and presence, which means "taking the time to be present and to listen deeply to the child, and not the voices in our own head that are pressing some kind of agenda" (Moore, 2017, p. 45). I have also begun to explore the topic of human development with parents and staff, and am helping people to understand the differences between traditional, modern, postmodern, and integral ways of parenting and teaching.

The key insight and transformation available to communities on the verge of integral values and perspectives is that they can whole-heartedly embrace a vision, mission, culture, and practice that is rooted in understanding human development and its implications, where adults appreciate where children are coming from, where they are going, and the context in which they are growing. As the director of Upland Hills School in Michigan—a similarly post-conventional school—explains:

> Children are developmental beings, always unfolding in awareness and capacity, and ever-evolving. They come into our lives as helpless, fragile, totally dependent, wide-open, complex, evolutionary extensions of our families, and our deep-time past. At the same time, they are our most essential bridge to our future. If we are to learn how to live in a global society, we will have to develop complex cognitive abilities that allow us to view the world from a multiplicity of perspectives. All children are living proof of how every one of us must move through distinct stages of growth as we construct and develop minds that are able to think beyond either/or and to reason from a perspective of both/and. (Moore, 2017, p. 90)

The difference in receptivity to my thinking, questioning, and leadership in the last two schools I have served has been a striking example of the very real and palpable differences in cultural norms, values, and consciousness. In a traditional or modern culture, post-conventional thinking can appear confusing, unproductive, or off-putting, but in a postmodern, or post-postmodern, and post-conventional culture, a new team member who brings excitement for change, big picture thinking, and pushing the envelope is likely to be met with mutual resonance, appreciation, and positive energy; at least that is my interpretation of my experience over the course of working in different schools.

In light of the whole that this study comprises (which is just a part of a larger personal story, and a broader field of inquiry), positionality takes on new and greater importance. Positionality—understood as an imperfect yet approximate Kosmic address—is the keystone. That is the underlying realization that led me to problematize and re-assess this study. I was unable to feel at peace with my interpretation of school leadership without somehow trying to locate the positionality of myself and my research participants in a more illuminating way. I realized I did not understand Weatherbee or Matthews well enough to establish a valid portrayal of their leadership. The key to understanding and explaining their cases would lie in a fuller understanding of how they perceived and understood their context, their work, their aims, and other people. I therefore presented Integral Theory as a way to explain why that is important, how it fits within a broader context, and how researchers can work to avoid overly partial approaches to research. I presented it also as an entry point into the terrain of growth and development, which I maintain is a crucial ingredient in educational leadership.

Having done this reflective work, I can attest to the ways in which the researcher is implicated in the process and outcomes of research and interpretation. An essential aspect of the postmodern turn was an attempt to come to terms with the positionality, subjectivity, and influence of individuals as constituted perspectives—as opposed to objective, passive observers who can proclaim truths for others. For me, engaging in a post-postmodern attempt to incorporate and account for that realization, while pursuing my own lines of thought regarding trends and patterns in individual, cultural, and social development, means having to account for myself within that work, not separate from that work. It means having to acknowledge that my perspective is in process, and is inevitably partial, as is everyone else's. It means having to engage in the meta-cognitive work of situating my own theorizing amongst others, and continuing to question and refine my own interpretations in dialogue with others, and being willing to change and improve my theories and views accordingly. This process is both humbling and energizing, and being able to see this work as developmental and progressive impels me to continue to strive for better views, maps, and theories, while also working to find new ways to share with others in ways that will be helpful. As a researcher and as a leader, it means perpetually trying to account for as many perspectives as possible, and incorporating and processing as much data as possible, while making decisions with an eye toward the ways in which the systems I am enmeshed in can continue to evolve in increasingly healthy and positive directions.

Ultimately, I see the expansion of frameworks and the conscious work of development as part of a broader social evolution to create improved educational environments that foster overall growth and transformation, where education is "understood as the exposure to what is different... such that new ways of doing things than are currently found in the world can actually be brought into being" (Osberg, 2010, p. 164). If we agree with Maslow, Piaget, Baldwin, Dewey, Habermas, Whitehead, Rawls, and countless others that the "Aristotelian Principle" is generally correct—that people universally prefer exercising increasingly complex skills in a context of non-alienated work—then we must continue to work toward creating educational environments where people can thrive under ideal conditions for creativity and self-actualization. In the language of systems, we need to create win-win, closed-loop systems of positive feedback and incentives oriented toward omni-positive outcomes (Schmachtenberger, 2018). Within win-lose structures (like our contemporary school systems), our innate drive toward agency and self-actualization will continue to manifest as competition. But within a win-win, non-competitive system (like my current school), that human impulse can manifest as a desire to go beyond current capacities in the spirit of service.

Given the anti-metanarrative, anti-hierarchy, materialistic, and reductive tendencies of the dominant language games and discourses of the early 21st century, post-postmodern, metamodern, and integral movements toward syntheses that transcend and include other discourses will not be well-received or welcomed. I expect that their importance will come to be known despite much resistance (while traditional, modern, and postmodern frameworks will continue to instigate and perpetuate social and discursive friction and culture wars). A key to this ongoing paradigm shift rests on the degree to which we can re-introduce and integrate narratives of development in ways that do not trigger and re-open the wounds and traumas of modernist, dominator hierarchies and power inequalities. As Torbert (2000a) and others emphasize, a sound developmental map

> will honour a variety of routes, and will commend each person to ground their development in their own inner light and life. And the map will, in principle and in every respect, be open to revision as a function of experiential and reflective inquiry. More radically, the ultimate rationale of the map is to empower people to make explicit their own maps grounded in their own experiential knowledge. (Heron, as cited in Torbert, 2000a, p. 264)

The theories we develop to describe the emergent territory of our growth will continue to change and improve over time, as must we. A map is never the territory, but that makes it no less crucial when navigating difficult terrain. We must remember that growth models involve trajectories of capacity, not designations of greater or lesser intrinsic human value; they denote a range of perspectives available to all people, not kinds or types of people. If we are engaged in ongoing growth, the words we use to describe the steps of our journey do not define us—they enable us to communicate to others how to traverse a path that all are invited to join.

POSTSCRIPT

Phronetic Social Science and Methodological Metacognition

I began this research wondering about the relationship between educational leadership and educational change, with a focus on how a leadership program for early-career principals was impacting the cultures and practices of participating schools. However, as my experience in these schools began to reveal problems and questions to me as a researcher, both my research questions and my approach to this ongoing inquiry evolved. As the complexity of these educational realities continued to disclose itself, the nature of my research and of my stance as a researcher continued to change. As time passed, the more I grew aware of and concerned about the persistent gaps between my initial analyses and the sum total of all that I perceived and understood about these schools. I knew that there were aspects and dimensions of these schools that my methods were not disclosing adequately, and I sought to surface and explain them.

In my research I sought to enact a "reflective" approach to social science, where I "look upon the external field as the conditions of existence of the locale within which research occurs. [And I] therefore move beyond *social processes to delineate the social forces* that impress themselves on the ethnographic locale" (Buroway, 1998, p. 15). This meant that different contexts of interpretation and domains of discourse needed to be accounted for and integrated, and that my perspective as a researcher—the one who decides what contexts and discourses are included and why—needed to be included as an ineluctable ingredient in the research. In sum, I had to account more fully for my own perspective, the differences between my perspective and the perspectives of the research participants, and the social forces that I understood to have a significant influence on these schools.

It was from this more reflective stance—thinking deeply about not just the data I collected, but about my stance and perspective as an interpreter of these schools—that I began to seek a more comprehensive framework for understanding what was happening in these cases in relation to their educational and social contexts. In this time it became clearer to me that I was not seeking to describe objectively what was happening, or what was good or bad in these schools, but that I was seeking to utilize the complex systems of these schools to help myself and others understand something about leadership, change, education, and/or human systems. The aim was to clarify and improve my thinking (and perhaps the thinking of others) regarding what was happening in these schools, and perhaps in other schools as well.

In regard to educational research, some may argue that one cannot generalize results from one system to another, due to constant change and a lack of controls; "structure determinism" amounts to a critique of most educational research because a truly emergent study cannot be duplicated. What can be replicated, however, "is the research attitude of mindful participation with a community around matters of shared concern" (Davis and Sumara, 2006, p. 101). Educational research must therefore be transdisciplinary and interdiscursive, leveraging qualitative data not to generalize results but to illuminate ideas, attitudes, and insights, and to contribute to ongoing dialogue between researchers, practitioners, and theorists. What is sought is not a final accounting or judgment, but a contribution to our interpretation of and thinking about matters of consequence in education and beyond. As Cremin (1990) noted,

> assessments... have been seriously flawed by a failure to understand the extraordinary complexity of education—a failure to grasp the impossibility of defining a good school apart from its social and intellectual context, the impossibility of even comprehending the processes and effects of schooling and, in fact, its success and failures apart from their embedment in a larger ecology of education that includes what families, television broadcasters, workplaces, and a host of other institutions are contributing at any given time. (p. viii)

Ideally, my efforts to bring an "attitude of mindful participation" into these schools was not a way to assess programs or people, but an attempt to enact what Flyvbjerg (2010) describes as a social science rooted in phronesis—an integrative approach that transcends and includes both analytical, scientific knowledge (episteme) and practical, technical know-how (techne). As Flyvbjerg argues, social sciences are not cumulative and predictive, and should not be predicated on the natural sciences as they often are. In the natural sciences, the exclusion of context is necessary for theory, but in the social sciences it is context that determines action and makes explanation possible—"context-dependence does not mean just a more complex form of determinism. It means an open-ended, contingent relation between contexts and actions and interpretations" (p. 43).

Phronetic social science aims to analyze and interpret not just behavior, but the values and aims of social practices as well—similar to how Jackson (2000) argues for the need for a critical systems thinking. It is "social science as public philosophy" (Bellah et al., 1986, p. 297), where "the boundary between social science and philosophy is still open" (Flyvbjerg, 2010, p. 64). However, it is erroneous to presume that cases cannot provide reliable information about a broader class of experience. In fact, generalizing from a single case is not only possible, it is done often and to great effect (a study of Galileo provides many good examples). As Beveridge argued, "more discoveries have arisen from intense observation of very limited material than from statistics applied to large groups" (in Flyvbjerg, 2010, p. 75). And as Rorty (1985) put it: "the way to re-enchant the world... is to stick to the concrete" (p. 173).

The attention to concrete particulars and context in qualitative research and social science dovetails theoretically with awareness of the historical, philosophical, and social context being studied and interpreted. Understanding history is a key element in phronetic social science, both in terms of a narrative of specific actors (Geertz, 1988), and in terms of a broader "historical sense," as in Nietzsche's philosophy (1968a, p. 35) and Foucault's social science. As MacIntyre (1984) surmises, "I can only answer the question 'What am I to do?' if I can answer the prior question 'Of what story or stories do I find myself a part?'" (p. 216).

The phronetic approach outlined by Flyvbjerg (2010) also dovetails nicely with complexity thinking in its ability to account for the dualisms of agency and structure. In a complex system, individuals are interdependent, and the interplay between individual actions and the ways in which individuals impact each other and are influenced by the dynamics of the system as a whole are constituents of a continual conversation of thinking and behavior. Similarly,

> Phronetic research focuses on both the actor level and the structural level, as well as on the relation between the two in an attempt to transcend the dualisms of actor/structure, hermeneutics/structuralism, and voluntarism/determinism. Actors and their practices are analyzed in relation to structures and structures in terms of agency, not so that the two stand in an external relation to each other, but so that structures are found as part of actors and actors as part of structures. (p. 137)

This is what Bourdieu (1977) called "the internalization of externality and the externalization of internality" (p. 72). Ultimately, the goal of such social science is to contribute to society's capacity for deliberation and action, through "a combination of concrete empirical analyses and practical philosophical considerations"—what Bourdieu called "fieldwork in philosophy" (Flyvbjerg, 2010, p. 167).

In this work I have found that the approach of phronetic social science, when combined with the analytical rigor of Integral Methodological Pluralism, provides a robust and fairly ideal approach to educational research, and to social science research more broadly. I implore others in these fields to experiment, play with, and enact these paradigms.

References

Alhadeff-Jones, M. (2010). The reduction of critique in education: Perspectives from Morin's paradigm of complexity. In D. Osberg & G. Biesta (Eds.), *Complexity theory and the politics of education*. Rotterdam, the Netherlands: Sense Publishers.

Alsbury, T. L. (2008). The crucible of reform: The search for systemic leadership. In B. Despres (Ed.), *Systems thinkers in action: A field guide for effective change leadership in education*. Lanham, MD: Rowman & Littlefield.

Anyon, J. (1980). Social class and the hidden curriculum of work. *Journal of Education, 162*, 7–92.

Anyon, J. (1981). Social class and school knowledge. *Curriculum Inquiry, 11*, 3–42.

Anyon, J. (2005). What "counts" as educational policy? Notes toward a new paradigm. *Harvard Educational Review, 75*(1), 65–88.

Apel, K. (1984). *Understanding and explanation: A transcendental-pragmatic perspective*. Cambridge, MA: MIT Press.

Apple, M. W. (1979). *Ideology and curriculum*. Boston, MA: Routledge & Kegan Paul.

Apple, M. W. (2001). Markets, standards, teaching, and teacher education. *Journal of Teacher Education, 52*(3), 182–196.

Apple, M. W. (2006). *Educating the right way: Markets, standards, god, and equality* (2nd ed.). New York, NY: Routledge.

Argyris, C., & Schon, D. A. (1974). *Theory in practice: Increasing professional effectiveness*. San Francisco, CA: Jossey-Bass.

Arnold, R. D., & Wade, J. P. (2015). A definition of systems thinking: A systems approach. *Procedia Computer Science, 44*, 669–678.

Atteberry, A., & Bryk, A. S. (2010). Centrality, connection, and commitment: The role of social networks in a school-based literacy initiative. In A. J. Daly (Ed.), *Social network theory and educational change* (pp. 51–76). Cambridge, MA: Harvard Education Press.

Aurobindo, S. (1955). *The life divine*. Pondicherry, India: Sri Aurobindo Ashram Press.

Bambrick-Santoyo, P. (2012). *Leverage leadership: A practical guide to building exceptional schools*. San Francisco, CA: Jossey-Bass.

Barnard, P. A. (2013). *The systems thinking school: Redesigning schools from the inside-out*. Lanham, MD: Rowman & Littlefield.

Bathurst, R., & Monin, N. (2010). Shaping leadership for today: Mary Parker Follett's aesthetic. *Leadership, 6*(2), 115–131.

Bausch, K. C. (2001). *The emerging consensus in social systems theory*. New York, NY: Springer.

Beabout, B. R. (2012). Turbulence, perturbance, and educational change. *Complicity: An International Journal of Complexity and Education, 9*(2), 15–29.

Beatty, B. (2005). Emotional leadership. In B. Davies (Ed.), *The essentials of school leadership*. Thousand Oaks, CA: Sage Publications.

Beck, D. E. (2014). Don Beck: Back from South Africa. *Integral Leadership Review, January-February*, 1–6. Retrieved from http://integralleadershipreview.com/11160-don-beck-back-south-africa/

Beck, D. E., & Cowan, C. C. (2006). *Spiral dynamics: Mastering values, leadership, and change*. Malden, MA: Blackwell Publishing.

Beck, D. E., & Linscott, G. (1991). *The crucible: Forging South Africa's future*. New York, NY: New Paradigm Press.

Bellah, R. N., Madsen, R., Sullivan, W. M., Swidler, A., & Tipton, S. M. (1986). *Habits of the heart: Individualism and commitment in American life*. New York, NY: Harper & Row.

Bergson, H. (2005). *Creative evolution*. New York, NY: Barnes & Noble. (Original work published 1907)

Bhaskar, R. (2002). *From science to emancipation*. New Delhi, India: Sage Publications.

Bhaskar, R. (2012). *The philosophy of MetaReality: Creativity, love and freedom* (2nd ed.). New York, NY: Routledge.

Biesta, G. (2010). Five theses on complexity reduction and its politics. In D. Osberg & G. Biesta (Eds.), *Complexity theory and the politics of education*. Rotterdam, the Netherlands: Sense Publishers.

Blake, R. R., & Mouton, J. S. (1964). *The managerial grid*. Houston, TX: Gulf Publishing.

Bostrom, N. (2014). *Superintelligence: Paths, dangers, strategies*. Oxford, UK: Oxford University Press.

Bourdieu, P. (1977). *Outline of a theory of practice*. Cambridge, UK: Cambridge University Press.

Bower, D. F. (2008). Leadership and the self-organizing school. In B. Despres (Ed.), *Systems thinkers in action: A field guide for effective change leadership in education*. Lanham, MD: Rowman & Littlefield.

Bowers, C. A. (2012). Questioning the idea of the individual as an autonomous moral agent. *Journal of Moral Education, 41*(3), 301–310.

Bowers, J. S., & Nickerson, S. D. (2001). Identifying cyclic patterns of interaction to study individual and collective learning. *Mathematical Thinking and Learning, 3*, 1–28.

Bowles, S., & Gintis, H. (1976). *Schooling in capitalist America: Educational reform and the contradictions of economic life*. New York, NY: Basic Books.

Bowles, S., & Gintis, H. (1986). *Democracy and capitalism: Property, community, and the contradictions of modern social thought*. New York, NY: Basic Books.

Boyatzis, R. E. (1982). *The competent manager: A model for effective performance*. London, UK: John Wiley & Sons.

Bronk, W. (1983). *Vectors and smoothable curves: Collected essays*. San Francisco, CA: North Point Press.

Brown, B. (2011). *Conscious leadership for sustainability: How leaders with a late-stage action-logic design and engage in sustainability initiatives* (Unpublished doctoral dissertation). Fielding Graduate University.

Brown, B. (2012). Leading complex change with post-conventional consciousness. *Journal of Organizational Change Management, 24*(4), 560–577.

Brown, J. (2012). *Systems thinking strategy: The new way to understand your business and drive performance*. Bloomington, IN: iUniverse.

Brown, S. (2013, April 9). At occupy the DOE, A push for democratic, not corporate, education reform. *The Nation*.

Bryk, A. S., & Schneider, B. (2002). *Trust in schools: A core resource for improvement.* New York, NY: Russell Sage Foundation.

Burawoy, M. (1998). The extended case method. *Sociological Theory, 16*(1), 4–33.

Capra, F., & Luisi, P. L. (2014). *The systems view of life: A unifying vision*. Cambridge, UK: Cambridge University Press.

Carter, S. C. (2001). *No excuses: Lessons from 21 high-performing, high-poverty schools.* Washington, DC: The Heritage Foundation.

Charmaz, K. (2000). Grounded theory: Objectivist and constructivist methods. In N. K. Denzin & Y. S. Lincoln (Eds.), *Handbook of qualitative research* (pp. 509–535). Thousand Oaks, CA: Sage.

Chaudhuri, H. (1977). *The evolution of integral consciousness*. Wheaton, IL: The Theosophical Publishing House.

Checkland, P. (1999). *Systems thinking, systems practice; Soft systems methodology: A 30 year retrospective*. Chichester, UK: John Wiley.

Cilliers, P. (1998). *Complexity and postmodernism: Understanding complex systems*. New York, NY: Routledge.

Cilliers, P. (2010). Acknowledging complexity: A foreword. In D. Osberg & G. Biesta (Eds.), *Complexity theory and the politics of education*. Rotterdam, the Netherlands: Sense Publishers.

City, E. A., Elmore, R. F., Fiarman, S. E., & Teitel, L. (2009). *Instructional rounds in education: A network approach to improving teaching and learning*. Cambridge, MA: Harvard Education Press.

Coburn, C. E., Choi, L., & Mata, W. (2010). "I would go to her because her mind is math": Network formation in the context of a district-based mathematics reform. In A. J. Daly (Ed.), *Social network theory and educational change* (pp. 33–50). Cambridge, MA: Harvard Education Press.

Cochran-Smith, M., & Lytle, S. (2009). *Inquiry as stance: Practitioner research for the next generation*. New York, NY: Teachers College Press.

Cohn, M., & Kottkamp, R. (1993). *Teachers: The missing voice in education*. Albany, NY: State University of New York Press.

Cole, R. P., & Weinbaum, E. H. (2010). Changes in attitude: Peer influence in high school reform. In A. J. Daly (Ed.), *Social network theory and educational change*. Cambridge, MA: Harvard Education Press.

Collins, J. C. (2001). *Good to great: Why some companies make the leap... and others don't*. New York, NY: HarperCollins.

Cook-Greuter, S. (2004). Making the case for a developmental perspective. *Industrial and Commercial Training, 36*(7), 275–281.

Coombs, P. H. (1968). *The world educational crisis: A systems analysis*. New York, NY: Oxford University Press.

Cotton, K. (2003). *Principals and student achievement*. Alexandria, VA: Association for Supervision and Curriculum Development.

Cremin, L. A. (1990). *Popular education and its discontents*. New York, NY: Harper & Row.

Creswell, J., Hanson, W., Plano Clark, V., & Morales, A. (2007). Qualitative research designs: Selection and implementation. *The Counseling Psychologist, 35*(2), 28.

Cunningham, C. A. (2014). *Systems theory for pragmatic schooling: Toward principles of democratic education*. New York, NY: Palgrave Macmillan.

Daft, R. L., & Lengel, R. H. (1998). *Fusion leadership: Unlocking the subtle forces that change people and organizations*. San Francisco, CA: Berrett-Koehler Publishers.

Daly, A. J. (2010). Mapping the terrain: Social network theory and educational change. In A. J. Daly (Ed.), *Social network theory and educational change*. Cambridge, MA: Harvard Education Press.

Daly, A. J., & Chrispeels, J. (2008). A question of trust: Predictive conditions for adaptive and technical leadership in educational contexts. *Leadership and Policy in Schools, 7*, 30–63.

Davey, M. (2012, September 18). Teachers end Chicago strike on second try. *The New York Times*.

Davies, B. (Ed.). (2009). *The essentials of school leadership* (2nd ed.). Thousand Oaks, CA: Sage.

Davis, B., & Sumara, D. (2001). Learning communities: Understanding the workplace as a complex system. *New Directions for Adult and Continuing Education, 92*, 85–95.

Davis, B., & Sumara, D. (2006). *Complexity and education*. Mahwah, NJ: Lawrence Erlbaum Associates.

Davis, B., Sumara, D., & D'Amour, L. (2012). Understanding school districts as learning systems: Some lessons from three cases of complex transformation. *Journal of Educational Change, 13*, 373–399.

Davis, B., Sumara, D., & Iftody, T. (2010). Complexity, consciousness and curriculum. In D. Osberg & G. Biesta (Eds.), *Complexity theory and the politics of education*. Rotterdam, the Netherlands: Sense Publishers.

Dawkins, R. (1989). *The selfish gene* (2nd ed.). Oxford, UK: Oxford University Press.

Dawson, T. L. (2017a). *National leaders' thinking: How does it measure up?* Retrieved November 16, 2018, from https://medium.com/age-of-awareness/the-complexity-of-national-leaders-thinking-how-does-it-measure-up-d848d5ee53b8

Dawson, T. L. (2017b). *The complexity gap.* Retrieved November 30, 2018, from https://medium.com/@theo_dawson/the-complexity-gap-faad87e0bb5f

Dawson, T. L. (2018a). *National leaders' thinking: What we've learned so far....* Retrieved February 1, 2019, from https://medium.com/@theo_dawson/national-leaders-thinking-what-we-ve-learned-so-far-12751e37bdbe

Dawson, T. L. (2018b). *What PISA measures. What we measure.* Retrieved February 4, 2019, from https://medium.com/@theo_dawson/what-pisa-measures-what-we-measure-e083621f2c87

Dawson, T. L., & Stein, Z. (2011a). *Virtuous cycles of learning: A digital revolution.* Paper Presented at the International School on Mind, Brain and Education, Erice, Italy.

Dawson, T. L., & Stein, Z. (2011b). We are all learning here: Cycles of research and application in adult development. In C. Hoare (Ed.), *Oxford handbook of reciprocal adult learning and development* (pp. 447–461) Oxford University Press.

de Chardin, T. (1965). *The phenomenon of man.* New York, NY: Harper & Row.

Despres, B. (Ed.). (2008). *Systems thinkers in action: A field guide for effective change leadership in education.* Lanham, MD: Rowman & Littlefield.

Diamond, J. (1999). *Guns, germs, and steel: The fates of human societies.* New York, NY: W.W. Norton and Company.

Doll, W. (1993). *A post-modern perspective on curriculum.* New York, NY: Teachers College Press.

Dreyfus, H. L., & Rabinow, P. (1983). *Michel Foucault: Beyond structuralism and hermeneutics* (2nd ed.). Chicago, IL: University of Chicago Press.

Duffy, F. M. (2008). Open systems theory and system dynamics: The twin pillars of transformational change in school districts. In B. Despres (Ed.), *Systems thinkers in action: A field guide for effective change leadership in education.* Lanham, MD: Rowman & Littlefield.

DuFour, R., DuFour, R., & Eaker, R. (2008). *Revisiting professional learning communities at work: New insights for improving leadership.* Bloomington, IN: Solution Tree.

Dweck, C. S. (2007). *Mindset: The new psychology of success.* New York, NY: Ballantine Books.

Education Research Service. (2000). *The principal, keystone of a high achieving school: Attracting and keeping the leaders we need.* Alexandria, VA: National Association of Elementary School Principals, and National Association of Secondary School Principals.

Edwards, M. G. (2010). *Organizational transformation for sustainability: An integral metatheory.* New York, NY: Routledge.

Egan, K. (2002). *Getting it wrong from the beginning.* New Haven, CT: Yale University Press.

Elm, J. P., & Goldenson, D. R. (2012). *The business case for systems engineering study: Results of the systems engineering effectiveness survey.* Pittsburgh, PA: Carnegie Mellon University.

Elmore, R. (2000). *Building a new structure for school leadership.* Washington, DC: Albert Shanker Institute.

Erickson, F. E. (1986). Qualitative methods in research on teaching. In M. Wittrock (Ed.), *Handbook of research in teaching* (3rd ed., pp. 119–161). New York, NY: Macmillan.

Esbjorn-Hargens, S. (Ed.). (2010). *Integral theory in action.* Albany, NY: SUNY Press.

Esbjorn-Hargens, S., Reams, J., & Gunnlaugson, O. (Eds.). (2010). *Integral education: New directions for higher learning.* Albany, NY: SUNY Press.

Esbjorn-Hargens, S., & Zimmerman, M. (2009). *Integral ecology.* Boston, MA: Integral Books.

Evans, R. (1996). *The human side of school change.* San Francisco, CA: Jossey Bass.

Fenwick, T. (2010). Normalizing standards in educational complexity: A network analysis. In D. Osberg & G. Biesta (Eds.), *Complexity theory and the politics of education.* Rotterdam, the Netherlands: Sense Publishers.

Finkelstein, S. (2004). *Why smart executives fail: And what you can learn from their mistakes.* New York, NY: Portfolio Trade.

Fischer, K. W. (1980). A theory of cognitive development: The control and destruction of hierarchies and skills. *Psychological Review, 87,* 477–531.

Fischer, K. W. (2009). Mind, brain, and education: Building a scientific groundwork for learning and teaching. *Mind, Brian, and Education, 3,* 3–16.

Fischer, K. W., & Bidell, T. R. (2006). Dynamic development of action, thought, and emotion. In W. Damon & R. M. Lerner (Eds.), *Handbook of child psychology: Theoretical models of human development* (6th ed., pp. 313–399). New York, NY: Wiley.

Fleener, M. J. (2005). Chaos, complexity, curriculum and culture: Setting up the conversation. In W. E. Doll, M. J. Fleener, D. Trueit, & J. St. Julien (Eds.), *Chaos, complexity, curriculum and culture.* New York, NY: Peter Lang.

Flood, R. L. (1990). Liberating systems theory: Toward critical systems thinking. *Human Relations, 43*(1), 49–75.

Flood, R. L. (1999). *Rethinking the fifth discipline: Learning within the unknowable.* New York, NY: Routledge.

Flyvbjerg, B. (2010). *Making social science matter.* Cambridge, UK: Cambridge University Press.

Forman, J. P., & Ross, L. A. (2013). *Integral leadership: The next half-step.* Albany, NY: SUNY Press.

Foucault, M. (1984a). Politics and ethics. In P. Rabinow (Ed.), *The Foucault reader.* New York, NY: Pantheon.

Foucault, M. (1984b). Nietzsche, genealogy, history. In P. Rabinow (Ed.), *The Foucault reader.* New York, NY: Pantheon.

Foucault, M. (1994). *The order of things: An archaeology of the human sciences.* New York, NY: Vintage.

Foucault, M. (1997). Polemics, politics, and problematizations. In P. Rabinow (Ed.), *Ethics: Subjectivity and truth. The essential works of Michel Foucault* (Vol. I). New York, NY: New Press.

Freinacht, H. (2017). *The listening society: A metamodern guide to politics.* Columbia, SC: Metamoderna.

Freinacht, H. (2019). *Nordic ideology: A metamodern guide to politics, book two.* Columbia, SC: Metamoderna.

Fuhs, C. (2008). Towards a vision of integral leadership: A quadrivial analysis of eight leadership books. *Journal of Integral Theory and Practice, 31,* 139–162.

Fukuyama, F. (1992). *The end of history and the last man.* New York, NY: Avon Books.

Fullan, M. (2005). *Leadership and sustainability: System thinkers in action.* Thousand Oaks, CA: Corwin Press.

Fullan, M. (2007). *The new meaning of educational change.* New York, NY: Teachers College Press.

Gage, N. L. (1989). The paradigm wars and their aftermath: A "historical" sketch of research on teaching since 1989. *Teachers College Record, 91*(2), 135–150.

Garrison, J. (2000). *Civilization and the transformation of power.* New York, NY: Paraview Press.

Gebser, J. (1991). *The ever-present origin.* Athens, OH: Ohio University Press.

Geertz, C. (1973). *The interpretation of cultures.* New York, NY: Basic Books.

Geertz, C. (1988). *Works and lives: The anthropologist as author.* Palo Alto, CA: Stanford University Press.

Giddens, A. (1984). *The constitution of society.* Berkeley, CA: University of California Press.

Gilstrap, D. L. (2005). Strange attractors and human interaction: Leading complex organizations through the use of metaphors. *Complicity: An International Journal of Complexity and Education, 2*(1), 55–69.

Giroux, H. A., & Purpel, D. (Eds.). (1983). *The hidden curriculum and moral education.* Berkeley, CA: McCutchan.

Glaser, B. G., & Strauss, A. L. (1967). *The discovery of grounded theory: Strategies for qualitative research.* Chicago, IL: Aldine.

Goldstein, J., Hazy, J. K., & Lichtenstein, B. B. (2010). *Complexity and the nexus of leadership: Leveraging nonlinear science to create ecologies of innovation.* New York, NY: Palgrave Macmillan.

Goleman, D. (1988). *The meditative mind: The varieties of meditative experience.* New York, NY: Jeremy P. Tarcher.

Goleman, D. (2004). *Primal leadership: Learning to lead with emotional intelligence.* Cambridge, MA: Harvard Business Review Press.

Goodman, J. (2013). Charter management organizations and the regulated environment: Is it worth the price? *Educational Researcher, 42*(2), 89–96.

Graves, C. W. (2005). *The never ending quest: A treatise on an emergent cyclical conception of adult behavioral systems and their development.* Santa Barbara, CA: ECLET Publishing.

Gronn, P. C. (2003). *The new work of educational leaders: Changing leadership practice in an era of school reform.* London, UK: Paul Chapman.

Gutmann, A. (1999). *Democratic education.* Princeton, NJ: Princeton University Press.

Habermas, J. (1971). *Knowledge and human interests.* Boston, MA: Beacon Press.

Habermas, J. (1984a). *The theory of communicative action: Reason and the rationalization of society* (Vol. 1). Boston, MA: Beacon Press.

Habermas, J. (1984b). *The theory of communicative action: Lifeworld and system: A critique of functionalist reason* (Vol. 2). Boston, MA: Beacon Press.

Habermas, J. (1988). *On the logic of the social sciences.* Cambridge, MA: MIT Press.

Habermas, J. (1994). The critique of reason as an unmasking of the human sciences: Michel Foucault. In M. Kelly (Ed.), *Critique and power: Recasting the Foucault/Habermas debate.* Cambridge, MA: MIT Press.

Habermas, J. (1996). *Between facts and norms: Contributions to a discourse theory of law and democracy.* Cambridge, MA: MIT Press.

Hallinger, P. (2011). Leadership for learning: Lessons from 40 years of empirical research. *Journal of Educational Administration, 49*(2), 125–142.

Hamilton, M. (2012). Leadership to the power of 8: Leading self, others, organization, system and supra-system. *Integral Leadership Review, 12*(5), October.

Harari, Y. N. (2015). *Sapiens: A brief history of humankind.* New York, NY: HarperCollins.

Hargreaves, A. (2011). Fusion and the future of leadership. In J. Robertson & H. Timperley (Eds.), *Leadership and learning* (pp. 227–242). London, UK: Sage Publications.

Hargreaves, A., & Fink, D. (2006). *Sustainable leadership.* San Francisco, CA: Jossey-Bass.

Hargreaves, A., & Fullan, M. (2012). *Professional capital: Transforming teaching in every school.* New York, NY: Teachers College Press.

Hargreaves, A., & Harris, A. (2011). *Performance beyond expectations: Executive summary.* Nottingham, UK: National College for School Leadership.

Hargreaves, A., & Shirley, D. (2012). *The global fourth way: The quest for educational excellence.* Thousand Oaks, CA: Corwin.

Harris, A. (2008). Distributed leadership: According to the evidence. *Journal of Educational Administration, 46*(2), 172–188.

Harris, L. S., & Kuhnert, K. W. (2008). Looking through the lens of leadership: A constructive developmental approach. *Leadership and Organization Development Journal, 29*(1), 47–67.

Harvey, D. (2007). *A brief history of neoliberalism.* New York, NY: Oxford University Press.

Healy, J. (2004). *Your child's growing mind*. New York, NY: Broadway.

Heck, R. H., & Hallinger, P. (2010). Testing a longitudinal model of distributed leadership effects on school improvement. *The Leadership Quarterly, 21*, 867–885.

Heckscher, C. (1994). Defining the post-bureaucratic type. In A. Donnellon & C. Heckscher (Eds.), *The post-bureaucratic organization: New perspectives on organizational change* (pp. 14–63). Newbury Park, CA: Sage.

Heifetz, R. A. (1994). *Leadership without easy answers*. Cambridge, MA: Harvard University Press.

Heifetz, R. A., & Linsky, M. (2002). A survival guide for leaders. *Harvard Business Review, June*, 5–12.

Heifetz, R. A., Grashow, A., & Linsky, M. (2009). *The practice of adaptive leadership: Tools and tactics for changing your organization and the world*. Boston, MA: Harvard Business Press.

Helsing, D., Howell, A., Kegan, R., & Lahey, L. (2008). Putting the 'development' in professional development: Understanding and overturning educational leaders' immunities to change. *Harvard Educational Review, 78*(3), 437–465.

Hemmings, A. (2012). *Urban high schools: Foundations and possibilities*. New York, NY: Routledge.

Herzberg, F., Mausner, B., & Snyderman, B. B. (1959). *Motivation to work*. New York, NY: John Wiley & Sons.

Heskett, J. (2011). *The culture cycle: How to shape the unforeseen force that transforms performance*. Upper Saddle River, NJ: FT Press.

Hobban, G. F. (2002). *Teacher learning for educational change*. Philadelphia, PA: Open University Press.

Howe, K. R. (2009). Epistemology, methodology, and education sciences: Positivist dogmas, rhetoric, and the education science question. *Educational Researcher, 38*(6), 428–440.

Howe, K. R., & Meens, D. E. (2012). *Democracy left behind: How recent education reforms undermine local school governance and democratic education*. Boulder, CO: National Education Policy Center.

Hursh, D. (2008). *High-stakes testing and the decline of teaching and learning*. New York, NY: Rowman & Littlefield.

Jackson, M. C. (2000). *Systems approaches to management*. New York, NY: Kluwer Academic/Plenum Publishers.

Jackson, M. C., & Keys, P. (1984). Towards a system of systems methodologies. *Journal of the Operational Research Society, 35*(6), 473–486.

Jantsch, E. (1976). Evolution: Self-realization through self-transcendence. In E. Jantsch & C. H. Waddington (Eds.), *Evolution and consciousness: Human systems in transition*. Reading, MA: Addison-Wesley.

Jantsch, E. (1980). *The self-organizing universe: Scientific and human implications of the emerging paradigm of evolution*. New York, NY: Pergamon Press.

Jolly, R. (2015). *Systems thinking for business: Capitalize on structures hidden in plain sight.* Portland, OR: Systems Solutions.

Kaomea, J. (2001). Dilemmas of an indigenous academic: A native Hawaiian story. *Contemporary Issues in Early Childhood, 2*(1), 67–82.

Katz, M. B. (2008). *The price of citizenship: Redefining the American welfare state.* Philadelphia, PA: University of Pennsylvania Press.

Kegan, R. (2001). *The evolving self: Problem and process in human development.* Cambridge, MA: Harvard University Press.

Kegan, R. (2003). *In over our heads: The mental demands of modern life.* Cambridge, MA: Harvard University Press.

Kegan, R., & Lahey, L. (2001). *How the way we talk can change the way we work: Seven languages for transformation.* San Francisco, CA: Jossey-Bass.

Kegan, R., & Lahey, L. (2009). *Immunity to change.* Boston, MA: Harvard Business Press.

Kegan, R., & Lahey, L. (2016). *An everyone culture: Becoming a deliberately developmental organization.* Cambridge, MA: Harvard Business Review Press.

Klein, N. (2007). *The shock doctrine: The rise of disaster capitalism.* New York, NY: Picador.

Kozol, J. (2005). *The shame of the nation: The restoration of apartheid schooling in America.* New York, NY: Crown Publishing.

Kuhn, T. S. (1970). *The structure of scientific revolutions* (2nd ed.). Chicago, IL: University of Chicago Press.

Kumashiro, K. (2012). *Bad teacher!* New York, NY: Teachers College Press.

Kurzweil, R. (2005). *The singularity is near.* New York, NY: Viking Penguin.

Ladson-Billings, G. (2006). From the achievement gap to the education debt: Understanding achievement in U.S. schools. *Educational Researcher, 35*(7), 3–12.

Lagemann, E. C. (2000). *An elusive science: The troubling history of education research.* Chicago, IL: University of Chicago Press.

Lahann, R., & Reagan, E. M. (2011). Teach for America and the politics of progressive neoliberalism. *Teacher Education Quarterly, Winter,* 7–27.

Lambert, L. (2009). Constructivist leadership. In B. Davies (Ed.), *The essentials of school leadership.* Thousand Oaks, CA: Sage.

Lasch, C. (1991). *The culture of narcissism: American life in an age of diminishing expectations.* New York, NY: W. W. Norton.

Leithwood, K., Harris, A., & Hopkins, D. (2008). Seven strong claims about successful school leadership. *School Leadership and Management, 28*(1), 27–42.

Lemke, J. L., & Sabelli, N. H. (2008). Complex systems and educational change: Towards a new research agenda. *Educational Philosophy and Theory, 40*(1), 118–129.

Lewin, K. (1943). Psychological ecology. In D. Cartwright (Ed.), *Field theory in social science* (p. 118). London, UK: Social Science Paperbacks.

Lewin, R. (1992). *Complexity: Life at the edge of chaos.* New York, NY: Macmillan.

Lichtenstein, B. B., & Plowman, D. A. (2009). The leadership of emergence: A complex systems leadership theory of emergence at successive organizational levels. *The Leadership Quarterly.* doi:10.1016/j.leaqua.2009.04.006

Lichtenstein, B. B., Uhl-Bien, M., Marion, R., Seers, A., Orton, J. D., & Schreiber, C. (2006). Complexity leadership theory: An interactive perspective on leading in complex adaptive systems. *Emergence: Complexity and Organization, 8*(4), 2–12.

Likert, R. (1961). *New patterns of management.* New York, NY: McGraw Hill.

Lynch Leadership Academy. (2010). *Mission and vision statement.* Chestnut Hill, MA: Boston College.

Lyotard, J. F. (1984). *The postmodern condition: A report on knowledge.* Manchester, UK: Manchester University Press.

MacIntyre, A. (1984). *After virtue.* Notre Dame, IN: University of Notre Dame Press.

Marris, P. (1974). *Loss and change.* New York, NY: Pantheon Books.

Marshall, K. (2005). It's time to rethink teacher evaluation. *Phi Delta Kappan, 86*(10), 727–735.

Martineau, S. (2007). Humanity, forest ecology, and the future in a British Columbia valley: A case study. *Integral Review, 4,* 26–43.

Marzano, R. J., Waters, T., & McNulty, B. A. (2005). *School leadership that works: From research to results.* Alexandria, VA: Association for Supervision and Curriculum Development.

Mascolo, M. F., & Fischer, K. W. (2010). The dynamic development of thinking, feeling, and acting over the life span. In W. F. Overton (Ed.), *Biology, cognition, and methods across the lifespan* (Vol. 1, pp. 149–194). Hoboken, NJ: John Wiley & Sons.

Maslow, A. H. (1968). *Toward a psychology of being* (2nd ed.). New York, NY: D. Van Nostrand.

McCombs, B. L. (2001). What do we know about learners and learning? The learner-centered framework: Bringing the educational system into balance. *Educational Horizons, 79*(4), 182–193.

McGregor, D. (1960). *The human side of enterprise.* New York, NY: McGraw Hill.

Meadows, D. (2008). *Thinking in systems.* White River Junction, VT: Chelsea Green Publishing.

Meier, D., & Wood, G. (Eds.). (2004). *Many children left behind: How the no child left behind act is damaging our children and our schools.* Boston, MA: Beacon Press.

Merriam, S. B. (2009). *Qualitative research: A guide to design and implementation.* San Francisco, CA: Jossey-Bass.

Merseth, K. K. (2009). *Inside urban charter schools: Promising practices and strategies in five high-performing schools.* Cambridge, MA: Harvard University Press.

MetLife. (2012). *The MetLife survey of the American teacher: Teachers, parents and the economy.* New York, NY: MetLife Inc.

Miller, M., & Cook-Greuter, S. (Eds.). (1994). *Transcendence and mature thought in adulthood*. Lanham, MD: Rowman & Littlefield Publishers.

Montuori, A. (2008). Foreword. In E. Morin (Ed.), *On complexity*. Cresskill, NJ: Hampton Press.

Moolenaar, N. M., & Sleegers, P. J. C. (2010). Social networks, trust, and innovation: The role of relationships in supporting an innovative climate in Dutch schools. In A. J. Daly (Ed.), *Social network theory and educational change*. Cambridge, MA: Harvard Education Press.

Moore, P. (2017). *The future of children: Providing a love-based education for every child*. Philadelphia, PA: Emergence Education Press.

Morgan, G. (2006). *Images of organization*. Thousand Oaks, CA: Sage Publications.

Morin, E. (2001). *Seven complex lessons in education for the future*. Paris, France: UNESCO.

Morin, E. (2008). *On complexity*. Cresskill, NJ: Hampton Press.

Murgatroyd, S. (2010). 'Wicked problems' and the work of the school. *European Journal of Education, 45*(2), 259–279.

Nadler, R. S. (1993). Therapeutic process of change. In M. Gass (Ed.), *Adventure therapy: Therapeutic applications of adventure programming* (pp. 57–69). Dubuque, IA: Kendall/Hunt Publishing.

Nagel, T. (1989). *The view from nowhere*. New York, NY: Oxford University Press.

Neumann, E. (1973). *The origins and history of consciousness*. Princeton, NJ: Princeton University Press.

New England Complex Systems Institute (NECSI). (2000). *What is the study of complex systems?* Retrieved from http://necsi.org/guide/whatis.html

New Leaders for New Schools. (2010). *Principal effectiveness: A new principalship to drive student achievement, teacher effectiveness, and school turn-arounds*. New York, NY: New Leaders for New Schools.

Nietzsche, F. (1968a). *Twilight of the idols*. Harmondsworth: Penguin.

Nietzsche, F. (1968b). *The anti-christ*. Harmondsworth: Penguin.

Nietzsche, F. (1969). *On the genealogy of morals*. New York, NY: Vintage Books.

Noguera, P. (2003). *City schools and the American dream: Reclaiming the promise of public education*. New York, NY: Teachers College Press.

Noguera, P. (2009). The achievement gap and the future of education policy in the Obama administration. *New Labor Forum, 16*(Spring).

Oliver, P. E., & Johnston, H. (2000). What a good idea: Frames and ideologies in social movements research. *Mobilization: An International Journal, 5*(April), 37–54.

Olivier, R. (2002). *Inspirational leadership*. London, UK: Spiro Press.

Opfer, V. D., & Pedder, D. (2011). Conceptualizing teacher professional learning. *Review of Educational Research, 81*(3), 376–407.

Osberg, D. (2010). Taking care of the future? The complex responsibility of education & politics. In D. Osberg & G. Biesta (Eds.), *Complexity theory and the politics of education*. Rotterdam, the Netherlands: Sense Publishers.

Osberg, D., & Biesta, G. (Eds.). (2010). *Complexity theory and the politics of education*. Rotterdam, the Netherlands: Sense Publishers.

Page, S. (2010). *Diversity and complexity*. Princeton, NJ: Princeton University Press.

Pang, N. S., & Pisapia, J. (2012). The strategic thinking skills of Hong Kong school leaders: Usage and effectiveness. *Educational Management Administration and Leadership, 40*(3), 343–361.

Penuel, W. R., Frank, K. A., & Krause, A. (2010). Between leaders and teachers: Using social network analysis to examine the effects of distributed leadership. In A. J. Daly (Ed.), *Social network theory and educational change*. Cambridge, MA: Harvard Education Press.

Peyser, J. A. (2011). Unlocking the secrets of high-performing charters: Tight management and "no excuses." *Education Next, 11*(4), 36–43.

Picketty, T. (2014). *Capital in the twenty-first century*. Cambridge, MA: Harvard University Press.

Pink, D. H. (2011). *Drive: The surprising truth about what motivates us*. New York, NY: Riverhead Books.

Porter, T. M. (1995). *Trust in numbers: The pursuit of objectivity in science and public life*. Princeton, NJ: Princeton University Press.

Pratt, S. S., & Stringer, A. (2008). Strange attractors in school leadership. In B. Despres (Ed.), *Systems thinkers in action: A field guide for effective change leadership in education*. Lanham, MD: Rowman & Littlefield.

Pryor, F. L. (2008). System as a causal force. *Journal of Economic Behavior & Organization, 67*(3–4), 545–559.

Puhakka, K. (1995). Restoring connectedness in the Kosmos: A healing tale of a deeper order. *Integral World: Exploring Theories of Everything*. Retrieved from www.integralworld.net

RAND. (2010). *Reauthorizing no child left behind: Facts and recommendations*. Arlington, VA: RAND.

Ravitch, D. (2011). *The death and life of the great American school system*. New York, NY: Basic Books.

Ravitch, D. (2013). *Reign of error: The hoax of the privatization movement and the danger to America's public schools*. New York, NY: Alfred A. Knopf.

Rawls, J. (1996). *Political liberalism*. New York, NY: Columbia University Press.

Reich, R. B. (2007). *Supercapitalism: The transformation of business, democracy, and everyday life*. New York, NY: Vintage Books.

Reich, R. B. (2011). *Aftershock: The next economy and America's future*. New York, NY: Vintage Books.

Reigeluth, C. M. (2008). Chaos theory and the sciences of complexity: Foundations for transforming education. In B. Despres (Ed.), *Systems thinkers in action: A field guide for effective change leadership in education.* Lanham, MD: Rowman & Littlefield.

Rhee, M. (2013). *Radical: Fighting to put students first.* New York, NY: HarperCollins.

Riddell, D. (2005). Evolving approaches to conservation: Integral ecology and British Columbia's great bear rainforest. *World Futures: The Journal of General Evolution, 61*(1–2), 63–78.

Robinson, V. M. J., Lloyd, C. A., & Rowe, K. J. (2008). The impact of leadership on student outcomes: An analysis of the differential effects of leadership types. *Educational Administration Quarterly, 44*(5), 635–674.

Rooke, D., & Torbert, W. R. (2005). 7 transformations of leadership. *Harvard Business Review, April,* 67–76.

Rorty, R. (1985). Habermas and Lyotard on postmodernity. In R. J. Bernstein (Ed.), *Habermas and modernity.* Cambridge, MA: MIT Press.

Rothstein, R. (2004). *Class and schools: Using social, economic, and educational reform to close the black-white achievement gap.* New York, NY: Teachers College Press.

Rowan, B. (1990). Commitment and control: Alternative strategies for the organizational design of schools. *Review of Research in Education, 16,* 353–389.

Sacks, P. (1999). *Standardized minds: The high price of America's testing culture and what we can do to change it.* Cambridge, MA: Perseus Press.

Sahlberg, P. (2011). *Finnish lessons: What can the world learn from educational change in Finland?* New York, NY: Teachers College Press.

Samuels, C. A. (2011). Report details "culture of cheating" in Atlanta schools. *Education Week, 30*(36), 1–22.

Saphier, J., & King, M. (1985). Good seeds grow in strong cultures. *Educational Leadership, March,* 67–74.

Sarason, S. (1971). *The culture of the school and the problem of change.* Boston, MA: Allyn & Bacon.

Schein, E. H. (2004). *Organizational culture and leadership.* San Francisco, CA: Jossey-Bass.

Schmachtenberger, D. (2017). *Global phase shift with Daniel Schmachtenberger.* Future Thinkers Podcast, Episode 36. Retrieved from http://futurethinkers.org/daniel-schmachtenberger-phase-shift/

Schmachtenberger, D. (2018). *Mitigating existential risks.* Future Thinkers Podcast, Episode 46. Retrieved from http://futurethinkers.org/daniel-schmachtenberger-existential-risks/

Schwab, K. (2017). *The fourth industrial revolution.* New York, NY: World Economic Forum.

Senge, P. M. (1994). *The fifth discipline: The art and practice of the learning organization.* New York, NY: Doubleday.

Senge, P. M., Cambron-McCabe, N., Lucas, T., Smith, B., Dutton, J., & Kleiner, A. (2000). *Schools that learn: A fifth discipline fieldbook for educators, parents, and everyone who cares about education.* New York, NY: Doubleday.

Senge, P. M., Scharmer, C. O., Jaworski, J., & Flowers, B. S. (2004). *Presence: Human purpose and the field of the future.* Cambridge, MA: The Society for Organizational Learning.

Sergiovanni, T. J. (2005). The virtues of leadership. *The Educational Forum, 69*(2), 112–123.

Sheldrake, R. (1981). *A new science of life: The hypothesis of formative causation.* Los Angeles, CA: J.P. Tarcher.

Showers, B., & Joyce, B. (1996). The evolution of peer coaching. *Educational Leadership, 53*(6), 12–17.

Simon, E., Gold, E., & Cucchiara, M. (2011). The prospects for public engagement in a market-oriented public education system: A case study of Philadelphia, 2001–2007. In M. Orr & J. Rogers (Eds.), *Public engagement for public education: Joining forces to revitalize democracy and equalize schools* (pp. 276–302). Stanford, CA: Stanford University Press.

Skabursis, A. (2008). The origin of 'wicked problems.' *Planning Theory and Practice, 9*(2), 277–280.

Sleeter, C. E. (2008). Teaching for democracy in an age of corporatocracy. *Teachers College Record, 110*(1), 139–159.

Smith, B. (2013, December 4). *The education you deserve: An open letter to my students at a "no excuses" charter school in Boston.* Retrieved from http://edushyster.com/?tag=match-charter-public-school

Smith, H. (1992). *Beyond the post-modern mind.* Wheaton, IL: Quest Books.

Smith, L. T. (1999). *Decolonizing methodologies: Research and indigenous peoples.* New York, NY: Zed Books.

Smith, R. (2018, January 4). *Never been better, never felt worse: Inside the rise of an Integral global operating system for the 21st century.* Keynote address at What Now? Conference. Boulder, CO. Retrieved from https://integrallife.com/never-better-never-felt-worse-inside-rise-integral-global-operating-system-21st-century/

Smitherman, S. (2005). Chaos and complexity theories. In W. E. Doll, M. J. Fleener, D. Trueit, & J. St. Julien (Eds.), *Chaos, complexity, curriculum and culture.* New York, NY: Peter Lang.

Smylie, M. A. (1995). Teacher learning in the workplace: Implications for school reform. In T. R. Guskey & M. Huberman (Eds.), *Professional development in education: New paradigms and practices* (pp. 92–113). New York, NY: Teachers College Press.

Southworth, G. (2009). Learning-centered leadership. In B. Davies (Ed.), *The essentials of school leadership.* Thousand Oaks, CA: Sage.

Spillane, J. P. (2005). Distributed leadership. *The Educational Forum, 69*(2), 143–150.

Spring, J. (2012). *Education networks: Power, wealth, cyberspace, and the digital mind.* New York, NY: Routledge.

St. Julien, J. (2005). Complexity: Developing a more useful analytic for education. In W. E. Doll, M. J. Fleener, D. Trueit, & J. St. Julien (Eds.), *Chaos, complexity, curriculum and culture.* New York, NY: Peter Lang.

Stake, R. (2006). *Multiple case study analysis.* New York, NY: Guilford Press.

Starratt, R. J. (2009). Ethical leadership. In B. Davies (Ed.), *The essentials of school leadership* (2nd ed.). Thousand Oaks, CA: Sage Publications.

Stein, Z. (2013). Ethics and the new education: Psychopharmacology, psychometrics, and the future of human capital. In *Proceedings of the 3rd Bi-annual integral theory conference* (pp. 1–37). San Francisco, CA.

Stein, Z. (2016). *Social justice and educational measurement: John Rawls, the history of testing, and the future of education.* New York, NY: Routledge.

Stein, Z., Dawson, T. L., & Fischer, K. W. (2010). Redesigning testing: Operationalizing the new science of learning. In M. S. Khine & I. M. Saleh (Eds.), *The new science of learning: Computers, cognition, and collaboration education* (pp. 207–224). Springer Press.

Stein, Z., Dawson, T. L., Van Rossum, Z., Hill, S., & Rothaizer, J. (2014). Virtuous cycles of learning: Using formative, embedded, and diagnostic developmental assessments in a large-scale leadership program. *Journal of Integral Theory and Practice, 9*(1), 1–11.

Stein, Z., & Heikkinen, K. (2008). On operationalizing aspects of altitude: An introduction to the lectical assessment system for integral researchers. *Journal of Integral Theory and Practice, 3*(1), 105–138.

Stein, Z., & Heikkinen, K. (2009). Metrics, models, and measurement in developmental psychology. *Integral Review, 5*(1), 4–24.

Stewart, J. (2000). *Evolution's arrow.* Canberra, Australia: The Chapman Press.

Stiglitz, J. E. (2007). *Making globalization work.* New York, NY: W.W. Norton.

Stone, D. (2012). *Policy paradox: The art of political decision making* (3rd ed.). New York, NY: W.W. Norton.

Stone, M. K. (2010). A schooling for sustainability framework. *Teacher Education Quarterly, 37*(4), 33–46.

Supovitz, J. A. (2008). Instructional influence in American high schools. In M. Mangin & S. Stoelinga (Eds.), *Effective teacher leadership: Using research to inform and reform* (pp. 144–162). New York, NY: Teachers College Press.

Surie, G., & Hazy, J. K. (2006). Generative leadership: Nurturing innovation in complex systems. *E:Co, 8*(4), 13–26.

Swimme, B., & Berry, T. (1992). *The universe story.* San Francisco, CA: Harper.

Taleb, N. N. (2014). *Antifragile: Things that gain from disorder.* New York, NY: Random House.

Taylor, C. (1989). *Sources of the self: The making of the modern identity.* Cambridge, MA: Harvard University Press.

Taylor, C. (2007). *A secular age.* Cambridge, MA: Harvard University Press.

Tegmark, M. (2018). *Life 3.0: Being human in the age of artificial intelligence.* New York, NY: Vintage Books.

Tillich, P. (1958). *Dynamics of faith.* New York, NY: Harper.

Toch, T. (2006). *Margins of error: The testing industry in the no child left behind era.* Washington, DC: Education Sector.

Torbert, W. R. (2000a). A developmental approach to social science: A model for analyzing Charles Alexander's scientific contributions. *Journal of Adult Development, 7*(4), 255–267.

Torbert, W. R. (2000b). Transforming social science: Integrating quantitative, qualitative, and action research. In F. T. Sherman & W. R. Torbert (Eds.), *Transforming social inquiry, transforming social action: New paradigms for crossing the theory/practice divide in universities and communities.* Boston, MA: Kluwer Academic Publishers.

Torbert, W. R. (2004). *Action inquiry: The secret of timely and transforming leadership.* San Francisco, CA: Berrett-Koehler Publishers.

Torre, C. A., & Voyce, C. (2008). Shared accountability: An organic approach. In B. Despres (Ed.), *Systems thinkers in action: A field guide for effective change leadership in education.* Lanham, MD: Rowman & Littlefield.

Tozer, S., Senese, G. B., & Violas, P. C. (2013). *School and society: Historical and contemporary perspectives.* New York, NY: McGraw-Hill.

Tyack, D. B. (1974). *The one best system: A history of American urban education.* Cambridge, MA: Harvard University Press.

Tyack, D. B., & Cuban, L. (1995). *Tinkering toward utopia: A century of public school reform.* Cambridge, MA: Harvard University Press.

Uhl-Bien, M., Marion, R., & McKelvy, B. (2007). Complexity leadership theory: Shifting leadership from the industrial age to the knowledge era. *The Leadership Quarterly, 18*(4), 298–318.

Ulrich, W. (1994). *Critical heuristics of social planning: A new approach to practical philosophy.* New York, NY: John Wiley and Sons.

Ulrich, W. (1998). *Systems thinking as if people mattered: Critical systems thinking for citizens and managers* (Working paper number 23). Lincoln, UK: Lincoln School of Management, University of Lincoln.

van Schaik, P. (2016). Urban hub 3: Integral theory, thrivable cities. *integralMENTORS.* https://paulvanschaik.wixsite.com/integralmentors/urban-hub-1

Wagner, T., & Kegan, R. (2006). *Change leadership: A practical guide to transforming our schools.* San Francisco, CA: Jossey-Bass.

Waldrop, M. M. (1992). *Complexity: The emerging science at the edge of order and chaos.* New York, NY: Simon & Schuster.

Wallace, B. A. (2000). *The taboo of subjectivity*. Oxford, UK: Oxford University Press.

Wallace Foundation. (2011). *The school principal as leader: Guiding schools to better teaching and learning*. New York, NY: The Wallace Foundation.

Walsh, R. (2018). *Unitas multiplex: A more integral approach to diversity*. Retrieved February 15, 2018, from https://integrallife.com/unitas-multiplex-a-more-integral-approach-to-diversity/?utm_source=Integral+Life+Newsletter&utm_campaign=0d769a0885-EMAIL_CAMPAIGN_2018_02_16&utm_medium=email&utm_term=0_de2cfb3770-0d769a0885-50207683&mc_cid=0d769a0885&mc_eid=cd9e9de6da

Watkins, A., & Wilber, K. (2015). *Wicked and wise: How to solve the world's toughest problems*. Kent, Great Britain: Urbane Publications.

Weathers, J. M. (2011). Teacher community in urban elementary schools: The role of leadership and bureaucratic accountability. *Education Policy Analysis Archives, 19*(3). Retrieved from http://epaa.asu.edu/ojs/article/view/887

Weedon, C. (1987). *Feminist practice and poststructuralist theory*. Oxford, UK: Blackwell.

Weick, K. E. (2009). *Making sense of the organization: The impermanent organization* (Vol. 2). New York, NY: John Wiley.

Wells, C., & Keane, W. G. (2008). Building capacity for professional learning communities through a systems approach: A toolbox for superintendents. *AASA Journal of Scholarship & Practice, 4*(4), 24–32.

Westheimer, J. (2007). Politics and patriotism in education. In J. Westheimer (Ed.), *Pledging allegiance: The politics of patriotism in America's schools* (pp. 171–188). New York, NY: Teachers College Press.

Wheatley, M. J. (2006). *Leadership and the new science: Discovering order in a chaotic world*. San Francisco, CA: Berrett-Koehler Publishers.

Whitehead, A. N. (1979). *Process and reality*. New York, NY: The Free Press.

Whitman, D. (2008). *Sweating the small stuff: Inner-city schools and the new paternalism*. Washington, DC: The Thomas B. Fordham Institute.

Wilber, K. (1995). *Sex, ecology, spirituality: The spirit of evolution*. Boston, MA: Shambhala.

Wilber, K. (2000a). *A theory of everything*. Boston, MA: Shambhala.

Wilber, K. (2000b). *Integral psychology*. Boston, MA: Shambhala.

Wilber, K. (2006a). *Excerpt A: An integral age at the leading edge*. Retrieved from http://www.kenwilber.com/writings/read_pdf/83

Wilber, K. (2006b). *Excerpt B: The many ways we touch—Three principles helpful for any integrative approach*. Retrieved from http://www.kenwilber.com/writings/read_pdf/84

Wilber, K. (2006c). *Excerpt D: The look of a feeling: The importance of post/structuralism*. Retrieved from http://www.kenwilber.com/writings/read_pdf/86

Wilber, K. (2006d). Introduction to integral theory and practice: IOS basic and the AQAL map. *Journal of Integral Theory and Practice, 1*(1), 1–36.

Wilber, K. (2017). *The religion of tomorrow: A vision for the future of the great traditions.* Boulder, CO: Shambhala.

Williams, B., & Hummelbrunner, R. (2011). *Systems concepts in action: A practitioner's toolkit.* Stanford, CA: Stanford Business Books.

Wilson, B., & Van Haperen, K. (2015). *Soft systems thinking, methodology and the management of change.* London, UK: Palgrave.

Wolin, S. S. (2010). *Democracy incorporated: Managed democracy and the specter of inverted totalitarianism.* Princeton, NJ: Princeton University Press.

Wright, R. (2000). *Nonzero: The logic of human destiny.* New York, NY: Pantheon Books.

Yin, R. K. (1981). The case study crisis: Some answers. *Administrative Science Quarterly, 26*(1), 58–65.

Yin, R. K. (2014). *Case study research: Design and methods* (5th ed.). Thousand Oaks, CA: Sage Publications.

Ylimaki, R. M., & Brunner, C. C. (2011). Power and collaboration-consensus/conflict in curriculum leadership: Status quo or change? *American Educational Research Journal, 48*(6), 1258–1285.

Young, R. (1990). *A critical theory of education: Habermas and our children's future.* New York, NY: Teachers College Press.

www.ingramcontent.com/pod-product-compliance
Lightning Source LLC
Chambersburg PA
CBHW051524230426
43668CB00012B/1733